Praise for Stephen Coonts'
THE CANNIBAL QUEEN

"Coonts shares his passion. . . . His account is that of a fellow in love with aircraft and at home in the sky. His writing style is friendly, frank and engaging. . . . His views are outspoken and interesting. . . . Coonts offers a good-humored account of an adventure very few pilots would even attempt."

—*Rocky Mountain News*

"THE CANNIBAL QUEEN is a pleasure, a delight to read. . . . I thought many times that Coonts is a little like William F. Buckley, but he flies instead of sails. . . . The book is a keeper."

—*Chattanooga News–Free Press*

"THE CANNIBAL QUEEN opens a whole new world. . . . This is a much different book from *Flight of the Intruder* or *Under Siege,* but it's likely Coonts fans will enjoy this real-life adventure as much as his novels."

—*Sacramento Bee*

"Enjoyable . . . breezily written . . . fun to read. . . . A travelog of small-town America, a walk through American aviation history, a look at contemporary family life and a lot of stream-of-consciousness musings about everything from sailing to weather reports. . . . THE CANNIBAL QUEEN should have broad appeal. . . . Coonts will leave his readers wanting more."

—*Chicago Tribune*

The culture of the private plane comes delightfully to life as Coonts marvels at a country where every little town has its strip, its laconic air controller, its cheap, clean motel just down the road. . . . The descriptions of flight and the portrait of an America seemingly trapped in a time-warp are arresting."

—*Kirkus Reviews*

Books by Stephen Coonts

FICTION

Flight of the Intruder*
Final Flight
The Minotaur
Under Siege*
The Red Horseman*

NONFICTION

The Cannibal Queen: A Flight into the Heart of America*

*Published by POCKET BOOKS

STEPHEN COONTS

A FLIGHT INTO THE
HEART OF AMERICA

THE CANNIBAL QUEEN

POCKET BOOKS

New York   London   Toronto   Sydney   Tokyo   Singapore

POCKET BOOKS, a division of Simon & Schuster Inc.
1230 Avenue of the Americas, New York, NY 10020

Copyright © 1992 by Stephen P. Coonts

Originally published in hardcover in 1992 by Pocket Books

All rights reserved, including the right to reproduce
this book or portions thereof in any form whatsoever.
For information address Pocket Books, 1230 Avenue
of the Americas, New York, NY 10020

ISBN: 0-671-03849-4

First Pocket Books trade paperback printing August 1999

10 9 8 7 6 5 4 3 2

POCKET and colophon are registered trademarks of
Simon & Schuster Inc.

Cover design by Iskra Johnson
Cover art by William S. Phillips

Printed in the U.S.A.

For Rachael, Lara and David

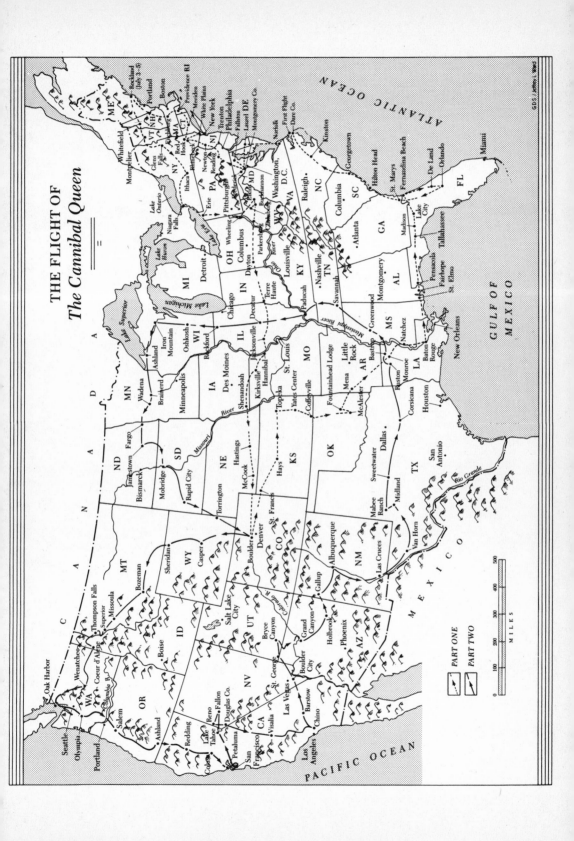

THE FLIGHT OF
The Cannibal Queen

PART ONE

Oh, that I had wings like a dove,
for then would I fly away,
and be at rest.

Psalms 55:6

1

———————

ALL REALLY GREAT FLYING ADVENTURES BEGIN AT DAWN—THE
dawn patrol, takeoff from Roosevelt Field for the flight across
the Atlantic to Paris, launch at first light for a strike on Rabaul,
and so on. Unfortunately this adventure was scheduled to begin
at noon. It actually got under way at 1:35 P.M. on a clear, sunny
Saturday afternoon in June, late, as most things in my life are.

That was what my watch read when I took a deep breath and
looked at the top of my son's head in the front cockpit of the
Stearman. Our few bags, a laptop computer and a camera bag
were stuffed into the luggage bay aft of the rear seat. The coffeepot at home was off.

For the next three months I would be flying this 1942 Stearman open-cockpit biplane around the United States. I had
shamelessly maneuvered my publisher into buying a book
about this adventure, and now it was time. Time to fly.

David, age fourteen, had agreed to accompany me for the first
two weeks, as far as Disney World in Orlando. He had never
been there so he agreed to go with the pilgrim's enthusiasm.

The plane was fueled, I had checked everything personally,
sectional charts were ready at hand, the sky looked good, my
ex-wife, Nancy, and our two daughters were on hand to wish

the adventurers a safe journey, the usual photos had been snapped, I had signed a new will at my lawyer's three days previous . . . What else?

John Weisbart, the guy who taught me how to fly the Stearman, is also on hand. "You checked everything?" he calls.

"Yeah."

"The oil dipstick cap?" David asks.

"Yep. Even that." I had forgotten to reinstall it on one previous flight with David. Oil sloshed all over the left side of the plane on landing.

"Clear," I call, flip on the master switch and engage the starter. The long prop swings. Six blades, then the mag switch to both. The big radial engine coughs out a gray cloud of oil, then catches with a throaty rumble.

With oil pressure up and the mixture knob and throttle retarded to idle, I reach for my helmet and headset and pull them on. As I am fumbling with the chin strap David's mother, Nancy, runs over to the side of the plane, kisses her fingers, then touches her fingers to my lips. It is a wonderful gesture.

With waves to everyone, we taxi out. After a few minutes of warming the engine and running it up, we taxi onto the runway and add power. The engine responds willingly. As I lift the tail off the runway I glance at the gauges—23 inches of manifold pressure and 2,250 RPM, which represents full power at 5,300 feet above sea level, the field elevation here in Boulder, Colorado.

I pull her nose off at 65 miles per hour and we are flying. She accelerates to 75 and I ease the stick back to hold that airspeed. Up we go at about 300 feet per minute.

We turn downwind and sail along parallel to the runway at 800 feet above the ground. Now the base leg, throttle back like we were going to land, then final but offset right. I level off a hundred feet above the ground and shove the throttle forward to the stop. Nancy and the girls are waving as we swoop overhead with the engine roaring mightily. I love that song.

We head east. First stop will be St. Francis, Kansas, the ninth annual Stearman fly-in, which by happy chance is this weekend, the second weekend in June. Level at cruising power at 7,500 feet and properly trimmed, David wants to fly her. I turn the stick over to him and search the sky for other traffic as I try to put it all into perspective.

"We're on our way," I tell him.

He soon gives the plane back to me. I gently waggle the stick and rudder and think of all the scheming and errands and planning that went into this aerial odyssey. This will be three months of flying around the country, three months of writing about it. The product will be my fifth book, and probably the most difficult one of the bunch. The flying will be the easy part.

Dave and I talk nervously on the intercom about this and that, pointing out landmarks, other airplanes, just talking. Finally we calm down and watch the land roll by beneath us.

The engine is humming perfectly. I sit drinking in the yellow wings against the blue sky and green land.

The plane's a big yellow Stearman open-cockpit biplane, a primary flight trainer built in the summer of 1942 by Boeing in Wichita, Kansas, for the Royal Canadian Air Force, one of three hundred built that summer for the Canadians under Lend-Lease. Like most Stearmans, when delivered this bird wore a 220-horsepower Continental engine, a big round radial.

The Canadians returned their Stearmans to the U.S. Army that fall. Apparently the rigors of open-cockpit flying in the Canadian winter were more than dedicated flight instructors and students could endure, even for king and country. So this beauty served out the remainder of the war in American colors.

After the war she was sold as surplus for $500 and acquired civil registration number N58700. Two owners later she was flying in Washington state for the Atomic Energy Commission. Why the AEC needed a Stearman is a mystery that will probably never be solved.

After that second tour of government service this plane was once again declared surplus and joined thousands of her sisters flying the American plains as a crop duster, then a sprayer as chemical technology changed. There she flew for over thirty years as the decades rolled by, the 1950s, the '60s, the '70s, and into the '80s.

Ready for the scrap yard in 1987, N58700 was purchased by Robert Henley, an airplane enthusiast from Denver, and restored by his father, Skid Henley, in McAlester, Oklahoma.

5

Skid installed a 300-horsepower Lycoming R-680 engine in the old girl, one that still wears a plate that notes that the U.S. government accepted delivery of this engine on August 2, 1942. So engine and plane are of equivalent age.

Restoring N58700 was obviously a labor of love. Skid gave her new threads of Stits fabric and painted her yellow. He added a gorgeous brown accent stripe that circles the lip of the cowling—he installed a cowling because he liked the look of it—and runs the length of the fuselage on both sides. The workmanship is superb throughout.

In May 1990 the thought occurred to Robert Henley that he had too many toys. The fact that he is a family man may have been a factor. Temporarily insane with this delusion, he showed me his Stearman. It was lust at first sight.

She was sitting primly in a tee-hangar at Front Range Airport, east of Denver. Standing in the sun and looking into the darkness of the hangar, you saw the yellow and the wings and the gleaming metal prop.

We rolled her out into the sun as Robert's wife, Ann, told me how they had worked all morning washing and waxing.

The sunlight on that yellow fabric was physically and emotionally overpowering, so brilliant, so bright, so beautiful. I stood there awed as a gentle breeze played across her and stirred the ailerons. She was big, yellow all over and greasy and oily in all the right places. She reeked of those wondrous smells that promise flight.

Stroking that taut yellow fabric, caressing the voluptuous, sensuous curves, sitting in the cockpit and staring at the motionless instruments and waggling the stick of laminated hickory as I ran my fingers along the throttle and mixture and propeller control levers, I fell madly in love.

The engine . . . ah, that big, round nine-cylinder radial is a work of art, its crankcase a battleship gray, the perfect background to display that engine placard that so proudly proclaims "1942." Not a fleck of rust anywhere. A film of oil on the pushrod bushings and on the bottom of the cowling. That morning thirteen months ago I reached in and got some on my fingers and felt that feeling of good, clean oil against precision-machined steel.

Staring into the shadows of that engine at the massive

machined parts, so clean, so ready, you knew. As you rubbed your oily fingers together you knew how that big radial would sound when it coughed into life. You knew how she would stumble and shudder and spray oil everywhere as white smoke belched from her stack and the gleaming, polished prop spun into a blur. You knew how the cough would subside into a throbbing growl that would echo off the hangars and drift away over the prairie.

I stared at my reflection in the mirror-smooth propeller hub. My hairline is receding and the years have etched lines into my face. Over my shoulder hung the sun's fireball, too bright to look at, shining down from a deep, deep blue sky.

"How much you want for her?" I asked Henley.

He told me.

"Worth every penny," I admitted, and bought that big yellow Stearman before he had time to change his mind.

John Weisbart taught me to fly her that summer. John has over a thousand hours in tail-wheel airplanes and took some refresher lessons in the Stearman from Henley, who is also a flight instructor. Then he began the frustrating job of transitioning a pilot with 2,500 hours in tricycle-gear planes into the most unforgiving tail-wheel airplane extant.

"She'll ground-loop on you at the drop of a hat," he told me, for the first of a hundred times. "When you flare to land you have to really work the rudder to hold her straight, keep the upwind wing down with aileron, hold the tail wheel on the ground with back stick. Fly her until you shut the engine down."

I nodded, pretending to understand.

"I'm telling you, Steve—she's so big, with her center of gravity so far aft, she'll take a bite out of your ass if you let her."

Sure, John. Sure.

I found out what he was talking about one afternoon in October. I was flying with my secretary's husband and paying more attention to other aircraft in the pattern than I was to flying my own plane, and just as I touched down the four-knot crosswind from the right weathercocked the Stearman. In the blink of an eye the left wingtip kissed the asphalt. Now, too late, I got busy with the rudder and stick. No ground loop, thank heavens, but a tattered wingtip and left aileron. I was a sadder and wiser man, especially when I got the bill. A little bit of fabric, glue and paint and the labor to properly install it set me back $320. Not a fortune, but *Aaagh!*

That incident was still in my future as John Weisbart began to initiate me into the mysteries of the Stearman. He decided that I should begin my lessons in the front cockpit while he monitored the proceedings in the rear one. Even I knew this was not the way it was done. "The instructor sits in front, John, and the student sits in back. I'm the student."

"I know that, but I'll feel a lot more comfortable with you up there and me back here. Trust me."

John was rapidly developing his own love affair with my new flame. Like a jealous teenager, I found this difficult to endure. Especially after five or six flights when I began to think I was getting the hang of this tail-wheel stuff. "Hey, John. Why don't you let me try it from back there?"

"Ahh, Steve, ol' buddy, it'd be a crime against nature to ding this Stearman. She's a beaut!" He glanced at the seductive wings, the glistening yellow paint, the shiny prop waiting to turn, then cast a vastly experienced eye upon me. "A couple more with you up front; then we'll see."

I finally got him in the front seat by embarrassing him in front of the mechanic, Steve Hall, who wandered out of the hangar one morning to watch us strap in. "Gonna have to put a stick of dynamite under John to get him out of that rear cockpit," I told Steve, with John listening.

"I feel more comfortable in back," John explained.

"Umm," Steve Hall said, ever the diplomat.

"Well, I guess maybe it's time." John looked me over for telltale signs of hangover or decrepitude. Seemingly satisfied, he sighed. "Okay, okay. I'll sit in the front."

He slowly climbed up onto the wing and made his way forward as I wondered if I was up to flying this yellow bird from the aft office, the captain's seat. Now I wished I hadn't been so hasty. I strapped in and sat there staring at the switches while John talked me through an engine start. With my stomach fluttering we taxied out, S-turning as usual, but from back here I could see better around the fuselage and engine.

Once in the air I discovered the rear cockpit is more wind-blown than the front. Here you are completely behind the wings and farther from the center of gravity, so any movement of the aircraft in pitch feels more pronounced. The look is different too. Although it is more difficult to see straight forward—especially with John's head in the way—the view to the sides is better when you flare. I decided it is also easier to detect any lateral movement of the nose in the landing flare, movement that you must use rudder to counter—the nose must go straight regardless of the crosswind.

Eventually John let me take her around the patch by myself, and one gorgeous, windless Colorado morning he signed me off as safe for solo. I haven't felt such a sense of accomplishment since my first solo in a U.S. Navy T-34 at Saufley Field in 1968.

And John told me again, "You've got to fly this thing every second in the landing pattern or she'll bite you on the ass."

In October I found out how right he was. Which is why I named the old gal *Cannibal Queen* and had a woman of appropriate demeanor and endowments painted on the right side, right above her name.

Today, thirteen months after I bought the *Queen*, David and I are aloft and on our way. I watch the engine instruments and refer to the sectional chart occasionally. We are flying true east, right down a section line over high plains still green from a wet spring. We have talked ourselves out and David is looking around, watching occasional puffy clouds floating over our heads. Then he looks out the right side of the plane awhile, then the left.

The first hour has barely passed when he announces, "I'm bored."

I sit silently pondering the amusement quotient of fourteen-year-olds. Was I like that when I was fourteen? My God, was it really thirty years ago?

More cumulo-puffballs are building in a layer above us. David is still reclining his head to watch them pass overhead. With St. Francis in sight dead ahead, I start to climb. At 8,200 feet we are even with the bottoms.

"You're not going to go through those, are you?" the bored one asks with a tinge of concern in his voice.

"Just between," I assure him.

Up another hundred feet and we slice through a narrow canyon between two puffballs. Damp gray wisps of nothingness off each wing. Then we are through and the small town of St. Francis, Kansas, lies before us.

I cut the power and let the Stearman descend as I call on the radio. No one answers on Unicom, 122.8. I listen. The altimeter setting would be nice, but I really want to know the wind. I learn from the radio calls that another Stearman is in the landing pattern. Finally I figure out he is using the grass runway that parallels runway 13, the only paved runway. I cross above the field and turn left downwind, only to be cut out of the pattern by a Cessna 182. Around again, only this time on base leg the sky is full of parachutists. I veer off to the right and add power for another trip around the circuit. Now the Unicom guy gets on the radio—wind about 20 knots from 120 degrees— the wind socks are standing straight out.

This time I plant the Queen in a mediocre three-point landing that the grass actually makes look good. Grass is like that. It is so forgiving that most tail-dragger pilots prefer it. On asphalt the large main tires of the Stearman stick and track without any sideways give, yet on grass both tires can slip sideways while the aircraft remains pointed straight. And sod has more give, more absorbency than asphalt. Occasionally after a too-enthusiastic arrival on asphalt or concrete the bird will return to the air with an unsightly and embarrassing bounce, propelled aloft in spite of the pilot's wishes by the action of the shock absorbers in the landing gear struts. Grass absorbs some of this shock absorber thrust, so the plane seems more willing to stay planted.

There are nine other Stearmans in St. Francis and the Cannibal Queen makes ten. A new record for the fly-in, we are told by the official greeter as he fills out my name and address. He takes a photo of David and me and points out a place to tie down the Queen.

With three grass runways, St. Francis is one of the finest fields in the country for tail-wheel airplanes. And the place is jumping. Ten Stearmans, all painted brightly with whatever color scheme struck the owner's fancy, another fifteen or twenty light planes, skydivers, three or four balloons, and a crowd of a hundred or so local spectators still lingering after a long day in the early summer sun. When you are tired of watching the noisy biplanes or scanning the sky for parachutes you can amuse yourself by inspecting sunburns, your own included. This is the great American airshow at a little town in the heartland. There are no paid aerobatic acts; the Blue Angels haven't been invited because they wouldn't come. This is just a bunch of old airplane enthusiasts, balloonists, jumpers, and their families, and the spectators who came to watch it all. This fly-in is put together every year by Robert Grace of Grace Flying Service, the local fixed-base operator (FBO).

David and I wander and look. I recall attending a local, do-it-yourself airshow at the grass field in my hometown of Buckhannon, West Virginia, when I was just a small boy. I remember the big acts were a guy who did aerobatics in a yellow J-3 Cub and two guys who leaped out of an airplane and floated earthward in surplus military chutes. That is about all I recall of that day, except for the fact my brother and I spent most of it running through the crowd playing hide-and-seek with each other. I must have been five or six then, maybe 1951 or '52. Strange that I should remember it so well.

To get to the cotton-candy stand we pass three farmers in identical bib overalls sitting on a bench smoking corncob pipes, not a one of them under the age of seventy. They sit without smiles, the smoke wisping from their pipes, their eyes focused on the airplanes from the past.

And we meet the people who belong to the biplanes. After we have the Queen fueled and tied down out in the grass between two of her sisters, a fellow named Kirk and his wife offer to drive us the three blocks to the motel in the twenty-year-old Cadillac courtesy car the motel provided. We agree, then wait for half an hour while Kirk does something or other at the other end of the flight line.

We sit in the grass in the shade under the wing and watch a white-and-blue Stearman arcing above us in the blue sky. Two Stearman pilots near us are giving rides—$30 for 15 minutes—so there are the usual squeals and trepidation as the neophytes are strapped into the front cockpits. One of the planes lacks an electrical system, so we watch the aviator hand-prop the engine. It starts easily on the first mighty swing of the big polished-metal prop. Another planeload of skydivers leaps into the arms of Jesus and floats earthward as the throb of radial engines surrounds and engulfs us.

11

At last Kirk is ready, and we climb into the ancient Cad for the three-block jaunt to the motel where we have a room reserved.

An hour later David and I walk the six blocks to the St. Francis City Park. The residential streets are lined with modest homes with huge trees in the yards. This is the Madison Avenue version of America, the stable, middle-class dream America of contented married couples with two kids and a friendly mongrel dog and a Chevy in the driveway. This myth pulls on our heartstrings even though we well know that small-town America is already an anachronism, even though we know that these farming communities on the prairie are dying as the families leave one by one for better jobs and better schools in the big cities, even though we know life here is as hard as it is anyplace else, or even a little harder.

The houses have porches and people sitting on them visiting with their neighbors on this gorgeous early-summer evening. When was the last time a developer in California or Colorado built a house with a porch on it?

So we walk along, this fourteen-year-old boy and I, looking at the houses and talking of what these people do to earn a living. David is curious about what kids his age do in a town this size "for fun" on a Saturday night.

I tell him they get in the family car or pickup and drag Main Street, like they did in Longmont, Colorado, in the summer of 1977 when I was on the police force there. And as they still do in every town in Colorado, including Denver. The kids drive up and down the street all evening, seeing who is in the other cars, occasionally stopping in a parking lot and sitting on the hood as the parade goes by. And they throw beer and pop cans. The whole scene infuriates the merchants, who still complain to the police as vigorously now as they did in 1977, and 1967, and 1957. Why the merchants get no wiser I don't know.

In the park a wheat farmer who barbecues commercially is cleaning up. He is finished cooking—all the meat is in large pots ready for serving. As he cleans his grill—a large boilerlike contraption that he tows behind a pickup—he tells a story about a woman in a bikini (from out of town, probably wicked Denver) who attended the fly-in two years ago. Right before his very eyes there on the sidewalk in the heart of St. Francis she

12

skinned out of the bikini she had worn all day and quickly donned shorts and tank top. "That recharged my batteries," he tells his listeners as he stones the grill clean of grease.

At last we line up to heap disposable plates full of barbecued beef, mashed potatoes and gravy, and home-style green beans. It is a feast. The evening sun is still above the horizon when the master of ceremonies thanks everyone for coming to the ninth fly-in and promises a bigger whing-ding for the tenth fly-in next year.

Then we are entertained by a barbershop quartet from Sterling, Colorado, a town on the high plains very similar to this one. The baritone is the Stearman owner who organized the first St. Francis fly-in, so he gets a round of applause. And when the singing is over we applaud the couple who got engaged today when a Stearman flew by towing a banner with the proposal LUELLEN MARRY ME JOHN. After we applaud the couple who were married at last year's fly-in, David and I walk the perfect streets back to our motel.

It has been a great day. We are on our way. The whole country is out there, the *Cannibal Queen* is ready and willing.

I am still glowing when David attacks me in the motel for our usual evening roughhouse. It's a congenital defect; he has to be tickled before he can sleep. I conk before he does. Later I wake up and find he has turned out the lights and is in bed asleep.

It's going to be a good summer.

13

2

_____

WE LIFT OFF THE GRASS RUNWAY AT ST. FRANCIS ON SUNDAY morning with more roar and vigor than I thought the Lycoming R-680 engine capable of. I glance at the gauges. Glory hallelujah, the manifold pressure reads 26 inches. Aha, St. Francis is 3,000 feet above sea level, and I have been flying out of Boulder, Colorado, which is at 5,300 feet. So *this* is what happens when you get a little closer to sea level.

A 70-mile-per-hour climb speed works out to about 12 degrees nose up. We soar skyward. Yee-haaa!

After we level out I turn the stick over to David. He ignores the rudders, as he has done on flights in the past when he tried this piloting gig. I keep him generally headed in the right direction, southeast toward Colby.

We are on our way again, probably the first Stearman to leave the fly-in. We had breakfast with an interesting group of flyers from Colorado and the pilot who had flown his plane the longest distance to reach the fly-in—from Florida. He flies to Bartlesville, Oklahoma, every year for the biplane fly-in, then comes to St. Francis the following weekend. After breakfast David and I walked the three blocks to the airport carrying our bags. After an hour or so of loafing and watching other

14

Stearmans give rides, David was ready to go. He was bored. Then two skydivers in full regalia mounted their trusty Cessna 182 to be transported aloft. David wanted to wait to see them come down.

We sat on the grass in front of the plane leaning back against the main wheels, me on the left, David on the right. The weather is fantastic here again today—severe clear—although it is supposed to be foggy toward the east. The FAA Flight Service Station briefer assured me the fog would burn off by the time we managed to arrive. I ran my fingers through the grass and looked at the *Queen's* wings arranged like pieces of sculpture above me against the blue.

Now we are a part of that sky. After a while the interstate highway that runs from Denver to Kansas City, I-70, becomes distinctive. We motor on and cross it just west of Colby, Kansas. We keep heading southeast to cross the highway again when it zigs south to Oakley, Kansas, then intercept it for the third time east of Oakley. I tell David to follow it.

This he can do well. Following a highway is much easier than flying a compass course and more fun since you get to look outside most of the time. Finally David gets tired and I take over.

We are not talking much today, just sitting silently watching the Kansas wheat fields and pastures roll by below. I break the silence occasionally to tell him the name of a town or village. My knowledge comes from the sectional chart that I use for navigation. The *Queen's* only navigation instrument is a wet compass: she has no VOR, no ADF, no Loran, no nothing. The gadget masters who spend thousands on the latest gizmo for their aerial pride and joy would have a stroke if they saw the *Queen*.

We will cross the country the same way the barnstormers flew their Jennys—with a map and a compass. We will follow highways, railroad lines, rivers, use the compass to go from one prominent landmark to another. This is the most basic navigation skill and goes by the name of pilotage. Add a watch and the method becomes dead reckoning. Amazingly enough, with nothing but a compass, watch and chart Charles Lindbergh flew from New York to Paris.

Yet pilotage has its limits. You must be able to see the ground and you must correctly identify what you see. At night the level of difficulty increases dramatically since all landmarks except towns and cities are hidden by darkness.

And since the *Queen* also lacks a turn-and-bank indicator, I cannot fly her into a cloud. Anything that obscures the ground or the horizon deprives you of your sense of when the aircraft is level. In the Stearman you are like a bird—your inner ear is your primary attitude reference and your brain is your navigation aid.

At St. Francis we saw a few Stearmans outfitted with all the gadgets and certified for instrument flight. At night. In my opinion a Stearman so equipped is just another airplane, although a funny-looking one. The only thing left to do is add a canopy and voilà! you'll have the world's most inefficient airliner.

But to each his own. If VOR and DME and ILS and Loran instruments make them happy, why not? Airplanes are like women—pick what you like and try to get it away from the guy who has it, then dress it out to the limit of your wallet and taste.

As David follows the interstate eastward, I sit back in the rear cockpit and luxuriate in the warmth and glow of a brilliant summer sky. An open cockpit makes you a part of that sky. You can reach out and grab a handful, sit up straight and let the wind play with the top of your helmet, or put your elbows on the padded edges of the cockpit and ride along in your winged chariot like a modern-day Caesar.

Here above the farms and ranches of the Great Plains, aviation lives up to the promise that inspired dreamers through the ages. Here you are truly separate from the earth, at least for a little while, removed from the cares and concerns that occupy you on the ground. This separation from the earth is more than symbolic, more than a physical removal—it has an emotional dimension as tangible as the wood, fabric and steel that has transported you aloft.

We humans need to belong, to be a part of a family, to have a circle of friends and work that occupies our hands and brains. Yet we also need some means to place our daily concerns and our lives in proper perspective. Flying provides that. Cockpits are our mountaintops, our seats above the clouds where we can see into forever. The machines lift us into a pristine wilderness on journeys that strengthen, refresh and renew.

*   *   *

Hays, Kansas, becomes visible about 15 miles away. We circle the lone runway and land to the north. Taxiing in, the little terminal–FBO office looks different somehow. "We tore the old one down and built a new one," the line boy tells me.

Oh. "Well, I haven't been here in three or four years." Not since the last time I took a Cessna 172 from Denver to Topeka.

This is our first real fuel stop on our aerial odyssey and David wants to pump the gas in. Standing on the back of the seat in the front cockpit, he fills the tank in the center of the upper wing. Like stock Stearmans, the Queen holds 46 gallons of gas and 6.6 gallons of oil. She burns about 12 gallons of gasoline and 1 quart of oil per hour, so her maximum range with a reserve is three hours. Watching David handle the fuel nozzle, I resolve to attempt no leg longer than two and a half hours. Gasoline to an airplane is like air to a diver—when you're out, you've got a major problem.

Two and a half hours at about 80 knots works out to 200 nautical miles in calm air, a great deal less if you are flying directly into a strong prairie wind. But I have no fixed schedule and the entire summer to fly in.

Since I first learned to fly I have wanted to make a long flight, to fly as far and as long as I could stand it, then to eat and sleep and fly again. Just fly, watching the world roll beneath, listening to the engine, watching the clouds drift past and the sun arc westward in the blue sky above.

This is the summer of my long flight. This will be my Stearman summer.

I climb back into the cockpit eager to fly on. We will take off to the south and then turn east to follow the four-lane interstate. At the hold-short line I ease the Queen to a halt and run the engine up to 1,600 RPM. Cycle the prop twice to get hot oil into the prop hub, then check the mags. As usual I get a 125 RPM drop on the right mag and 50 on the left. She has done that since the day I acquired her and Steve Hall, the mechanic, can find nothing wrong. The Queen has an idiosyncrasy. I can live with that. I have several.

Taxi onto the runway and line the Queen up with the center line by putting an equal amount of runway on both sides of the nose. On the ground the Queen sits on her tail wheel with her nose pointed toward heaven, so the pilot cannot see directly forward. In this regard she is exactly like so many of the World War II airplanes that she and her sisters trained tens of thousands of pilots to fly—the B-17, P-40, P-47, P-51, Hellcat, Corsair, Avenger, and so on. When Harold Zipp and Jack Clark of Stearman Aircraft designed this masterpiece in 1933 by modifying Lloyd Stearman's C-1 design, *all* military aircraft had tail wheels.

I smoothly push the throttle and mixture knob forward with my left hand—the mixture knob goes about halfway and the throttle goes all the way to the stop. Today at Hays, 2,000 feet above sea level, the manifold pressure increases to 28 inches and the RPM goes to 2,250. As we go east toward the Mississippi we will come down off the high plains and each field will be lower than the last.

Simultaneously with the power increase, I tweak in some right rudder to counter the torque effect of the swirling air striking the rudder, and push the stick full forward. The tail must come off the ground as soon as possible so I can see where I am going and adjust our course down the runway with rudder.

Today at Hays the tail comes up within 10 seconds. In Boulder it takes about 15. As the tail comes up another rudder adjustment is required to counter the P-factor of the prop arc moving downward. With the tail up the plane is in the proper attitude to fly, running along on just its two main wheels, and I move the stick slowly back toward neutral as the load on the control surfaces changes with increasing airspeed.

Looking forward through the two little glass windshields, around the top of David's head, I can see the entire runway and the center line. I jockey the rudder to hold us straight and today add some right stick into the prevailing crosswind to hold the right wing down.

Airspeed increasing nicely, 40 MPH . . . 50 . . . a glance at the engine gauges while I jockey the rudder . . . 60 . . . 65 and stick back a little to let the elevators bite and the wings take the weight of people, gasoline and airplane, all 3,000 pounds of it, controls constantly moving as necessary to keep the wings level and the nose rising in the unstable air.

She's flying. Stop the nose coming up with forward stick and start giving her some forward trim.

Up we go away from the earth.

Once David asked, "When the tail comes up like that, what keeps the plane from going right on over on its nose?"

"Aerodynamics. As the tail rises above a streamlined position it becomes an airfoil with a downward lift vector, which pulls the tail back down to where it should be."

"Oh," he says, visualizing it and understanding. I think.

The Wright brothers' greatest contribution to heavier-than-air flight was the realization that the machine would be flying in an unstable medium, the atmosphere, so it had to be designed in such a way that the pilot could make the constant adjustments necessary to counter the vagaries of the moving air, adjustments that birds make by altering the position of feathers, thereby changing the curvature and shape of their wings. They grasped the fact that a successful flying machine would have to be an artificial bird. It would have to climb, turn, and descend in unstable air under the absolute control of the person who flew it. No fools these American-Gothic originals, they decided to emulate the birds and achieve control by changing the shape of the machine's wings. We still do that today, although we use ailerons or flaperons instead of wing warping, the Wrights' technique.

The Wrights' insight and solution solved the problem that had baffled and stymied all the experimenters before them, all those crazy dreamers through the ages who had tinkered and tried. It had stymied the Wrights' contemporaries too, who immediately copied or tried to improve on the Wright technique once they grasped its implications.

The technical solution to the problem of controlled flight is more than a history lesson. It has profound implications. Flying an airplane is more complex than operating a boat: you merely steer a boat and occasionally push or pull on the throttle to go faster or slower. To fly an aircraft you must constantly alter the shape of the wings, you must use stick and rudder to climb or descend or turn to counter the swirls and vertical motion of the air; you must judge your height and speed and progress through the air and alter these factors as necessary to return to earth in a controlled manner. To fly an airplane you must truly fly as the birds do, an ironic truth that would have made the ancient dreamers smile.

Thank you, Orville. Thank you, Wilbur, wherever you are.

Flying is a skill, of course, like riding a bicycle, one that can be learned by anyone of modest intelligence and physical gifts who has the ability to take instruction. But when truly mastered and the aircraft becomes a part of you, an extension of your physical abilities, then flying is an art. And by happy coincidence, this mastery of the skill can occur with any airplane—indeed, with any craft that leaves the ground—if the pilot will only work at it long enough and hard enough.

I don't have anywhere near that skill level yet in the *Cannibal Queen*. Maybe by the end of the summer I'll get a taste of it again. I had it once, back in my twenties when I flew A-6 Intruders for Uncle Sam. After a thousand hours or so I could really fly that machine, make it do precisely what I wanted it to do in any flight regime. I could hold altitude like the altimeter needle was glued to the dial, nail an airspeed, bring the plane right to the edge of the stall and hold her there with whatever power setting I chose. I could feather it onto the runway or plant it, as I chose, where I chose, with whatever sink rate I chose. I could *fly* that airplane.

That is the feeling I want again. Flying is the only skill in life that I have ever mastered to that degree of proficiency. Some musicians have that level of skill, as do champion race car drivers, motorcycle riders, golfers, tennis players, and so on. It *can* be acquired if one works hard enough and has a little bit of talent.

Forbes Field in Topeka is a former military base with three or four long, wide runways and a huge parking mat with weeds growing up through the cracks in the concrete. The Kansas Air National Guard flies KC-135 tankers from one end of the field. One was busy making approaches as we taxied in.

It's a long taxi, about halfway across Kansas, so I added power and raised the tail and steered with the rudder. Occasionally the prop whacked off a tall weed.

David and I got a motel room at an establishment on South Topeka Avenue that I often stayed in when I was in the Naval Reserve and commanded a reserve unit here. I like Topeka. Although it's the capital of Kansas, it's really just a small town on the eastern plains. It has lots of neat little houses owned by working Americans and lots of older cars and comfortable, tree-lined streets. There are also a couple of good barbecue places where the prices are very reasonable.

The following morning at 8 A.M. the clouds were low and dark. A thunderstorm loomed to the northwest. And this was the day a professional photographer would take our picture. We had arranged to meet at a small, private grass field to the north of town, so David and I prepared the Stearman for flight and took off. As we flew north over the west side of the city the clouds ahead looked nasty.

"Rain," David announced.

"Terrific."

We go into it at a thousand feet. Visibility drops somewhat but not too much. And we stay relatively dry in the cockpit, which is nicer.

The field is right where the sectional has it spotted, so I drop down for a low pass to look it over. A mudhole with standing water is about 500 feet from the approach end, and there is another at midfield. The taxi areas in front of the one tee-hangar look like quagmires. I make another pass then head southeast for Billard Field.

Billard belongs to the city of Topeka and has a non-federal control tower. It is small in comparison to the faded grandeur of Forbes and has a really neat little terminal that houses the FBO and a restaurant that serves decent coffee and hamburgers, although the person who wrote the menu gave the sandwiches cutesy names like Baron Burger and Cherokee Favorite. We order breakfast in the restaurant and settle in to wait. I suspect the photographer will go out to the grass field and then come here when he discovers we aren't there. And that is what happens.

Luckily the storm bypasses Billard. The photographer, David Zlotky, snaps away. Soon David and I are back in the airplane while Zlotky waits with his camera beside the runway. I plan for a dozen landings unless he waves me in sooner.

The landings are fun. I come in high and slip the plane some, do some wheel landings, some full stall, really work at flying the Queen. Like a fine horse, she responds to every twitch of the controls, absolutely obedient, seemingly trying to please the man with the reins. This quality is what made the Stearman such a fine trainer.

21

If only I were better at it. But I guess if competence came too easily it wouldn't be worth much.

Here we come on base leg, intentionally high and five miles-per-hour fast, carrying a smidgen too much power. Wind off the left side, with maybe five knots crosswind component. On final, still high and fast, I crank in a ton of right rudder and apply left stick. She comes down like a brick in the slip.

Now! Straighten her out, little right rudder for the crosswind, power just so, glide angle okay . . . coming down nicely . . . begin the flare by reducing power and pulling the stick back while the rudder is adjusted and more left aileron is applied. Correct for the burbling air and shifting wind, increase the backstick, watch the nose . . . and she touches down slightly tail first. The mains fall a good six inches. Darn!

I let her slow while working the rudder to hold her straight.

"He wasn't waving," David tells me, so I smoothly advance the throttle and mixture and lift the tail. 50 . . . 60 . . . 65, and we're off to do it again!

I like flying. I like getting up early in the morning and looking out the window at the sky, the feeling of the breeze on my face as I preflight the airplane, the look and smell and feel of the airplane. I like anticipating the flight to come and imagining how it will be. I like thinking about it afterward. I like everything about flying.

The next morning we fly south from Topeka through a sunny sky dotted with scattered puffy clouds. As soon as David takes over the controls he tells me, "The airspeed's a hundred miles an hour."

"We're in an updraft. The aircraft is actually descending in a column of rising air, so it goes faster. We'll be out of it in a bit."

We soon are. Now we enter a downdraft. Our airspeed decays and we start a descent. I tell David to pull back more on the stick. He does and our airspeed falls to 80. A little thermal activity has a big effect on your airspeed when you don't have much to play with.

David tells me from the front cockpit, "This is the only way to travel." This comment draws a wide grin from his old man. The boy feels the magic too.

He is following the highway. And today he is using the rudder to keep the plane in balanced flight. We talked about it last night and today he is working at it. I sit in the back cockpit studying the sectional. Hmm, Yates Center has a grass field southwest of town.

"You wanta land at a grass field?" I ask my chauffeur.

"Sure." He is agreeable to most of my suggestions, so I try to reciprocate by being agreeable when he advances his. We get along very well, I think, for father and teenage son.

He has no brothers but he has two teenage sisters, both older. Lara is eighteen and Rachael nineteen. They include him in most of their activities, so in many ways David seems older than he is. He knows what's cool and what isn't—he avoids what isn't like a Pentecostal avoiding sin.

Lara paid him the ultimate compliment one day in my presence while talking to a boy her own age who wanted to take her somewhere. Lara wanted David to go along. I didn't hear what her male friend said to that, but I heard Lara's reply: "My brother is the coolest guy I know."

I have high hopes that the three of them will remain close friends all their lives. I won't have a say, of course, but like all parents I have hopes. And like all parents I worry about each of them too much. They will grow up and do just fine as they find their own way in life. I know this and fret anyway.

I am still musing along these lines when Yates Center looms into view. The grass airport is easy to spot—the grass appears short and there is an ag sprayer parked at one end. No hangars or other buildings though.

I make a pass over the field and study the wind sock. Now a left downwind and power back, airspeed at 80. We touch down in as nice a landing as I have made in a while and taxi to the end of the field, up a gentle incline, to where the ag plane is parked.

The ag pilot is pumping chemicals into his plane from two big tanks mounted on a trailer. We get acquainted and study the wind sock. The wind is out of the southwest, about eight knots. "We've been waiting to see if this wind is gonna hold," he tells me. "Been trying to spray the weeds in this pasture west of here for two days."

After a bit he decides to give it a try. He climbs up into the

Cessna Ag Truck and straps in. The engine comes to life with a rumble and he taxis away without preliminaries, his prop blast raising a cloud of clippings from the fairway-short grass.

In a few moments the Ag Truck comes over the swell in the runway at full throttle climbing gently. He's got a load on that plane. He levels at 50 feet or so above the ground and lays the plane into a right turn, then levels the wings heading west. He is soon out of sight.

I sit on a rail and talk to the pilot's son, a boy of sixteen or seventeen. "Nice plane you got there," he says, nodding at the *Queen.* In a moment he continues, "We got a plane, an Aeronca. Rebuilt her last year. Painted her three colors." He looks me in the eye and grins shyly. "That's hard to do, you know, putting on three colors. We had a heck of a time getting it right. But she looks real good now."

The sun on my back is very pleasant, as is the smell of cut grass carried on the warm Kansas breeze under this blue June sky. I sit soaking it in as the young man tells us of his Aeronca and how she flies. The wind sock is steady. The smoke from my pipe rides away upon it.

Sitting in the grass, caressed by the sun and wind, the *Queen* patiently waits. The sun gleams on her polished prop.

It is difficult for us today to imagine the excitement that our grandparents and great-grandparents felt the first time they saw an airplane fly, actually saw the miracle performed.

That this insubstantial stuff we call air would actually support the weight of a heavy machine—well, the thing defied reason.

You read about the flights and the daredevil flyers in the newspapers and magazines, but when your chance came to see the miracle with your own eyes, it was probably at a field much like this—a pasture on the edge of town. And the plane was much like the *Queen,* an open-cockpit affair with two wooden wings and canvas stretched taut. If you were lucky you got a chance to touch it, which didn't strengthen your faith. Canvas? Stretched over a framework of wooden ribs?

And then it happened. For every person there was that moment when the wheels of the double-decked canvas contraption lifted out of the grass. The spokes spun slower and slower as the machine continued to accelerate and climb.

It flies—my God, it flies! And I have lived to see it!

I have never tired of it. Airplanes taking off have fascinated me ever since I can remember.

With David in the front cockpit and me in the rear, the *Cannibal Queen* performs the miracle yet again. She lifts her wheels from the grass and soars on the prairie wind.

We eat lunch at the Coffeyville, Kansas, airport, also an ex-military airfield. Next to the FBO is a short-order lunch counter that has a table full of back issues of *Sport Aviation*, the Experimental Aviation Association's publication. I peruse an issue from 1972 while we eat hamburgers.

This issue has a story about a fellow who flew a home-built single-seat aerobatic plane to all of the lower-48 states to promote the EAA. A map depicts his route, which is filled with right angles. It looks as if he hit most states on the corners. What would be the fun in that? The article doesn't say much about fun. Maybe that's implicit.

Perhaps I should hit every state. It would give my publisher something to put in the press kit they send the reviewers and it would give the reviewers something to write about. As it is the book reviewers may merely dismiss my scribbles as "How I Spent My Summer Vacation," by Stephen Coonts, who is old enough to know better but obviously doesn't.

I started in Colorado and now I'm in Kansas. Only 46 states to go.

I look at the nifty pictures in the magazine as I mull over the idea. This guy flew his home-built around the country in 1972, when the Vietnam War was in full swing. I spent seven months that year flying A-6s in combat. That December Rachael had her first birthday, but I missed it. I was on Yankee Station, the same place I had been when she was born.

The hamburger is good. As for the route, I'll have to think about it. If I manage to land in all of the contiguous 48 states, I could brag about this summer for the rest of my life.

Only one other plane, a Cessna, takes off in the hour we spend on the ground. The big empty airfield with its dilapidated hangars and cracked asphalt is all ours when we taxi out and give the *Queen* full throttle.

25

3

S KID HENLEY IS A TALL, LEAN MAN WITH A LITTLE WHITE MUS-
tache on his upper lip. His face is tan and weathered, as befits
a man who has spent his life flying airplanes. He admits to
seventy-seven years of age and 15,000 hours in the cockpits of
Stearmans. I goggle.

David and I landed in McAlester, Oklahoma, after flying
down from Coffeyville. Now we are standing on the ramp at
the airport looking at the *Cannibal Queen*. Skid Henley restored
her. He started in the fall of 1987 and finished a year later.
"Did two of them, one right after the other. They're a little
different. Yours has the headliner behind the rear cockpit."

"Why'd you do that?" I ask. The headliner was not stock.
In fact, mine is the only Stearman I have ever seen with a
headliner.

"Well, I'll tell you." He grins and walks over to the plane.
"See these wing leading edges? They're one-piece metal. I
bought five of them 'cause I usually mess one up. But I didn't
this time. Had one left over and was looking at the plane and
thought why not? So I turned it down some and spread it a
little and fixed it on top of the fuselage behind the rear cockpit.
Looks pretty good, I think. Of course, then I had to alter the

door to the baggage compartment. Sawed it in half and moved the hinge to accommodate the headliner."

He spoke quickly, the words and thoughts tumbling out. "This plane was a PT-27, made for the Canadians. When I first saw it, it was trashed out, no engine, wings two feet longer than they are now. The tail was torn off in a tornado or something, and Frank Dear got it and worked on one wing, but it was too big a project. He sold it to me, then I sold it to an engine shop. They let it sit for three years; then Frank Dear got it again. Then my boy Robert decided he had to have a biplane, and he called Frank and made a deal and it ended up over in my workshop.

"Got the engine up in Indianapolis. It was off an AT-10—they weren't much of an airplane—and the ring cowl was with it, right off an AT-10. Went up to Indianapolis and brought it down on a pickup truck."

Finally I steered Mr. Henley to his life in aviation. "First airplane I ever saw to get to know was a Heath Parasol. Then I got to flying a Gypsy Moth. Finally a fellow signed me off for solo in it even though I'd been flying it without papers since I was fourteen. Got my license as an airplane mechanic after I had an eye injury, but my eye finally healed up and it's the best one I got now."

He went on, detailing an aviation career that included ten years as an airline pilot, test pilot flying SBD Dauntless dive bombers for Douglas Aircraft, civilian flight instructor for the U.S. Army Air Corps during World War II, and after that, owner of an agricultural applicator service headquartered in Alice, Texas, that operated Stearmans from New Brunswick to Nicaragua. He even flew rice in the Philippines.

"Only time I ever crashed a Stearman was on the side of a volcano in Nicaragua. Had a 450 Pratt in it [that's the 450-horsepower Pratt & Whitney R-985 engine], and I slowed that thing until she was hanging on the prop and mushing down onto a grove of trees. Had to put her there because just beyond the trees the side of the volcano went straight up. Just mushed her down and pulled the mixture off right before I hit. That Stearman is still up in those trees on the side of that volcano.

"But a Stearman will take anything. Boeing tested an airframe to seventeen Gs without any deformation. If you hit the ground

27

at anything less than thirty degrees of dive, you'll walk away. Guaranteed."

The sky was clearing as Mr. Henley talked and occasional shafts of sunlight made the yellow Stearman glow. Beyond it on the east side of the airport rose a low wooded ridge. McAlester lies on the edge of the eastern Oklahoma hill country. Mr. Henley saw me looking at the tree-covered ridge, the first relief from flat country I'd seen since leaving Colorado. "Sprayed all over that country east of here. Know it pretty well. Nowadays this southeast corner of Oklahoma produces more marijuana than anyplace else in the world."

I nod, somehow saddened. Mr. Henley changes the subject. I ask him if he wants to go for a ride in the *Queen*, but he declines. He tells me that he has no medical certificate, which is really no excuse since I am a licensed pilot, but I know he has had medical problems the last few years and accept his excuse without protest, though not without regret. I would have really liked to sit in the front seat and let the pro show me how it should be done from the captain's chair back aft. But he probably knew that.

Finally it is time to go. We shake hands and say good-bye in the terminal as I pay for my gas. David and I man up and taxi out without an audience. I know Mr. Henley is still in the terminal, perhaps watching through the window, so as we lift off I wave at the terminal with my left hand.

As we climb out to the north I finger the lump of the wallet that contains my Second Class medical certificate. Hell, Skid Henley is only 33 years older than I am. He rejuvenated the *Queen*—made her better than new. Why can't they do that to a man?

We spend the night at the Fountainhead Lodge on Lake Eufala, thirty or so nautical miles north of McAlester. We had passed it on the way south and noted that the parking lots were relatively empty. The lodge has a spiffy asphalt runway and tie-down mat on the hill above it. We tie down the plane and use the phone mounted on a post to call the lodge. They send a car.

The young woman at the desk speaks with a crisp British

accent. I wonder how in the world she ended up at the reception desk of a lodge on Lake Eufala in the Indian Nations. Probably married a Yank. Or perhaps she's an adventurer working her way around the world and it has taken her three years to get this far. That would be a very British thing to do. I don't ask. She probably gets asked that question ten times a day. I like to think she is an original adventurer.

Dave and I don swimming suits and head for the pool with me lugging the laptop computer along. After five minutes I am ready to get out and type, but he wants me to "play." I linger in the water for a few more minutes, then get out and turn on the computer. After five minutes he comes over to the edge. "See the fountain? The water comes out of it through two outlets. I'll plug up one and you plug up the other and we'll see if we can make it overflow."

How would Hemingway have handled this? Steinbeck? Tom Clancy? Unfortunately I refuse, then watch him try to raise the water level by using his forearm to plug just one outlet. An hour later I wish I had accepted the invitation.

The next morning as we taxi out I tell David to follow me through on the controls as we take off. I talk him through the takeoff, explaining what I am doing as I do it. When I get the plane level at 2,000 feet I turn it over to him. We are heading 120 degrees magnetic, a course that will take us right across the Ouachita Mountains, the rugged southeast corner of Oklahoma that Skid Henley said produces a lot of marijuana. With David flying I scan the hills and ravines below, trying to spot a pot field amid the trees and brush. No luck. As if I would know one if I saw it.

David sees the ridges coming at us and we consult. Under my direction he pushes the prop lever to full increase RPM, then adds throttle. When we reach 3,000 feet we level off. As he readjusts the controls and trim, we creep up another 200 feet. I let him fly. The heading wanders as much as twenty degrees. The wet compass swings backward, as all wet compasses do, but in the Stearman it's the only directional indicator we have. Until one gets accustomed to it, it is disorienting to see that the course one wants lies to the right on the instrument, but one must turn left to get to it. David does fine for a neophyte.

29

Puffy little cumulus clouds float a hundred feet above us. The visibility is excellent, maybe 12 or 15 miles, and the sun is quite pleasant. The saturated air is relatively smooth this morning.

After 45 minutes or so David tires of flying and turns the stick over to me. We are just about out of the mountains, yet the clouds are increasing. The bases seem a little lower so I slowly descend to 2,500 feet. Since we flew for a half hour the day before and could not get gas at the lodge airport, I decide to land at Mena, Arkansas, which our route will take us directly over.

Par for the course, no one answers on Unicom, 122.8 for this airport. After three tries I give up. The attendant is probably out fueling an airplane, or in the restroom, or whatever. Unicom isn't a tower, and I like that.

The haze is getting thicker and now the clouds above us cover about fifty percent of the sky. When the airport comes into view at about eight miles, I swing around to come across the runway. David and I search for the wind sock without success.

"The wind should be out of the south," I tell him, and make a left downwind turn for runway 18. I have Dave put his hands and feet on the controls and talk him through the landing. I misjudge the flare and fall the last twelve or eighteen inches. An arrival. Ah me . . .

Taxiing in we finally find the wind sock, a faded little rag hanging limp from the airport beacon tower. We pull up in front of the Fixed Base Operator who sports a Phillips 66 sign. Parked south of the building is a C-130 Hercules with an engine missing. The fuselage looks to be in good shape.

After fueling I make an intersection takeoff, level at 2,500 feet, and turn the controls over to David. He flies for five minutes, then says, "You take it."

"You feeling alright?" I ask.

"Yeah. Just sleepy."

And he wedges his helmeted head into the right rear corner of the cockpit and falls asleep as the plane jounces and bounces in light chop. Amazing! This may be a first—the first guy to fall asleep in a Stearman!

For the first time this trip I have no one to talk to. I turn off the intercom so as not to disturb him and concentrate on the flying. We are over southern Arkansas crossing a section of low

30

hills, wild, rugged terrain with few roads and no houses or farms that I can readily see. One forgets that there are still places like this in the United States. In the future as the nation urbanizes, the marginal farms will probably go to the counties for unpaid taxes and most of them will be reclaimed by nature. In West Virginia such places are often acquired for pennies by investors and eventually sold to major corporations, which are content to pay the pitifully low property taxes and use the land as tree farms. So the rural counties lose population and get ever poorer in a vicious cycle of budget cutting and decline.

We are making 93 MPH on the airspeed indicator, but I am running 2,050 RPM and 22 inches of manifold pressure to get it. The thicker the air, the more power it takes to fly through it.

Or is this an engine problem? I must consider that possibility. Is the engine making its usual power? Once again I scan the oil temp, oil pressure and cylinder head temp gauges, the only engine gauges I have. By nature I fret, a personality quirk that my military flight instructors honed and polished into a personality defect. Flying is composed of a myriad of small details; those people who seem to do best at it pay strict attention to each and every one of them.

I listen carefully to the beat of the engine.

I have not been paying a lot of attention to navigation, and now I get the payback. With the clouds looming higher and the air so saturated that there is a rainbow around the sun—when I can see it—I start looking for the town of Gurdon, Arkansas. We hit the reservoir a while back right on the money and the town should be coming up any time. I expect to see Interstate 30, which crosses from southwest to northeast at a 90-degree angle to my course, which is still 120.

The minutes tick by. No town. I know we have a headwind from the south, but how much?

Heck, I should have timed the leg. I search the sectional chart for another landmark. Nothing looks obvious. I look below. Featureless flat, wooded country, little wandering roads and occasional houses. Maybe I've overflown it.

How do you miss a four-lane interstate highway from less than a half mile above it?

Well, maybe you were busy listening to the engine.

I should have timed the leg. Dang! I remember the time Billy

31

Wagner and I didn't time the legs on our first night low-level strike over North Vietnam in an A-6 Intruder and got lost. Bill couldn't recognize the turn points on radar so we motored around over the Red River delta at 420 knots, 400 feet above the mud and water with a load of bombs. We almost hit a hill. We spent 45 minutes over the beach that night and never did find the target.

And I have just repeated that little mistake. Where in hell is that damn interstate?

Visibility less than eight miles, I guess. Clouds are pretty solid above. No more sunlight and shadow.

David rearranges his head against the left side of the cockpit and goes back to sleep.

How many minutes has it been? Well, maybe I've overflown it. I must have. So what is the next checkpoint? El Dorado. More relatively flat, featureless terrain between Gurdon and El Dorado, but there's a road from Gurdon down that way.

So if I've overflown Gurdon, where is this little highway going southeast to Camden and El Dorado? I crane my head right and left, scanning the ground below. Maybe I've drifted off course and the highway is too far left or right to be seen in this haze. That's certainly possible.

Just when I decide that I have overflown the interstate and Gurdon and am slightly lost, the four-lane highway looms into view. How did Ernest Gann say it in *Fate Is the Hunter*? "Here a fool found salvation."

Okay, where's the town? Is it right or left? Let's see, the airport is northeast of the town, the runway oriented east and west. . . . Heck, there it is at 11:30, right where it should be. Visibility five or six miles. I carefully check my watch and swing to the new heading, 150. This should take me to Camden or thereabouts; then I'll just truck down the four-lane to El Dorado.

And it works out that way. Why in the world was I sweating finding Gurdon? After all, who could miss an interstate highway from 2,000 feet over it?

I decide to land at the downtown airport at El Dorado, so I tune in the Unicom frequency and give them a call.

Nothing.

I try El Dorado Radio on 123.6. Still nothing. Maybe the radio's broken.

What the heck, Dave's still asleep; we've still got half a tank of gas; Monroe, Louisiana, is only 50 miles away. New course 135. Onward. Through the goo. Visibility is getting worse, but it's still way above legal minimums and Monroe approach can give me a steer if necessary. If the radio really works. Better find out.

The Monroe Automatic Terminal Information Service (ATIS) broadcast is garbled at first but it clears as I fly along. I get the altimeter setting and wind, 210 at five knots. I can hack it. Onward.

Monroe Approach is also garbled. They answer me but I can't understand them—too low and too far out. I tell them I will call back when I'm closer.

I fly on with David still asleep. Maybe he's sick. Never heard of a kid sleeping like that in an open cockpit.

Heading 135. That's the heading on the chart for the Victor airway from El Dorado to Monroe, so literally tens of thousands of people have successfully reached Monroe, Louisiana, from El Dorado, Arkansas, by flying that course. I will be the first that fails to do so. The weather is really getting gooey and this big lake or reservoir—Bayou D'Arbonne—remains hidden from my sight. I finally get Approach and they give me a discrete IFF squawk and cheerfully tell me to report the field in sight. Roger that.

Where is that dang lake? We're talking square miles here, folks, not acres. This thing is too big to miss. The problem is that I am used to flying out west, where the visibility is 90 miles plus. You can see things in Colorado. And I am used to flying a Cessna T-210 cross-country at a ground speed of three nautical miles per minute. I am making less than half that. Ninety-three statute miles per hour indicated is about 82 knots—nautical miles per hour—a little more when converted to true airspeed, so I am covering just a smidgen more than one and a quarter nautical miles every minute. I need to learn patience, which God knows was never my long suit. I will hop from foot to foot at the Pearly Gate waiting for St. Peter to check the list.

I could ask Approach for a steer.

Naw. I'll wait. More minutes tick by.

I fidget in the cockpit and listen to Approach talk to an airliner climbing out of Monroe. Some severe weather to the south of town, he says.

There! Way over on the right, isn't that water? Yep. Well, I'm way left of course. I alter heading twenty degrees right.

How did I get this far left? Wind?

We fly for a while and the lake becomes distinct in the haze. Near the south end I come back to a course of 135. I watch the clock. Seven minutes later Approach informs me that the field is at my 12 o'clock and ten miles. I ease the nose left and peer into the murk. Nothing.

Keep flying. David stirs, then sags back. Boy, that kid can sleep.

Now Approach gives me a vector, 090 for traffic.

The sensation is like flying in an inverted bowl. Only a circle of land and brown water is visible below me, and the airport and town are not within the circle.

New vector 080. Two more minutes pass. I am watching the clock carefully now.

"Stearman Seven Zero Zero, come right to One Eight Zero." I swing the plane. "The airport is at your twelve o'clock, four miles."

I look. Nothing. Is the visibility really this bad? Maybe . . . yes, that's the end of a runway. Okay, there it is. "Got it in sight," I announce on the radio. Visibility is down to about 3 miles.

"Squawk VFR and contact the tower," the controller tells me.

As I drift down toward runway 18, David wakes up and sits erect in the cockpit. I flip on the intercom. "We're here."

"Umm."

A large black cloud sits just southeast of the field. That is a thunderstorm if I've ever seen one. The runway and mat are wet as we taxi in and shut down.

Later I look at the chart and try to figure out why I had so much trouble finding Bayou D'Arbonne. Ah ha, the airway goes almost over the El Dorado downtown airport and I turned to the 135 heading when I was three or four miles to the northeast. So I was flying parallel to the airway but offset to the left, the north, in poor visibility. If the visibility had been just a little worse I would have completely missed seeing D'Arbonne.

I am learning. I tell myself it's just a matter of shifting gears, getting used to 82 knots and all this haze. And timing the legs.

Oh well, it's an adventure. And that's why I came.

4

THURSDAY MORNING AT THE HOLIDAY INN IN WEST MONROE, Louisiana, I stand looking at thick fog. Just to the southwest of the motel is a television tower that the chart says is 518 feet tall. The top is obscured. When I went to the restaurant at seven it was thicker than it is now, at 8:30 A.M., so the fog is slowly lifting. That is cheering.

David folded last night at 9 P.M. and is still sleeping eleven and a half hours later. The night before at Fountainhead Lodge in Oklahoma he watched *Dances With Wolves* until 9:30, then sat and watched me write until 11. Then he read what I had written and went cheerfully to bed at 11:30.

With the lights out the fun began. He crept from the bed and jumped me. Tickle, tickle, tickle. The horseplay subsided at midnight, but I got him up at 7. Even with his naps in the Stearman, he crashed last night at 9 after watching a half-hour television special and indulging in a short tickle session.

I have this sneaking suspicion that he isn't really as ticklish as he wants me to believe. His feet aren't ticklish at all. He doesn't even wiggle when you work on the soles of his feet with a finger; never has.

He is fourteen years old, five feet six and a half inches tall,

120 pounds. He shaves now about once a week. Very mature in many ways, but he still likes to roughhouse. He is a natural gentleman, always considerate of others, and has an inquiring mind. I suspect that he is the smartest person in the family. I know he is brighter than I am.

He grins a lot, unashamedly displaying his braces and their green rubber bands. I asked him, Why green? Because the last ones were black and he felt like a different color.

When he wakes up I will phone Flight Service and get a weather brief. I suspect this fog won't lift enough to be flyable until noon at the earliest. So we are in no hurry. Last night we decided to fly down to New Orleans today and spend at least a full day sightseeing—maybe ride a riverboat on the Mississippi and wander around in the French Quarter, America's tackiest tourist trap.

The quirk in the American psyche that draws people to places like the French Quarter also makes them pull off I-70 in Oakley, Kansas, and pay real money to see the world's largest prairie dog and a cow with five legs. Not that I have yet visited the hottest tourist draw in Oakley, Kansas, but I'll admit, I am curious. I have never seen a 250-pound prairie dog and the sight just might be worth five dollars.

David is waking up now. He looks around, then burrows back under the covers. Now he is examining the sheet situation. His lower one got pulled down and wadded up. He gives up. He flops back and closes his eyes. Another half hour of morning snoozing seems to be in the works. Nope, his eyes are open. He has just logged twelve straight hours of Zs.

I go outside and check the TV tower. The clouds are just above the top of it. Here and there patches of blue are visible. In a little while we can fly.

It is just 11:10 A.M. on my watch when I add power and push the stick forward to lift the tail. The field elevation here at Monroe, Louisiana, is only 79 feet above sea level but I am still surprised when the manifold pressure needle steadies at 29 inches. We are only losing one inch of pressure in the manifold system, which strikes me as excellent for a normally aspirated engine. That thought is worth a smile, and one spreads across my face.

The plane accelerates well with the tail up and I pull her off and let her climb at 80 MPH, which is still a nice angle in this thick air. I level at 1,000 feet and turn to the southeast.

The bases of the broken clouds are another thousand or so feet above and the visibility is about a dozen miles. The low flat country spreads away in all directions.

When Monroe Departure turns us loose, I climb to 1,500 feet and flip on the intercom. David has his head resting on the right side of the cockpit. "Sleeping already?"

"Playing a game." He brought his Nintendo Game Boy along on this trip. What did I do to entertain myself at age fourteen, back in the dark ages before electronic games?

I address myself to the chore of holding 135 degrees on the wet compass. It flops around as usual and I remind myself it rotates backward. The airspeed is more or less steady at 95 indicated.

Today I annotate the chart with the time as we pass prominent villages and road intersections. Back to basics. There will be no repeat of yesterday.

After 40 minutes of flying we strike the Mississippi River between Chamblee and Waterproof. I carefully annotate the chart and mark the time, 11:50.

I turn the flying over to David and tell him to keep us over the river heading south. "Where are all the boats and barges?" he asks.

"We'll see some."

In less than a minute we do, a group of fifteen barges pushed by one tug heading upriver. And another barge-tug combination a half mile behind the first.

David peers out one side of the cockpit, then the other. Ahead of us dark clouds are building. The forecast was for thunderstorms after one o'clock. They're early. Low, flat, wet terrain in every direction, a varying mixture of mud and water that would be tempting fate to try an emergency landing on. I survey the levees. Maybe on a levee if the engine quits.

The town of Natchez, Mississippi, comes into view ahead. I search off to the left for the airport and find it. We swing over the northern edge of town and I tell David to follow the four-lane going east. We had planned to go 30 miles east following this highway to a little grass field called Dixie, but now the

37

clouds ahead loom a dark gray, almost black. It still looks pretty good to the south, down the river toward Baton Rouge.

"I think we better land here at Natchez and get some gas. Look at those clouds."

A woman answers our call on Unicom. I fly a left downwind and land on runway 18. We have been airborne only 1.2 hours, but when the weather gets crummy a fellow can't have too much gas.

Three black men help us fuel the *Queen*: a heavyset man in his late fifties, a young man in his twenties, and a teenage boy. The young man laughs when he sees the artwork on the right side of the plane. "Come look at this," he tells the older man. "She's all right," he assures me with a broad grin.

"Snack bar upstairs," the older man informs me after a look at David, the bottomless pit. He had breakfast just two and a half hours ago, but he is indeed hungry again. The snack bar is a short-order grill manned by a large black woman with a friendly smile. The odor of grease is heavy in the air. David orders a hamburger and fries and gets a coke from the pop machine.

She cooks it to his order. No McDonald's, this. Pickles, onion and mustard on a big juicy burger. I watch him eat it with a touch of envy. All burgers were like this when I was a young-ster. I didn't see my first McDonald's until I was twenty years old, but I refrain from making this remark to David. He would just shake his head and mutter "old geezer" with a grin to take the sting off.

On the way back to the airplane he looks at the grass. "Not the same as Colorado," he announces.

"Too much rain and heat."

The black cloud is still obscuring the sky to the southeast, so we plan to fly south around it, down toward Baton Rouge. As we clear Natchez I see the highway leading south and point it out to David. With the plane cruising at 1,500 feet he takes over the flying and moves the plane to the left so as to keep the highway readily in sight without craning his neck. He is fighting to hold the nose down to keep from climbing. "A hun-dred miles an hour," he tells me.

"We're in an updraft."

We cross the Homochitto River at 1:12. Our indicated airspeed is down to 85 and he is losing altitude. We're in a downdraft now. I help him put in more back stick. Airspeed drops off to 80. Then we are out of it and the airspeed increases as the nose comes down. The storm is now off our left wing, forward and aft as far as I can see, and the way ahead is getting darker. Uh oh!

As we pass the Netterville Airport by Wilkinson, Mississippi, I can see a gap to the southeast in the rapidly developing wall of black cloud. "Head for the gap," I tell David, and point. He comes thirty degrees left and settles on a course of about 120.

By the time we reach Centreville twelve minutes later we are firmly in a cloud canyon, with black storms to the left and right, areas of lightness ahead and behind. I have David steer thirty degrees right, aiming for the lightest area in the sky. We cross Clinton, Louisiana, at 41 after the hour, 46 minutes after takeoff from Natchez.

The sky is lighter ahead. But only for a moment. We enter a hole. I can look up and see blue sky.

After a glance I give that up as a waste of time. Black clouds behind us to the north, to the southeast, and directly west. The only relatively clear area is to the southwest, toward Baton Rouge. And they have an airport radar service area.

I take over the flying and put the airplane in a circle. Jackson, Louisiana, is the nearest airport, but it is right under that boomer to the west. We could go back to Natchez, but the object of today's journey was to arrive sooner or later in New Orleans.

I swing the plane toward the west and the road that leads from Clinton to Baton Rouge. When I am near it, I swing to parallel and call Baton Rouge Approach.

I am too far out and too low.

We motor inbound awhile. Gray clouds ahead, undoubtedly with water in them. I descend to 1,000 feet, plenty high enough in this pancake-flat country. Now Approach assigns me a discrete IFF squawk and acquires me on their radar. I have no more than rogered them when we fly into a rain shower, which pours on the windscreens and across the wing surfaces. Thanks to some miracle or Lloyd Stearman's genius, the cockpits remain dry. We fly on, keeping the ground firmly in sight.

In less than a minute we are through the shower and entering another bright area. The Baton Rouge airport is visible from eight miles away against a backdrop of black cloud. We enter a left downwind for runway 4 and I make like a master flaring in a huge two-knot crosswind.

Inside the FBO office a corporate pilot is sitting in front of the television displaying the National Oceanic & Atmospheric Administration's weather broadcast. I note with professional interest that he is reading a technothriller and settle in to study the radar picture. Yuck! Level-one rain showers surround Baton Rouge, which is in the only hole for 50 miles. Some level-two and level-three activity down toward New Orleans, but New Orleans itself looks to be free of precipitation. I get David into the room and show him the chart.

Wanting to teach him to think in aviation terms, I ask, "What do you think we should do?"

He fires it right back. "What do you want to do?" Okay, Pop. You're the pilot!

On our way back to the ramp to tie down the *Cannibal Queen*, we pass the corporate pilot whose reading we disturbed. He is talking to two compatriots. "The thing that scares me," he says, "and I have read this in three separate places so it's probably true, is that the Russians have got this thing that drills a hole in . . ."

I go through the door and miss the rest of it. Today Boris Yeltsin is getting elected president of the Russian Republic and he wants to emasculate the Communist-controlled central government. Gorbachev would probably be amazed to hear that some Americans are still worried about the evil empire.

With the *Queen* tied down and the controls locked, we rent a car for the remainder of our journey to New Orleans. I've parked planes before when the weather got too bad, and a lot farther away from my destination. This is part of flying light airplanes and, I tell myself smugly, one reason I am still alive and kicking.

Ten miles out of Baton Rouge the deluge begins. "Glad we aren't flying."

David agrees with this sentiment.

"You sleepy?" I ask him.

"Naw," he says, then a minute later reclines his seat and goes promptly to sleep.

The downpour continues for an hour, until we are only fifteen miles west of New Orleans. David sleeps soundly through the whole thing.

After checking into the hotel right on Bourbon Street in the heart of the French Quarter, father and son set forth to see the sights. There are a lot more T-shirt emporiums than I remember from my visit four years ago, but about the same number of sex shows. The only businesses that are disappearing are the bars with live jazz bands. I only see two left. Pete Fountain's place is gone and so is Al Hirt's. Preservation Hall looks even filthier and more forlorn than it did in '87.

My first visit here was in 1968 when a bunch of guys and I drove over one Saturday from Pensacola, Florida. Somewhere at home I still have a black-and-white photo one of the guys took of me standing by a light pole on Bourbon Street the summer I turned twenty-two. The place had more mystique for me then. Now it strikes me as just plain tacky—the inscription on one of the T-shirts for sale to the boobs from Colorado and all points east and west captures the raw essence of Bourbon Street today: "Just suck it."

Maybe the place was tacky back in 1968 but I was too green to see it.

David is not interested in the square in front of the Louisiana Historical Museum or the statue of Andrew Jackson and he doesn't even glance at the paintings the artists have hanging on the wrought-iron fence. We climb the levee, sit in silent contemplation of the vast river for 30 or 40 seconds—the maximum period a fourteen-year-old can remain in one place motionless without the sword of school authority hanging over his neck—then walk westward down the levee to the paddleboat *Natchez*. A few moments later we are the proud possessors of two tickets for the seven o'clock dinner cruise.

"You want to lose these, or shall I?" I ask David, holding out the tickets.

"You do it," he says, grinning.

We walk around for an hour and ruin our dinner with ice cream cones. Going aboard at 6:15, we find dinner is served cafeteria-style and has already begun. We join the line and both choose the chicken instead of the fish. It is okay.

41

When the boat casts off we are standing back aft watching the giant paddlewheel flail the water and the sailor untying the ropes holding the stern to the pier. As he flakes down the ropes on the deck I explain to my son that the trick is to make the ropes uncoil without knotting or kinking. He nods silently. Through the years he has become resigned to the fact that his father is full of odd, worthless bits of information that will be bestowed upon his gratis for little or no reason.

The ship's whistle roars loudly—steam—and the wheel churns the water. We go to the bow and breathe deeply of the smell of the river and the sea carried by the breeze.

Coming back upriver an hour later David asks for something to toss into the paddlewheel. I give him a paper pipe filter. He throws it. Then he spits. "Wouldn't it be nifty to drop a water balloon and see it break on the paddle?"

I agree that that would indeed be nifty. Water balloons fascinate him. He was disappointed that we were assigned a second-floor room in our hotel: water balloons have to fall a lot farther than that to be worth the trouble.

We pass alongside the minesweeper fleet moored at Navy Supply Center New Orleans. I explain that the little ships are made of wood so that they won't influence magnetic mines. We are deep into a discussion of the technology of mines as we pass by the ships. People are visible on the bridges. I can see an Officer of the Deck in whites greeting sailors in civilian clothes coming back from liberty. It would really be fun to spend a few years on a little ship like one of these minesweepers, everyone knowing everyone, sailing here and there, charging ashore on liberty. I was a naval aviator and the smallest ship I served aboard was USS *Enterprise*—just me and the captain and five thousand other guys. Okay, maybe I envy the little-ship sailors.

Walking back to the hotel after dark we find the streets full of people drinking beer from plastic cups. This still looks like the Bourbon Street crowd I remember from my youth—families on vacation, young couples glued to each other, teenagers out for a toot and an occasional knot of sailors in civilian clothes—but something is different. On the corner of Bourbon and St. Peter it hits me. The sound has changed.

Twenty years ago the background beat was jazz. Now it is

rock music. Today the place has the look and feel and sound of North Beach in San Francisco.

David examines the window displays of the sexual paraphernalia shops and the transvestite show. He peers around the door touts of the girlie clubs for a glimpse of the naked females cavorting within. "Let's go to see one of these shows," he pleads after scrutinizing the eight-by-ten publicity photos posted outside a club with the proud name of The Orgy.

I shake my head.

"You ever been in one of these places?"

"Yeah. A time or two."

"Well, let's go."

"No."

"Why not?"

"You're not old enough."

"How old do I have to be?"

"Older."

5

WE LEAVE BATON ROUGE ON A TYPICALLY HAZY SUMMER MORN-
ing by climbing to 1,000 feet and flying eastward above the
interstate. Those highway engineers did all the surveying years
ago, so why reinvent the wheel?

The drone of the Lycoming is a pleasant accompaniment for
singing or dreaming or contemplating the vicissitudes of life.
It's also a good background for flying.

I am flying up a storm when I spot a Cessna 152 at my 7
o'clock, at my altitude and also using the interstate to navigate
eastward. Before long the Cessna pulls even about a hundred
yards to my left. I wave wildly. The pair in the Cessna's cockpit
ignore me, if they see me at all. And they pull steadily away.

The ignominy of it! Passed by a Spam can!

I slump lower in my seat and scan the gauges listlessly. Ah
me. To find a flying machine slower than this one would be
difficult today. Most slower machines have been enshrined in
museums or left in weed patches to rust into oblivion. Occasionally some charitable soul hauled one of the rotted wrecks
to the junkyard and put it out of its misery in a smelter. But
most planes just surrendered atom by atom amid the weeds
where fate had abandoned them.

The reason is economics. Keeping an aircraft airworthy is an expensive undertaking, as Orville and Wilbur quickly learned. Technical progress in aviation has been driven by the demand for quicker, more fuel-efficient machines, ones able to carry a greater payload at less cost. Obsolete aircraft that could no longer pay their way were usually abandoned without ceremony.

And this Stearman, *Cannibal Queen*, is obsolete, by any measure. The ubiquitous Cessna 152 also holds two people, but it is faster, uses less fuel, and is much cheaper to maintain. It lacks the vices inherent in the tail-wheel configuration and so is easier for primary flight students to master. And it lacks a soul.

The Queen has one.

I'm sure of it.

Test pilot Chuck Yeager once noted laconically, "An airplane is an airplane," but Lordy, I hope there's more to a great machine than that. Don't the sweat, blood and tears of its creators count for anything? When steel and wood and aluminum become works of art, doesn't that matter? What about all the men and women who strapped themselves into the cockpit and there tried to master the secrets of flight, to fulfill this species' deepest yearnings? Surely all those hopes and dreams are somehow embodied in this inanimate thing. Surely.

David and I really didn't need to stop at St. Elmo, Alabama, a little one-runway paved strip just south of Mobile. Perhaps it was the stench that infuriated David as we flew past the refineries at Pascagoula, Mississippi, or perhaps all the coffee I drank earlier that morning, but I didn't think I could hold out another twenty minutes.

We swooped in to St. Elmo and taxied to the fuel pump; then I abandoned the plane in an undignified dash for the restroom. When I returned the plane was surrounded by a half dozen men and the girl from the desk. She helped David and me fuel while the men admired the plane.

They helped us push the Queen away from the pump, and with much waving David and I departed. We flew across Mobile Bay and alighted in Fairhope, Alabama. There we used the phone and called William E. Butterworth—Bill—who is better known under his nom de plume of W. E. B. Griffin as the author of the *Brotherhood of War* and *The Corps* series published by Putnam.

Bill answered the phone and readily accepted my invitation to go for a ride in the Stearman. But first he wanted to buy us lunch, which he did at the country club associated with the Marriott resort in which he lives at Clear Point.

Bill is in his early sixties and has made his living for almost forty years as a writer. He is the author of over 140 books written under fourteen pen names, adopted, according to his wife, because the libraries would only buy one William E. Butterworth book a year.

At lunch he tells us anecdotes of his early writing days and his latest trip to New York for the big thumb-your-nose-at-the-rest-of-the-publishing-world party that Phyllis Grann, Putnam's president and CEO, threw for her best-selling scribblers. He and Tom Clancy had lunch with Robert Gottlieb, who is also my agent, and Bill tells me about that. All in all, he concludes, he had a great time and he's glad he went.

Then he launches into a discussion of his upcoming duck-hunting expedition to Uruguay. "It's one of the few places left in the world," he says, "that doesn't have signs saying 'Welcome American Tourists' and 'Thank You for Not Smoking.'"

Back at the Butterworth home after lunch, Mrs. Butterworth, who has the flu, presents David with three of Bill's books and one of her own, for she is a writer too and a recognized expert on calligraphy.

A pilot who hasn't flown in years, Bill has trouble maintaining altitude in the Stearman. He persists in placing the nose too low even though I am coaching him on the intercom, which is truly lousy. Electronic wizardry is not yet up to the challenge of making a decent intercom for an open-cockpit aircraft. This is Bill's first ride in one and the newness of the sensations overrides his rusty piloting instincts. Finally I take the controls and do pirouettes a thousand feet above his house, then take him sightseeing along the east side of the bay.

Bill Butterworth is the writer so many of us aspire to be, a man who earned a living doing what he wanted to do. He is an original character, opinionated, self-confident, sure of himself. I bid him good-bye wondering if I have enough of that fire to sustain a career. Oh well, time will tell.

Flying on to Pensacola, Dave and I find the clouds are getting lower and the visibility deteriorating, a typical summer afternoon on the gulf coast. In these climes mornings are the time to fly, the earlier the better.

We cross directly over Saufley Field, the field where I learned to fly, and I point it out to David. The airplanes are all gone now, moved to the main Naval Air Station—"mainside"—and the old runways have been crisscrossed by new ones, so almost the whole square mile is paved. I went out there last year for a look-see during a Pensacola visit and was stunned to see the abandoned hangars and the empty parking mats with weeds growing up through the cracks. Today from the air we can't see the weeds.

Approach gives us a right base approach to runway 16 at Pensacola Regional. We swoop in and I manage a beautiful landing, the main wheels kissing just an instant before the tail. One of the old hands at the St. Francis fly-in recommended this as his preferred technique, but I can rarely do it this well. More practice—I need more practice.

We park at the FBO and fuel the plane with the help of two college students who are in awe of the big biplane. They provide rags for me to wipe the oil off the front of the fuselage and a screwdriver for David and me to remove the hubcaps so we can get at the inflation valves on the main tires. David has been complaining that the right main tire is low, and he is right. It has about ten pounds of air in it. After some sweating on the hot concrete, we manage to get the hub plates off both wheels and fill them to 35 PSI.

With the job done he tells me that my shirt is filthy with oil and sweat. I wipe my oily, greasy hands on my jeans and use a sleeve to swab my forehead. Then I grin at him. One of the first lessons I learned in this town is that flying is a sweaty business not for the fastidious. That is one of the things I like about it.

Inside the FBO the desk lady makes phone calls to every rental car agency in town and informs us there are no wheels to be had. A big whing-ding of World War II vets is down at the civic center. Then she tries the hotels. The civic center Hilton is full, but on her third call she finds us a room at a Holiday Inn at one of the malls.

The motel even sends a van, which turns out to be driven by a college student who tells us he is going to move to Denver. He's been all over the east coast, he says, and is ready for The West. I nod my understanding. I joined the Navy to get out of West Virginia, so I know how he feels. The worst mistake a young person can make is to whittle down his dreams to fit the size of his hometown.

After a dip in the motel pool, David and I trot across the parking lot to the mall and take in *Robin Hood* with Kevin Costner. The previews of coming attractions give me a jolt. Sandwiched in between the trailers on a Danny DeVito comedy and a cop shoot-'em-up is a farce about naval aviation. The logo is a direct rip-off of the *Flight of the Intruder* movie triangle artwork, which was taken directly from the Vietnam-era Intruder patches that still adorn the leather flight jackets of A-6 pilots and bombardiers. Did my book start this? I sigh as I listen to this Pensacola Navy crowd guffaw at the foolishness on the screen.

That evening before bed I remembered Bill Butterworth's remark about how much he enjoyed the big publishing blowout in New York, and I recalled the one I got invited to several years ago. It was Doubleday's ninetieth anniversary party and they held it in the ballroom of a swanky hotel on Fifth Avenue, just north of the southeast corner of Central Park. I wore one of my Denver oil-company-lawyer suits and my best tie.

All of Doubleday's heavy hitters were there. The booze was free and there were bushels of shrimp and crab legs and even caviar. I didn't know a soul except Nancy Evans, who was then the president of Doubleday, and David Gernert, my editor. Of course they knew everybody and had to mix and mingle.

I got a double scotch since the price was right and sat on one of the railings overlooking the entrance. I was perched there when Bill Cosby arrived in a blue jogging suit, two-piece. Must have set him back at least fifty bucks, but what the hey, he could afford it. He looked at me and I looked at him and then he recognized somebody and started talking to them. I spotted a woman with a truly awesome cleavage and started staring.

Then Jackie Onassis, Doubleday's best-known editor, arrived. Every eye in the place went to her. She is the only true celebrity

I know of—she doesn't have to hire a publicist or call the reporters when she's in Aspen to try to get her name in the papers. She doesn't have to sing, dance, write, act, or do the Carson show. And until the day she dies every living soul who sees her will gawk. I did.

Mrs. O stayed for ten minutes or so as the television cameras ground and the crowd milled around her, then when I turned my head to look for a waiter bearing another scotch, she vanished. Everyone was craning to see where she went but she made her exit slick as a pickpocket. Later I heard she had been escorted there by a man. He's the most anonymous guy on the planet. Nobody saw him.

I went over to the TV guys and watched them twiddle knobs and check lights. One of the cameramen and I mingled socially. "You here with the party?" he asked finally.

"Security."

"Oh."

"You see anybody pocketing the silverware, you let me know."

When I left I saw actress Betty White waiting alone on the sidewalk for a limo or taxi. I said, "Hi."

She said, "Hi."

She's a nice lady.

Pensacola, Florida, is one of my favorite cities. Here the dreams begin. When I first saw it in the summer of 1966, a month before my twentieth birthday, it was a small, sleepy southern town and my stay did not promise to be a good one. I arrived at the local airport at the end of my very first long trip on an airplane with a small suitcase and a set of mimeographed orders to report the following afternoon at 4 P.M. to Aviation Officers Candidate School (AOCS) at the Naval Air Station. The admirals had concluded that the Vietnam War might be long and bloody and trained pilots might become scarce, so they had resolved to increase the supply. I was to be a small morsel of their cannon fodder, although from my vantage point the Navy's need for pilots looked like an opportunity to learn to fly and fulfill my military obligation. If I lived through it, fine. If I didn't, well ... the grim reaper was still a long way away and who could say how a man's life would run?

I took a taxi from the airport, the first taxi ride of my life, and had the driver drop me in front of the biggest hotel in town—indeed, the only hotel in town. The San Carlos is gone now but in its day it was a beaut—six or seven stories, lots of velvet drapes and leather chairs and all in all, one hell of a fine place for a youngster who had just completed his sophomore year of college and was out adventuring for the first time.

I had read the orders word for word and made careful note of the hour of my required arrival. Instinctively I knew that it would be not wise to arrive early. After a fitful night's sleep, I spent the next morning wandering the streets of Pensacola and looking at the trains in the yard and glancing through the windows of the sailors' bars. It was hot that late June day in the deep south, with the heat rising in shimmering waves from the streets and a humidity that was truly oppressive to anyone not accustomed to it. Situated right on the Gulf of Mexico, Pensacola had its full share of humidity but was spared some of the heat that makes towns a hundred miles inland smoldering hells in late summer. But Pensacola was without doubt a southern town, full of loafers and farmers in bib overalls piloting pickup trucks. What it had that most towns didn't were sailors and airplanes out at the base, but these weren't very noticeable my first morning.

The day went too quickly as my mouth got dryer and dryer. At last I hailed a cab in front of the hotel and set off. Not very many minutes later I became rudely acquainted with my very first drill instructor, a U.S. Marine Corps staff sergeant. The officers candidate school received a supply of newly minted drill instructors every year from the drill instructor school at Parris Island, South Carolina. I thought it was nice of the Marine Corps to share with the Navy. Actually, in spite of the hell those combat veterans put us through, I found myself acquiring a deep respect, affection even, for those model soldiers who tried to make military men of us college boys. That feeling has continued to grow as the years have passed.

After six weeks of fun and games the sergeants sent me back to college via bus since the airlines were on strike at the time. I remember that bus station, dirty with the usual grimy patina and peeling paint of public buildings the world over, with one large fan suspended from the ceiling turning slowly, lazily, while the short-order grill filled the room with the odor of grease, a WHITES ONLY sign over one men's room and a COLORED over the other. Integration had just arrived in the Deep South in 1966 and they hadn't gotten around to repainting the signs.

The next summer I returned to Pensacola for another six-week visit with a few handpicked drill instructors. We saw Pensacola for only a few hours on Saturday and Sunday afternoons. The rest of the time was spend studying Navy stuff, marching and getting inspected and getting ready to get inspected again. The last week of AOCS I got to be a candidate officer, a term of art that meant that the academics and physical training were over and I got to march the other candidates around.

One night that week, while I was standing an all-night duty officer watch, I sneaked into my drill instructor's office, sat in his chair and put my feet up on his desk. It was a sublime moment.

Then I noticed a metal box filled with file cards on the desk. I confess, I looked.

Yep, each card had the name of a guy in my class. In the blink of an eye I had mine out. There were exactly three words on the card: "Lacks military bearing." That was it. Nothing else. Staff Sergeant Balyette had chosen those three words to summarize my twelve weeks of AOCS and to predict my future in the military. He was an expert, so I knew it was true. They can put it on my tombstone as my epitaph.

I came to Pensacola to stay and fell in love with the place in late May, 1968, as a spanking-new college-graduate ensign assigned to flight training.

AOCS was turning out thirty new ensigns a week, the Naval Academy was popping them out, and the Naval ROTC units around the nation were shipping them here. The town was awash in ensigns the summer of 1968, or so it seemed to me. The "gouge" on the best restaurants—cheap with edible food—and fun places swirled through the training classes. We cruised the streets and went over the causeway to Pensacola Beach and sparked what few single women there were. I never managed a date.

Still, we saw Pensacola as a great adventure, our first step into the real world after college, with a real paycheck and a real chance to succeed or fail solely on our own efforts. I still see her that way. I get a warm fuzzy every time I visit.

In the last twenty-five years the city has doubled in size and changed dramatically. Now it has four-lane highways, a big civic center with an attached Hilton Hotel sporting a cutesy old-timey railroad station for a lobby, all the usual malls and three-bedroom two-bath suburbs. Here and there in this homogenized glitz are a few remnants of Pensacola the way it was before the developers and improvers got their hands on the controls.

The saving grace is that the town is still full of young men—and now women—just out of college and trying to earn a place for themselves in naval aviation. For them the future is a bright glowing road that stretches ahead toward an infinite horizon. That is as it should be. Youth without optimism would be unbearable.

The two men who made the most impression upon me at Pensacola were Jimmy Hanks and George Dustin. Lieutenant Commander Jimmy Hanks was my first flight instructor. Like most naval aviators, he was a medium-sized fit man who spoke softly and meant what he said. Fate had played him a nasty trick: he owned a lumberyard in Pensacola but had been recalled to active duty by the Navy and assigned as a primary flight instructor at VT-1 at Saufley Field. So he flew students all day and managed his business at night—I don't know when he slept. It seemed to me that if the Navy was going to recall him to active duty, they should at least have the decency to ship him somewhere for an adventure. He seemed to regard his recall to active duty as another shit sandwich. Still, he was an excellent flight instructor.

I was one of three students Mr. Hanks was shepherding through primary, and I was perhaps his dullest and least promising. On the first flight in the T-34 I became deathly ill and filled the barf bag he had thoughtfully provided beforehand. Doped with Dramamine, I worked like a slave on subsequent flights yet acquired the skills so slowly that Job would have thrown his hat in the dirt.

Jimmy Hanks explained it for the sixth or seventh time, his voice low, trying to use nontechnical words so this bumpkin from West Virginia would finally comprehend and convert that comprehension to cockpit performance. But he wasn't a saint. The fifth time I taxied the airplane in after a flight and forgot which space we had taxied out of at the start, he didn't scream, he didn't shout—he just informed me curtly that if I didn't write the row and space number on my kneeboard from now on, he was going to shove my pencil up my ass.

One day he asked, "You want to fly jets?"

I admitted that I entertained that ambition. So he began to pad my grades, salt in some above-average marks that I hadn't earned. In those days a student needed above-average cockpit grades to qualify for the jet training pipeline.

Years later when I was a flight instructor on A-6 aircraft I came to understand the risk that Jimmy Hanks decided to run. Sending a marginal student to a challenging program just because he wants to try it is merely giving him a golden opportunity to fail. Failure for a student pilot usually means being washed out of the program, but occasionally the consequences are more catastrophic. Thirteen student pilots crashed fatally at the bases where I flew in the fifteen months it took me to earn my wings. Jimmy Hanks decided to give me the opportunity I wanted well knowing that I was going to have to learn to acquire the critical skills quicker or I was going to be washed out or dead.

I occasionally wonder what my life would have been like if I had not gone to jets, not gone to A-6s, not gone to Vietnam. I wouldn't have met the girl I married, I wouldn't have had the children I did, perhaps I would not have become a writer. Who knows? Maybe I would have married an heiress or be living in sin with a starlet with silicone tits.

George Dustin had an equally significant influence on my life. He was a lieutenant in his late twenties, a Spad pilot. The Air Force called their Spads A-1 Skyraiders but George Dustin never did. A Spad was a Spad was a Spad.

Mr. Dustin had a massive head that sported a square, handsome face, this atop a pair of broad shoulders and oak-tree arms. His voice was a hoarse, gravelly bass that carried even when he tried to speak softly. I got to know Mr. Dustin because he taught the pre-solo course that gave us students the basic information about the Alabama gulf coast peninsula where we

53

flew and he administered a multiple-choice examination on this body of knowledge. The fledgling had to pass the exam before he could solo. I failed it the first time around and got to spend extra time with Mr. Dustin reviewing the material—"stupid study" we called it.

Then my parents arrived in Pensacola for a vacation and I got busy squiring them around and not cracking the books. I failed my first retake of the exam. And the second. Now I needed a perfect score to pass this hurdle. To Mr. Dustin's and my dismay I failed the third retake by missing one question.

I was on the verge of flunking out of flight school. Nauseated, unable to eat, trying to be pleasant to my folks, I studied the material in my BOQ room until the wee hours—the names of all the outlying emergency fields that a solo student could use for an emergency landing, their shapes and dimensions and runway orientations, their precise locations, the shape and orientation of the landing patterns, the height and location of the tallest tower in gulf coast Alabama, and so on, rudimentary essential information that had to be acquired by rote memorization, which I loathed. But I had to do it.

On my fifth attempt at the test, the fourth retake, Mr. Dustin gave the answer sheet a cursory glance and marked "100%" on the top. He stared at me, gave his leonine head a slow shake, and rumbled, "Get outta here."

I found out later that the powers that be changed the rules after my record-breaking academic adventure. From this day forth, they decreed, a student would get only two retakes of the pre-solo examination if he failed it the first time. And failure to pass the second retake with a perfect score would be considered irrebuttable evidence that the student was incurably, hopelessly stupid, incapable of ever becoming a naval aviator. A wise and merciful course was mandated: since capital punishment was no longer in vogue and the jails were already full, the wretch would be washed out of the flight program and sent someplace where he would not need to operate any machine more complicated than a safety razor, with, of course, appropriate annotations in his service record to ensure that he would never be promoted.

The lesson I got out of all of this was that I had to study and be prepared for every flight, every written examination. I couldn't loaf in flight school as I had done in college, expect to read the book the night before the exam and waltz in and rack up an A or B. Uh-uh. So I dug in for the most demanding period of my life and never failed another written exam or had an unsatisfactory flight. And I became a jet pilot.

I don't know whatever happened to Jimmy Hanks or George Dustin. Neither is listed in the Pensacola telephone directory, which is too bad because I wanted to give them both a ride in the *Cannibal Queen*. If they ever read this they will probably be surprised to find their names here. They probably won't recall the incidents related here or remember my name. I can't remember the names of the students I instructed. But students remember instructors.

The next day, Sunday, Father's Day, David and I got a rental car and drove over to the Naval Aviation Museum at the Naval Air Station. This is quite a museum and it's worth the trip if you ever get the chance.

Among the planes that you will see nowhere else is the NC-4, the first aircraft to fly across the Atlantic Ocean, a feat this particular aircraft performed in 1919. It's a huge four-engine flying boat, an open-cockpit biplane with a boat hull. The size of this wood and fabric masterpiece will stun you.

The pre–World War II collection is superb. The World War II exhibit is, I believe, the most comprehensive collection of U.S. Navy aircraft of that era under one roof anywhere. The PBY Catalina is the best specimen I have yet seen.

Displayed without apology is a Stearman painted silver and two N3Ns, the Naval Aircraft Factory version of the Stearman company's masterpiece. The N3Ns have different landing gear, but they are yellow sisters to the *Cannibal Queen*. I bragged to David that the *Queen* looked as gorgeous as the two N3Ns before I started putting a lot of hours on her.

"You bought yours to fly," David said, "not hang in a museum." I think he sensed that I was apologizing for the *Queen*'s chipped paint and accumulating grime. This is not as perceptive as you might think since he has watched me carefully wipe her down after every flight.

The airplanes in the Naval Aviation Museum are in as good

a condition as those at the Air and Space Museum in Washington, D.C. In comparison, the planes at the Air Force Museum, in Dayton, Ohio, look like old airplanes that were merely defueled and rolled inside, a condition the Air Force refers to as "flight line ready." The Navy planes glisten and gleam, sparkle and shine.

I suppose one could argue that airplanes shouldn't be shined like a pair of drill instructor's inspection shoes since the lay tourist might get a false impression, but I contend they look better indoors when they are spotless and shiny. Ask the owner of any antique car why he put five layers of paint on his pride and joy, then waxed it to a high gloss. No fool thinks Model A Fords came from the factory that way. Women intuitively understand that looking one's best adds to the aura of romance, which is what aviation museums are all about. Flight *is* romance—not in the sense of sexual attraction, but as an experience that enriches life.

After touring the museum we drove out to Pensacola Beach. We forgot our bathing suits, so we took off our shoes and socks and waded into the surf with our jeans rolled up as high as they would go. They got wet anyway. In minutes David was in to his knees.

On the way back to town we stopped at a beach gear emporium and acquired goggles and a snorkle for David, then drove the twenty miles to the motel and tried out the new equipment in the motel pool. It worked fine.

At times David looks like a man to me, but sporting around in a pool he is half boy, half fish. "Come on in," he pleads, then gets upset that his middle-aged father needs only five minutes of water sport to tire of it. Why don't fathers stay boys for as long as their sons need them that way?

A thunderstorm drove us back to our room. As we looked out the window at the rain, he asked what we were going to do this evening. "We could get dressed," I suggested, "and go pick up a couple women. You get the short one."

"That's fine with me," he shot back, "but I get first choice."

We cogitated upon it and decided to go to dinner instead. It was 10 o'clock when we got back to the motel. I went to sleep while he was writing postcards. When I awoke at midnight to answer nature's call the lights were out and he was sound asleep.

6

I WOKE UP MONDAY MORNING AT 5:50. YESTERDAY WE STAYED in Pensacola because thunderstorms rolled in at 9:30 A.M. while David was still asleep. Today we want to fly east to a beach near Jacksonville on Florida's east coast. The weather will probably be just like yesterday's, so the sooner we take off and point the Queen east, the better. I roll David out as soon as I've had my shower. He wakes easily and jumps out without protest. He wants to go to the beach and he can always sleep in the plane.

"Where are we going today?" he asks.

"I dunno. We'll dodge the storms and find an airport someplace."

"Oh, Toto," he warbles, "this isn't Kansas."

At the airport David installs the wheel hub plates that we removed to get access to the tire inflation valves. We move the plane around to rotate the wheels and allow the screws to be installed easily.

I keep looking to the south at a huge thunderstorm coming this way. David seems to be going too slow. Better not push him. I break down the tie-downs and preflight the plane between glances at the oncoming storm. The sky to the northwest is relatively clear, just the usual puffy clouds and haze.

Ready not a minute too soon, we strap ourselves in and I crank the engine. As usual, she starts readily and emits her morning puff of gray, oily smoke. It is 7:02 A.M. The storm has an anvil on it that is blotting out the morning sun. The sky is growing dark. Welcome to Florida!

We lift off runway 16 heading straight for the approaching solid black wall. Approach gives me a vector of 050 degrees and I turn handily. As we level at 1,500 feet over the bay it is apparent the storm is still several miles away. It wasn't even a close call.

We motor up over Whiting Field and once we are north of I-10, turn to parallel it eastbound. The interstate highway is the rough boundary of the Eglin restricted areas, which lie south of the highway and go all the way to the southern coast of the barrier islands. Pensacola Departure switches me to Eglin Approach. A female controller is busy with Air Force traffic shooting practice approaches into Eglin: she acknowledges my existence and forgets about me as Pensacola fades into the haze behind.

David is doing something in the front cockpit, eating a candy bar I think. That's his breakfast. His mother would wring my neck if she knew. But she's in Colorado and that's a lot of miles behind us.

No other storms in sight. Ten to twelve miles visibility under a scattered layer of scud, the bottoms of which are several hundred feet above us. At about 10,000 feet is a thin broken layer. We fly in and out of occasional weak patches of sunlight, but mainly we are under clouds. The engine sounds strong, vigorous. I twitch the controls as David rests his head on the right side of the cockpit for a nap.

We are flying over a vast pine forest, have been flying over one, in fact, since we left Baton Rouge on the Mississippi River eastbound. The farmers of the Deep South have given up. The cotton plantations of the last century that were sharecropper farms in the first half of this one are now just pine tree farms. The forest is broken only by highways knifing through and occasional towns, here and there a pasture, a few meandering streams. The odd grassy area only emphasizes the vastness of this pine wilderness and how iffy it would be to find a safe emergency landing place. I would like to fly higher to increase my chances of finding an acceptable landing place if the engine craps out, but this haze and low scud would obscure the ground, which I must see to navigate.

Not that there is really anything to worry about. This big round Lycoming has been running strong for longer than I've been alive. Today is not its day to die. Nor is it our day.

Over De Funiak Springs Eglin Approach turns us loose after verifying that we are following the interstate eastward. The controller suggests we switch to Cairns Approach, so I do. Cairns is an Army helicopter base in the Fort Rucker, Alabama, complex somewhere north of us. After a few minutes on that frequency I tire of listening to Air Traffic Control and ask to leave the freq. The male controller readily agrees. I turn the radio off. Blessed silence.

I flip on the intercom switch and ask David how he's doing. "Fine."

"See that little cloud up ahead? Let's fly through it."

He's agreeable. "All right."

I add a couple inches of manifold pressure and climb three hundred feet. I boresight the cloud. It's dead ahead, growing larger as we thunder toward it at 95 MPH. Seconds from impact David screams over the intercom, "We're going to die!"

Then the gray stuff engulfs us, obscuring the ground. I hold the stick motionless, the rudder frozen. And I glance down. A glimpse of the ground—this is a little cloud—just where it should be, then we are out into the clear again.

"Drat," I tell David, "I think we're still alive. I feel alive, how about you?"

Crossing the Appalachicola River I tune the radio to the Tallahassee ATIS frequency as I inform David that we have entered the Eastern Time Zone. Even at 1,500 feet we pick up the ATIS broadcast clearly: broken layer at 14,000 feet and a solid layer at 25,000, instrument approaches to runway 27 and departures on 36, wind out of the west at ten knots. I can hack that.

Abeam Quincy I call Tallahassee Approach and tell them I am inbound. They stun me. "Tallahassee Municipal is IFR with two miles visibility in fog." I look east. It's gooey all right. The same to the south.

I consult the chart. "We'll land at Quincy." This airport is only two miles north of my position and I know the weather's good enough.

Approach suggests either Quincy or Tallahassee Commercial. I consult the chart again. The big airport is Tallahassee Municipal on the south side of the city, about twelve miles south of the VOR, the radio navigation aid. Commercial is a little airport due east of me and six or seven miles north of the city limits. The Tallahassee VOR is at their field. Okay, we'll go there.

I see the lake near Commercial's field at six miles and tell Approach I have the field in sight. I switch to Unicom and give them a call. A woman answers promptly: wind six knots favoring runway 16.

I pick out the field and descend on a right base, make the 90-degree right turn and drop the Queen in. I flare a foot too high and David comments. He is becoming a connoisseur. Commercial has one asphalt runway 3,000 feet in length. I use about half of it and turn around on the runway and taxi back to the turnoff. On one side of the mat a vigorous elderly man is waiting. He directs me toward a semitrailer painted white and labeled 100LL—fuel.

I shut down and check my watch. I started the engine in Pensacola an hour and 47 minutes ago. I climb out. "Gonna need gas."

David unstraps, takes his helmet off and stands in his seat. I pass the hose up to him. David also likes to add the oil the Queen needs after every flight to replenish the sump tank. Our host hands me the two quarts I ask for while David is still standing on the top of the front cockpit seat, and since I am busy craning my head to the south and wondering what Flight Service will say about the weather, I forget to wait to let him add it. I do it myself.

"Nice airplane," the man tells me.

"Thanks."

"Sure seen a lot of Stearmans in my time," he says. "Used to buy them surplus for six hundred dollars each."

"Six hundred bucks wasn't easy to come by back then, but that was still awful cheap."

"That it was. Them was good ol' planes."

"How long you been here at this airport?"

"Since '46. We opened it in '46."

"Didn't know you were here. I was going to stop over at the big airport."

"They pump lots of gas. You won't make any difference to them. You will to us."

With the Queen replenished with fuel and oil—Stearman blood—we go into the little one-story building that houses the office. There we meet the lady I heard on the radio.

On the phone Flight Service tells me the weather is 1,500 to 2,000 scattered, a broken layer at 14,000, all the way east across the peninsula to Jacksonville. No reported thunderstorms, although they will undoubtedly pop before too long. We'll have a tailwind of ten knots. But no pilot reports along that route. That bothers me. "What about this fog over Tallahassee?" I ask. "How far east does that go?"

"Pretty localized. A lot of it's smoke from a forest fire southwest of the field. And it rained an inch down here last night." Flight Service has their regional office at the municipal airport. "Always gets foggy after that much rain."

Reassured, I thank him and go to the little front office with the lady behind the desk. She is nearsighted and bends over the credit card form to fill it out. David is in one of the chairs in front of her desk so I take the other.

Her name is Emily Hinson. The man who helped us park and fuel is her husband, Jim. They bought the land for the airport right after World War II. "It was grass up until '67 when we paved it because too many people were just flying over. You'd be amazed—nowadays they won't even taxi on grass. And we used to have a charter operation off this grass field with twins. After we paved it our tire bill sure went up."

I like her. She is feisty and sharp as a tack. In several ways she reminds me of my mother.

She tells Dave and me how the feds are trying to condemn the 70 acres of land that the VOR sits on. This is land the Hinsons leased to the FAA for 30 years, but now they want to condemn it so the government can take advantage of rising property values in the future. She is indignant. The litigation has been going on for seven years and will finally go to trial next month. "They postponed the trial I don't know how many times. Seems they just want to wear you down, drag it out so long you'll just quit and take their money."

61

I agree. That is precisely what the government and big corporations do in litigation with individuals, especially those without deep pockets. I know. I used to be a lawyer with a moderately large oil company.

"I notice you have your fuel in a tank truck. Are you having trouble with the EPA?"

"Over there," she points, "we have two eight-thousand-gallon tanks. Been there for years. Going to have to hire one company to dig them up, another company to test the soil, and if it's bad, a third company to dig it out and treat it or haul it away. The state tells you what you have to do and gives you a deadline, and if you don't, the EPA comes after you. The fine for not doing it is *ten thousand dollars a day*."

"They're coming after you like you were Texaco."

"Going to put us out of business, that's what they're going to do. And they don't care. They don't know anything about aviation and they collect their paychecks regardless."

Several weeks ago I stopped in Virginia Dale, Colorado, which is merely a wide spot in the road 9,000 feet above sea level, at the only filling station–cafe between Ft. Collins, Colorado, and Laramie, Wyoming. I asked the proprietor why his gasoline pumps were locked up. He told me the same story Mrs. Hinson is telling now—the Environmental Protection Agency made the rules like he was pumping 200,000 gallons a month. They refused to differentiate between huge-volume businesses and tiny operations. "Screw everybody alike; that's their motto." Like small independent gas stations all over rural and urban America, he was going out of business. He and his wife would sell hamburgers and candy and try to survive, but there was no way he could get the money required to meet the demands of the EPA GS-2s who were hounding him. And he was bitter. A way of life was being eliminated by unelected bureaucrats because "environmentalists" want the government to get tough with "polluters." He was being put out of business even though there was not a shred of evidence his tanks ever leaked a drop of gasoline into the groundwater. A lifetime of work blown away by the wind. He was very bitter.

I refocus on Mrs. Hinson. She is telling me the EPA is putting the aircraft paint shops in southern and central Florida out of business. She asks if they are after the paint shops in Colorado.

I tell her I don't know. "Wouldn't surprise me." Nothing surprises me anymore.

As I taxi out Mrs. Hinson thanks me over the radio for stopping and invites me to come back. I tell her I will.

And I mean it. If Jim and Emily Hinson can find the courage to weather the storms, I will keep coming back. I owe them that.

A half hour later over Madison, Florida, David and I are craning our necks trying to find a public grass airfield depicted on my chart. The chart says it is 150 feet above sea level and 3,300 feet in length. No Unicom frequency. Right by a north–south road. I decide I have it and point it out to David. There is a strip oriented north and south one pasture west of the road and two empty hangars for airplanes. "That's it, I think." I pull the power back to let us descend.

"No," David says, and points. "Over there. There's some parked airplanes."

Sure enough. I swing the Queen in the right direction as David chortles, "You were going to land in some farmer's cow pasture!"

Such are the trials and tribulations of the world's finest aviator when he takes his fourteen-year-old son flying.

We cross above the real field and examine the wind sock. Out of the west. I swing out on a left downwind and pull the power. Down to 80 MPH, trimmed, a gentle left turn to bring us in over the trees for another mediocre landing. Damn!

We roll out to the western end of the strip and turn around. With the prop ticking over at idle we look at the five little airplanes tied in the sun. There's no shack, no fuel pumps. Not even a rusty old pump or a newly filled hole in the ground to show that the EPA has been by.

I gun the engine and we taxi back down the runway for takeoff. Soon we are airborne and climbing steeply. With 300 horsepower in this dense air the Queen climbs like a homesick angel.

We stop in Lake City for gas and food at another sprawling former military air base. I ask the man who helps us fuel the plane why the tower didn't answer my calls. "He's out to lunch," I am told.

I eye him. It's a nonfederal tower, but still . . . "He always out to lunch?" I ask.

"No. But it's ten after twelve."

I ask about food. The lunch counter is closed on Mondays. A man standing looking at the plane announces he is on his lunch hour and we can ride into town with him.

His name is James Rand. He is a mechanic for Emery-Riddle Worldwide, the air freight company, and he is in Lake City tending a sick DC-8 that I saw on the south side of the field as we circled in the pattern overhead.

He spends our time together talking about airplanes in the manner of a man who doesn't get to talk to many people in his work. He says he has read all my books. I instantly like him.

He is just back from a sojourn in Guam, where he wrestled some B-29 pieces from a wreck in the jungle and brought them back. One of the pieces is a top turret complete with two bullet holes. "All the better," I remark, and Mr. Rand readily agrees.

"Don't know what I'm going to do with this stuff, but I'll do something. It's amazing, but there's all kinds of stuff in that jungle over there if a fellow is willing to go into the brush and work like a slave getting it out. I saw a Val dive bomber over-turned in a big brush pile with its landing gear sticking out. It's a warbird restorer's paradise. Some of the metal is pretty corroded, but some of it is in surprisingly good shape."

All of which stirs my acquisitive juices. I begin to think about a trip to Guam to scout around. I could rescue two or three wrecks of the same type and ship them back and hope to get enough critical parts in restorable condition to build one good airplane. It would cost a fortune, of course, but with a couple more novels and maybe a movie, I could swing it. Sure I could.

What better thing could I do with the money? I have no desire to be the richest man in the graveyard, although there is little chance of that unless some heiress makes a total fool of herself by falling head over heels for me. And where am I ever going to meet a foolish heiress?

Maybe a Hellcat or gull-wing Corsair. I saw gorgeous examples of those types yesterday in Pensacola. Oh me oh my. I am musing along these lines when we say good-bye to Mr. Rand at the airport and he promises to read the book about my adventures with the *Cannibal Queen* when it is published.

Inside the terminal a fellow is leaning on the counter when I pay for my gas. "You going out?" he asks.

"Yep. East."

"Lots of buildups around Jacksonville up to ten thousand feet. That's why we landed here."

I eye him critically. A cloud with tops at ten grand is not anything to write home about. And I have been doing just dandy under this stuff at 1,500 feet above the ground.

I grunt noncommittally and stick the yellow credit card invoice in my wallet with all the others. When my wallet gets too thick I will throw them all away together. "Come on, David."

We pause by the plane and consult the chart. After some head scratching, we decide on Fernandina Beach as our destination. Neither of us has ever heard of the place, but it is on an outer island adjacent to the sea and a town is nearby, so presumably we can get a rental car and motel room.

The guy in the tower doesn't answer my radio calls. He probably isn't back from lunch yet. What the hey, it's only 1:30 P.M.

David wants to know how long this trip will take. I tell him an hour. He is wearing down. We have done three hours of flying already.

We pick up the interstate and head east to MacClenny. There I turn north and follow the highway to St. George, Georgia, which sits in the little finger of Georgia that pokes down into Florida. From St. George we fly the compass northeast toward Hilliard, Florida, on U.S. 1. I am going around the Jacksonville Airport Radar Service Area (ARSA) to the west and north because I don't want to talk to those guys unless I have to and because it looks as if a big thunderstorm is growing right over Jacksonville. It is dark and gloomy in that direction. As we fly toward Hilliard we can see a forest fire burning off to the northwest in Okefenokee Swamp. And a rain shower over that way.

Hilliard has a grass airfield right beside the highway. When we hit the highway I turn northwest and start looking. There it is, complete with airplanes. For a moment I toy with the idea of making a landing just for the heck of it, but we have been airborne for 37 minutes and David is wearing out. I swing the plane directly east toward the mouth of the St. Marys River, the dividing line between Georgia and Florida. In ten minutes we are over the estuary.

The sun is out and casting areas of light and shadow on the

winding river and the saltwater marshes that are so much a part of coastal Florida. The big thunderbumper is off our right wing. I ease the throttle back a smidgen and let the Queen drift downward.

"Where's the ocean?" David asks.

"Dead ahead, beyond those islands." The haze and the gray sea merge there into a vague nothingness.

"Beach bunnies," David roars. "I want beach bunnies."

I level at 500 feet, the mouth of the river dead ahead. Now we can see the ocean beyond. I swing off to the left to cut across Cumberland Island, then out over the surf I turn south past the mouth of the river. David waves madly to bathing-suit clad figures on the beach. Some of them wave back.

The airport is yet another former military base, sprawling, with three or four wide, paved runways. The Unicom man suggests runway 8, but on the downwind I get a good look at the wind sock and decide on runway 13. As we drift down final I can see two experimental airplanes on the taxiway surrounded by people. They look up as we float over with the engine almost at idle. The touchdown is acceptable.

A beach on the Atlantic.

We will stay here on Amelia Island for two nights and go on to Orlando on Wednesday where we will meet Nancy and the girls at the airport. They are flying in from Denver on an airliner for a visit to Disney World. As I tie down the *Cannibal* Queen and wipe the oil from the nose, the thunderstorm is only four or five miles away. It hits just as we check into a condo on the beach. The rain pelts down and the winds gust.

I go out on the porch, smoke my pipe, and sit watching the ocean. I have always liked the wildness of the sea.

7

SOMEDAY I'M GOING TO OWN A BOAT, A MOTORCYCLE, AN ATV, and a jet ski.'' With this definitive pronouncement David concluded his argument to the jury as we crossed the causeway to Pensacola Beach on Father's Day, two days ago. We had just passed a boat rental place a couple miles back when he launched into his let's-do-it routine. There ought to be a law against people that rent mobile suicide machines putting up signs where children riding in cars can see them. All parents have heard these pleas to the gods from their offspring and I am no exception. I refused his entreaty because I know next to nothing about boats. I told David so.

"But you were in the Navy!" You know, Dad, ships and water and all that stuff.

"I just flew the planes. Somebody else drove the ship."

"There's nothing to it." I let this pass. "I'll steer and you just ride." This comment also went unanswered. It was followed by the list of things he would acquire as soon as he became a millionaire.

Last night I resolved to prove to my son that his father is not a wimp. The secret fear of every father has become reality—my manhood is suspect to the seed of my loins, the scion of the

67

clan. I see no alternative—we will rent a jet ski. At least I don't have to beat up the father of the kid across the street!

I told David of my decision last night. "Rent two of them," he replied. "We'll race."

This morning he comes out of bed wide-eyed and ready. Why do parents do this to themselves?

The man on the dock at the harbor eyes me speculatively as I stand nervously inspecting the four jet skis he has tied alongside.

"I'll take the blue one," David says. His courage in the face of the unknown fills me with awe. This is the courage of youth, some juice God squirts into kids to help them face a world where everything is unknown. It leaks out as people age, which is why they get gray hair.

"You ever ride one of these?" the ski man asks me. He is short, rotund and bald and has an enviable tan on his bare legs. His tanned belly protrudes from an unbuttoned short-sleeve shirt.

"Uh, no, but I've been riding motorcycles for over twenty years. I should be able to handle it." That's the right note—confident, macho, fearless—to exorcise all those wimp doubts from that fourteen-year-old head.

"You won't have any trouble," the jet-ski mogul says reassuringly—it must be obvious that I need reassurance—and reaches for a life jacket, which he helps me don. "But I only rent to people sixteen and older. Your son can ride along behind you."

David takes it well, I think. He turns a shade paler and his shoulders sag. The instant the man turns away for a moment he asks, "You'll let me drive, huh?"

"We'll see."

I had visions of us cruising slowly up and down the St. Marys River and the inland waterway for an hour or so, but that expectation dies quickly. The brown jet-ski man points out the boundaries of the area we are to stay in. It's an area of the adjacent harbor maybe a quarter-mile long bounded on one side by the quay and the other by boats anchored out. "Avoid the oyster beds over there." He points. The area where he wants us is completely within his sight. He can watch us every minute.

I almost lose it the moment the engine is started. The choke sticks out. With the engine idling too fast we move smartly away from the pier. I am trying to steer, jab in the choke knob down by my left knee, and keep this damn thing right side up, all the while listening to Dave offer advice.

At last I get the choke in and the ski pointed in more or less the right direction and we cruise out of the harbor at idle, with the man who rents these infernal devices standing on the dock shouting advice. My left wrist is strapped to the ski in case I overturn. My stomach feels like I swallowed a rock.

Outside the harbor the water has a little wave action. Not too much. Actually it is flat as a plate, but the tiny swells make our craft bob and sway like a drunken horse. This thing is a personal injury lawyer's dream come true. I envision the happy faces of the lawyers listening to the heirs tell how their son-husband-daughter-fool fell off a jet ski and drowned while they watched in horror from terra firma.

I experimentally add a touch of throttle. Our craft responds and the bobbing motion becomes more pronounced. But I gradually get the hang of it and fearlessly crack the throttle another eighth of an inch.

We motor slowly down the anchorage, hitting some chop and staying upright, David remarkably silent. Perhaps he senses I am not yet ready for a backseat driver's comments. I steer over by some anchored yachts and David waves at the folks on deck. One is a beautiful two-masted wooden sailing vessel with peeling, faded paint. "That's a schooner," I tell David. He remains silent, unimpressed with the vast extent of my nautical expertise, which he knows I got out of books while my underwear remained dry.

We are halfway around the anchorage on our second circuit when the jet-ski mogul comes flying across the water on one of his craft. He wisely stays well away from me, but he cuts the throttle and shouts, "Give her full throttle and get up and plane."

Plane! Now there is a word I understand. What the hell! We can both swim and we're wearing life jackets—we'll bob like corks.

I cautiously squeeze the throttle to the stop. The jet ski accelerates and steadies out. The chop from the wake of the other ski now translates into an up and down pitching motion, not difficult to handle. Yeah!

We roar up and down the anchorage as I gain confidence. We blast through the wake of several passing boats and I even venture some S-turns. Around and around we go. Now I understand. This thing is a motorcycle on water and, like a motorcycle, gains stability with speed. The only difference is that it has its own unique handling characteristics since it's on water, not pavement.

After an age and a half at full gun I ask David how long we have been at it.

He consults his digital, waterproof watch. "Fifteen minutes."

Holy . . . We rented this thing for an *hour!*

This is a hoot. It's exhilarating and one must work every moment to keep the ski under control. It's pure fun. It's also boring going around and around this anchorage, so we come in after half an hour.

The mogul gives us a refund and returns the key to my rental car. I walk away grinning.

David is glum. I understand. It's hell when you're fourteen and want to get your hands on the controls and the world refuses. But his time will come.

That afternoon in the resort jacuzzi—we had rented a beach condo for two nights—I meet a banker from Warner Robins, Georgia, on vacation. His name is Ray Durham. After the usual polite conversation my mode of cross-country travel comes up.

"A Stearman," he says, savoring the word. "I grew up on a farm in Georgia and this ag operator had two Stearmans that he flew off a road right near my house when he was working our area. He took down the road signs and pumped the chemicals into his tanks from a beat-up old truck. Ah, those gorgeous old planes. Do you have the two-twenty Continental in yours?"

"Three-hundred Lycoming."

He nods. His son comes over and eases into the hot water. He is thirteen and his name is Corey. Ray suggests it's about time to go get dressed for dinner. Corey doesn't want to leave yet.

"If they get ready and we aren't there, they'll fuss at us," Ray tells his son. Poor devil, I think. Women are the same everywhere.

They sit silently in the hot water, apparently contemplating the prospect of fussing women. I ask Ray if he has ever ridden in a Stearman. One thing leads to another and we make a date for 7 P.M. at the local airport.

Ray is my first passenger. David helps him strap in and adjusts the cloth helmet, the headphones, and the goggles. The sky is overcast and the wind calm. A while ago a rain shower went through, but it's well past, out to sea. I fire up the Queen and taxi out. "This your first Stearman ride?"

"Yep."

"First ride in an open cockpit?"

"Yep."

"You'll love it."

We take off to the east and I take the Queen past the beach and out over the ocean. The air is absolutely still—our craft cleaves through it like something from a dream. Every twitch of the stick brings just the anticipated response. I pray for days like this.

I swing her south and turn her over to Ray. He gingerly begins making turns. He loses a couple hundred feet, dropping us to 500. He wanders aimlessly around savoring the experience, the throbbing engine, the sea and beach below. I have my elbows parked on the edges of the cockpit.

Finally I take her and make a couple of two-G turns to give him the taste of it, then head back for the field. On the downwind we fly over a Little League ballpark with four fields arranged like pie quarters. The lights are on and the teams are on the fields. We float overhead under the overcast.

I decide to land on the grass runway they have mowed to the right of the east-west paved one. As I float in, the man on Unicom tells me that we have two spectators, so I should wave. I ask if they are out on the grass. When he doesn't respond I add power. We fly down the runway at fifty feet as I repeat the question. I feel absolutely confident David knows not to leave the area of the parking mat, but this could be someone else. The Unicom man says, No, they are on the mat.

I put her down on the next approach and taxi in. David assists Ray from the cockpit and straps in Corey while I keep the engine running. This time I take off from the grass. Corey tells me this is his very first airplane ride.

71

Thirteen and never been up in a plane? I am stunned. I took my first airplane ride at the age of six in an Aeronca Champ without an electrical system. I can still remember my Dad hand-propping the engine while the pilot, my Dad's law partner, grinned at me. I was too small to see over the instrument panel, so I looked at the gauges and listened to the engine and savored the weird sensations. I recall looking out the window at the trees below and thinking how wonderful it all was. The flight lasted seventeen minutes. Didn't matter. I was hooked.

I let Corey fly the *Queen.* We go north around the end of the island, make the turn up the St. Marys River, then drift south over the anchorage where David and I had our jet-ski adventure this morning. Two pulp mills are pouring their fumes into the still evening sky.

I enter the pattern for the grass runway on a left base. On final we are ten miles per hour fast, so I lower the nose. When I flare we float along above the grass like cottonwood fluff drifting on a breeze. At last we alight and I use the remainder of the strip to get stopped.

I am furious with myself. Why didn't I slip her down, scrub off that excess airspeed? What was I thinking about?

I am still seething at myself as we say good-bye to Ray and Corey and watch them leave. Damnation! Am I ever going to learn to fly this plane?

"Corey said flying in a Stearman has been a lifetime ambition for his dad," David tells me. "He told me so while we were waiting." This makes me feel better.

We are sitting in a Pizza Hut when the last of the twilight fades. In minutes some of the Little League crowd comes in, two complete teams and their parents. They are boisterous, happy. The last of my frustration leaks away.

David is smiling, the crowd is raucous, I am content. A summer evening in small-town America. I like it more than words can express. My life is passing too quickly, but by God I am spending it well.

The next morning I wake up David at seven o'clock. I want to arrive in Orlando by noon before the usual Florida afternoon thunderstorms get cooking. The morning here is foggy. The briefer at the Flight Service Station tells me that Jacksonville airport just a few miles east is 200 feet and a quarter mile in fog. "This stuff looks localized in the Jacksonville area, though. Gainesville is clear and so is Orlando. It should burn off before long."

I thank him and go out onto the lawn that leads to the beach and look at the sky. Fog floating eastward in strands, with patches of blue above.

David and I turn in the car at the airport FBO and I get a cup of coffee from the courtesy pot. I leave a quarter in the kitty. Out on the mat where the Queen is tied down we can see the goo westward toward the Jacksonville airport. I look south. That's the way we will go, south along the beach, through the Mayport Naval Station airport traffic area, flying just off the beach until we near Daytona Beach, where we will strike a little southwest for Orlando. More blue sky to the south.

We untie the airplane and load our stuff into the baggage bin behind the rear cockpit; then I go back inside for another cup of coffee. As I sip it I decide the sky to the south is definitely clearing. I throw the styrofoam cup in a trash can by the fuel pump and climb into the cockpit. David is already seated up forward.

This morning the surface wind is out of the south at five or six knots, so I use runway 18. These abandoned military fields were a real bonanza to small towns, providing them with first-class airports that small communities could never afford to build. And some can't afford to even maintain.

Eleven hundred feet puts us just on top of the scattered, patchy fog layer. I turn the flying over to David and get on the radio to Mayport tower. They cheerfully let us fly through their airspace. We spot an aircraft carrier, hull number 60, lying tied to the Mayport carrier pier. I try to remember which ship that is, but can't. She is smaller than *Nimitz*-class boats, I concude, although not by much. Her decks are bare of aircraft but there is some heavy equipment by the catapults. They must be working on the cats. Four surface warships are also tied up there. They look to my rusty eye to be a couple destroyers and two guided missile frigates.

In minutes David turns the flying back over to me and rests his head on the right side of the cockpit. I ask him if he is going to sleep. No, he's just looking.

He's not in love with flying, as I am. Perhaps that is inevitable. He will fall in love with it only if he sweats bullets trying to come up with the money for aircraft rentals and instructors and gasoline, then lies awake nights wondering why the skills are so difficult to master and the money so hard to come by. We truly value only what we earn.

South of Jacksonville we leave the last patch of fog behind. The gauzy sky gives us plenty of soft, diffused sunshine and excellent visibility.

Off to the left the sea sparkles as the sun reflects off the swells. A few fishing boats trolling their nets are in sight most of the time. No other ships. To our right the beach shines like a golden ribbon in the sun. Between the dune and highway A1A sits a single endless row of beach houses side by side, all facing the sea, that stretches away to the south until it disappears in the haze. Has anyone ever counted the houses along the beach between Jacksonville and Daytona?

Nearing De Land, David has a suggestion. "Let's land at Orlando and get the camera out of the baggage bin, then fly over Disney World."

"Why don't we land at this next airport and get the camera out? Then we'll be ready."

He agrees that would save time.

We have been flying for an hour and sixteen minutes when I cut the engine by the fuel pump in De Land. We have gas to go on to Orlando, but we fuel and oil the plane anyway.

I put the camera around my neck and we depart heading southwest. I soon turn the plane over to David while I consult my sectional chart. Let's see. . . . There is an Airport Radar Service Area in Orlando. The FAA owns the air from the surface to 4,000 feet for five nautical miles in all directions around the tower, and from 1,400 feet to 4,000 for five more miles. If we stay outside that circle with a ten-mile radius, we will be okay. And luckily Disney World is marked on the chart as being southwest of the city, safely outside the circle. Maybe five miles outside it.

We will fly southwest across the northern approaches to the city to Lake Apopka. That will be a snap to find. Then we will head straight south to Disney World. No problem.

On the way to Lake Apopka David is busy in the front cockpit, though I can't see just what he is doing. Then he sticks his right arm out in the wind. A paper airplane is attached. He turns it loose. I sigh.

Leaving Lake Apopka I see a large silver ball sitting on the ground fifteen miles or so south and point it out to David. "I'll bet that's Disney World." It is. We later learn that's the geodesic dome at EPCOT Center.

So we fly toward it. I snap some pictures of David leaning out the left side of the front cockpit, then the right. Then I change rolls of film.

Over the sprawling Disney complex I search the sky for other aircraft, then gawk at the sights below. We are flying at 1,200 feet now. As David flies I photograph. Then we turn and start back north. Now I maneuver the plane with one hand while I use the camera with the other. The sunlight is streaming through the gaps in the cloud layer a thousand feet above us onto the bright yellow wing, so I want the wing in the picture with the Disney edifices so that everyone will know that this picture wasn't taken by a NASA satellite. I shoot the whole roll of film as we fly from sunlight to shadow back to sunlight.

Heading north back to Lake Apopka, I dial in the ATIS frequency for Orlando Executive. The radio is marginal at best and the transmission is scratchy, which is one reason I don't like to work with Approach controllers. I often miss a transmission or don't get their drift. Now I listen carefully. He says something about a TCA.

A *TCA?* A huge, sprawling Terminal Control Area? My God, I thought Orlando had a piddling little ARSA!

I listen to the recording again while I stare at the sectional. Yep, he said "TCA."

A shot of adrenaline whacks me in the heart. Have I violated restricted airspace because I didn't know it was there? I cuss without keying the intercom.

Holding the stick between my knees, I wrestle with the sectional chart until I find the date information. Lordy, this thing expired in September of last year! I'm flying with an outdated chart! Well, if I've just earned my first flight violation, it's too late to sweat it now. It's done.

Flying east from Lake Apopka, I switch to Executive Tower

and listen a while. Other aircraft are coming in VFR from the north. David releases two more paper airplanes before I give Tower a call. They answer routinely.

Will some FAA enforcer be waiting for me on the ground?

A fine and license suspension would be just perfect. I stew about this all the way in.

No one is waiting for us. We taxi around awhile and a guy in a truck leads me to a place to tie down the Queen. As I wipe the oil off the fuselage I curse my own foolishness for not checking the expiration dates on these charts more carefully. A thousand details to take care of and I only remembered 999.

I make a deal with a guy who works for the FBO to wash the plane sometime during the next five days. She needs a bath to get rid of this grime. Hell, so do I.

Inside the FBO is a pilot shop. I make a beeline for it and latch onto a Jacksonville sectional chart. Outside I unfold it. Relief floods over me. They gave Orlando a TCA all right, one with the usual circle with the 30-mile radius centered on Orlando International. But the airspace that is controlled down to the altitudes where I fly the *Cannibal Queen* is rectangular, the first rectangular TCA I have ever laid eyes on. And the airspace over Disney World is uncontrolled up to 3,000 feet.

That was a close squeak.

"Did you see me release those paper airplanes?" David wants to know.

"Yeah."

"I wrote messages on them."

"Like what?"

"I can't tell you."

I scrutinize his face. He wants me to think the messages were obscene, but if I ask him he'll deny it. He gives me a big, slow grin, his braces gleaming.

His mother will be here tonight. Thank goodness.

I throw down the newspaper just as David comes back into our hotel room. He has been downstairs feeding some of my hard-earned quarters into video games. He looks tired. We swam when we first got here, then I tried to nap and read the paper while he amused himself. He stacks the unused quarters on the dresser and falls into bed facedown. In minutes he is asleep.

We have four and a half more hours to wait before the plane is due with Nancy and the girls, at 10:16 P.M. I turn on the computer and get busy.

When I turn it off three hours later, he is still asleep. I wake him and we head for the commercial airport a mile away. The terminal is really snazzy, new and modern.

The plane will be more or less on time. As we eat a tasteless hamburger in the only airport grease shop still open, I thank him for flying with me these past ten days.

He grins.

"You glad it's over?" I ask, already knowing the answer.

"Yeah," he admits. "That's a lot of flying. But thanks for taking me."

What a fine young man he is. Walking down the concourse I am still glowing; then he sticks a finger in my ribs. The flying hasn't changed him.

8

DISNEY WORLD WAS BUILT BY PEOPLE WHO THOUGHT BIG. THIS monument to the American credo that Bigger is Better and Biggest is Best cannot be seen in its entirety by any one mortal, not if he is accompanied by youngsters who insist on sleeping until 11 A.M.

Fortunately, after a day or so of walking and standing in endless lines in the muggy Florida summer heat, you will lose any desire you might have had to see the *whole* thing. The thought will occur to you that the Disney folks have a lot of people on their staff who think the perfect family vacation resort is a place where everyone can do precisely the kind of things most moms like to do on Sunday afternoons—shop in quaint little doodad stores for worthless souvenirs, wander endlessly looking at faintly amusing architecture (Oh, wow! Here's the casbah in Tangiers without the dirt and squalor and Moslem fanatics ready to slit your throat), and occasionally invest in a soft drink at movie-theater prices to keep the kids pacified. You will survey infinite vistas of manicured, weed-free lawns and flower beds while you recall your scraggly little petunia patch back home. You will listen to zillions of young children squeal about thirst and bathrooms. All this you can do on a smaller scale in any large city.

What makes Disney World special are the continuous con-
veyor belts of little plastic cars that carry a cargo of up to eight
humans each through dark, winding tunnels filled with weird
stuff. So you go from building to building, shuffle slowly
through mind-numbing mazes of crowd-control railings, and if
your bladder holds out and a thunderstorm doesn't soak you,
you will see more weird stuff than you can hope to remember
for more than an hour. And to think the people who thought
this up work for a drug-free company!

Everyone should come here at least once and find they spent
twice as much money as they thought they would. Every good
parent should give this experience to his or her children, who
will grow up warped if they don't see a million acres of grass
without weeds and all the freaky educational stuff in the tunnels. That's what's wrong with me—I'm forty-four and this is
my first visit, and probably my last unless there's a procreative
accident lurking in my future.

The first day of our Disney adventure we "did" EPCOT Center. I don't know why they always capitalize all the letters in
EPCOT, but I think it stands for something abstruse.

Our hotel was nifty in that the monorail ran right through
the fourth-floor shop and restaurant area. From the outside it
sort of looked like an ancient Mayan temple, and as I climbed
the steps it occurred to me that I was making the pilgrimage
with a lot of good sacrifice material—one first-born son and two
virgins.

Anyway, we checked into our hotel, which the desk person
said had 1,036 rooms, dumped our bags and drained off the
slag, then boarded the monorail.

At EPCOT we charged through the surging crowd for the
geodesic dome, where we boarded a little plastic car and were
transported through the ubiquitous tunnel. I have already forgotten what we saw there. We immediately scurried to the next
building and had a similar experience. The same in the third
and fourth one. Nancy and the kids did the fifth one by themselves while I loafed outside.

They saw Michael Jackson do something that earned him
outrageous bucks and came out groaning. "Now I remember

why I detest Michael Jackson," Rachael whispered to me. Lara and David just rolled their eyes. Nancy liked it though.

Hungry, jaded with the Disney experience, we found grub in a fast-food joint where everything costs twice as much as it does "outside." We were smiled at yet again by the gracious employees.

We left our trash in a can like good citizens and joined the throng outside in the grotesque humidity. A short boat ride across the lake and we were in the midst of the international exhibits, the faintly interesting architecture of which I spoke, full of shops selling knickknacks like you buy a third cousin who is getting married and restaurants selling stuff that doesn't look like anything your mother ever made.

We took in a well-done concert by a band called the College All-Stars. They played some Broadway show tunes and a group of dancers cavorted appropriately. Then we went down the walkway and Lara tried her hand at playing a dulcimer. She could learn it if she worked at it.

Now a sidewalk portrait artist caught Nancy's eye. In a twinkling Nancy had contracted for three profile portraits, one of each of the kids, which turned out to be four because she was unhappy with the way Rachael's first one turned out. It was 9 P.M. by the time the pictures were all done.

We loafed for the next hour, strolling leisurely and sitting on a flower-bed retainer wall, while waiting for the 10 P.M. light show to start. David tried to get us to scoot to the front of the mob and stand for a half hour so we would be sure and see everything, but Nancy and I scotched that. We waited patiently on our retainer wall and watched the human parade while David stewed.

The light show involved a lot of fireworks and laser lights and classical music. I was hoping they would close with Lee Greenwood's *God Bless the USA* and use fireworks to emblazon the American flag in the sky, with lasers zigging around, but they didn't. Maybe the Fourth of July.

Then we joined the mob trying to get to the parking lot and monorail. At 11 we got back to our hotel.

The next day David, Rachael and Nancy went to the Disney-MGM theme park while I wrote. Lara slept most of the day, not feeling too chipper. When the adventurers returned, I asked

David how it had gone. "Well, everybody said the Star Tour is the thing to do—'Oh yeah, you'll really like it.' So we did that. But it's all over in three minutes. It's kinda stupid."

The following day was Saturday and, by mutual consent, water sports day. We rented Water Sprites, little boats with 10-horsepower engines, at the marina in front of the hotel and putted around the lake for an hour. Nancy and I shared one, but each of the kids had one of their own. David's went the fastest, a happy accident that tickled him no end. Lara's went okay. Rachael traded hers in twice trying to get a faster boat and ended up with one that ran out of gas in the middle of the lake. The boat Nancy and I shared plowed the water at the speed of a garbage barge.

Then we packed the car and went looking for a place that rented jet skis or wind surfers or water skis. We found a jet-ski merchant on a little lake in Kissimmee.

This mogul also refused to let David pilot one. I thought the kid took it well. I would have spit on the man's shoe.

Rachael drove one with David up behind and Lara drove the other with her mother as her passenger. Just when I think I know Nancy like a book I wrote myself, she does something to astound me. I should have known. The kids tell me she learned to wind surf in Hawaii last summer.

We signed up for 40 minutes of jet skiing, but after 15 the merchant waved them in. Storm coming. About the time everyone had concluded the warning was a false alarm, the storm hit, a torrential tropical downpour that reduced visibility to about a hundred yards. After it passed, Lara and Rachael and their passengers rode the jet skis around the little lake for their remaining 25 minutes.

That evening Nancy thought it would be a good idea to go to Pleasure Island for a sit-down dinner, so we rode the bus over. We selected an Italian joint, Portofino Yacht Club. David thought the sign looked like "Pot Belly Yacht Club."

The waiter was a young man from Danville, Virginia, a first-class nice guy. As Lara pondered her dinner selection, he explained about one of the specials, a shrimp concoction. I told him to save his breath—the girl hadn't let a shrimp touch her lips in 18 years and I doubted if she would tonight.

She glanced at me, asked about the other specials, then ordered the shrimp. After the Virginian disappeared with the orders, I asked her, "Did you order shrimp just to stick it to me?"

She ignored me. As I contemplated the magnitude of my faux pas the conversation swirled on, jokes and teasing and wry comments on the state of the universe and man's precarious place in it. They are acute observers, looking for places for themselves. This fall will be Lara's freshman year in college, Rachael's sophomore year. These girls are becoming women before I am ready. They are children no longer, nor are they mature adults. They are somewhere in that gray twilight zone between.

Babies should gestate for 18 months, childhood should last 40 years, and parents should have time to learn how to be parents before the whole experience is over. If the creator of the universe ever asks my advice, I am going to suggest these changes.

Moments like this are what family vacations are really about. The essence of parenthood is to see the child mature, and where better than on an expedition to a tourist attraction? Here you see them night and day for a week or so. Here you learn what they really think, who they really are.

Sunday we went to the Magic Kingdom. It is a first cousin of California's Disneyland and I understand it was the first theme park in Disney World.

When we got to Tomorrowland all three kids saw the sign, GRAND PRIX RACING, and lined up. They came out shaking their heads. The cars are on rails and the only real control is a foot pedal to make it go, though it doesn't go very fast. Rachael's refused to go at all. This ride should be avoided by anyone over the age of eight.

> *Warning!*
> To enter this ride,
> you must be in good health,
> with no heart conditions,
> motion sickness, weak back,
> or other physical limitations.

That's what the warning sign said at Space Mountain in Tomorrowland in the Magic Kingdom park. But the sign is just

82

inches from the place you board the indoor roller coaster for a fast ride through dark, twisty tunnels. It would have been nice if they had added "weak bladder" to their list of disqualifying infirmities and posted the list out front where a fellow could chicken out with a little dignity. Now as I stare at the sign I realize I am committed.

Rachael and Lara and Nancy are behind me staring at my broad, manly back. David is in front. He turns around with his grin and announces, "You're going in the front seat."

"Uh-uh. You are."

"Not me."

I try to get behind Rachael. "I'm not going in the front seat," she tells me without a trace of shame.

Her sister, Lara, says the same thing. So does Nancy. Women! And they want equal rights!

I merely walk toward the back of the six-person car and stand there. We arrange ourselves so the front seat is empty. At last I come to my senses. I'll never live this down. "I'll ride in front," I announce with simple dignity and move that way. I can just ride the whole trip with my eyes closed—there's nothing to see in a dark tunnel anyway. The attendant waves me toward the rear, bless him. He says to leave the front seat empty.

We are quickly seated and pull our safety bars down. Then we are off. A grind up the long incline, then headfirst down the chute in the dark, right, left, up, down, the Gs tugging first one way, then another, David screaming in front of me at the top of his lungs. It's over in about 90 seconds, about the same as every roller coaster.

I suspect roller coaster freaks will think Space Mountain pretty tame. Those wooden monsters around the country that have thrilled generations of youngsters—the Twister, the Rebel Yell, the Hurricane—will squeeze the juice out of a stone. Still, it's the best ride at Disney World.

Last year my brother, John, got deathly ill on the Body Wars ride in EPCOT. He described the room where everyone sits as a cross between a cocktail shaker and a vibrator bed gone crazy. After almost losing his lunch in that contraption, he staggered out to sit for an hour and a half before regaining control of his stomach. So some of the Disney World rides might be profitably avoided by people sensitive to motion sickness.

The rides in Fantasyland are all equivalent to the carousel that sits in the middle of the area. Fantasyland is for kids still in diapers. A woman in the laundromat told me that the Thunder Mountain ride in Frontierland is pretty good, but my tribe never got that far. She said her family was from Chicago and this was their sixth Disney World vacation. "But the kids are getting too big," she said with hope in her voice, "so next year I'm voting for Colorado." I told her that made sense to me.

After the Magic Kingdom, we came back to the hotel for lunch, then got our swimming gear and drove to Typhoon Lagoon. I rented a locker and got on my swim suit, then we trooped through the wall-to-wall bodies to the beach. There is a real beach, with real sand, around a giant man-made pool with a surge device that produces one large wave every 90 seconds. I sat down behind a palm tree on the only empty pool chair we could find to guard our stuff while the kids and their mom sported in the water.

Modern swimwear hides nothing, and with a crowd of thousands to examine, I saw every imaginable body type and size known to medical science. Big guts, big butts, big thighs, little guts, little butts . . . I qualified there as an expert witness able to swear that people come in all shapes and sizes. Which I already knew. The only excitement I had was watching a tartlet in a teeny-weeny bikini that barely contained her truly mammoth assets light a cigarette and suck on it with puckered, painted, Lolita lips.

Did I make such a fool of myself when I attempted to claim an adult's estate?

After a half hour sweating in the oppressive heat and humidity trying to remember, I was ready for the baby-urine and chlorine mixture they advertise as water in these parts. Just then an announcement came over the loudspeaker that a storm was coming—this is Florida, folks—and the pool was closed. Everybody out!

More time passed and so did the crowd. Just when I had decided my brood was missing in action, they arrived. After ten minutes in the water they had elected to make the pilgrimage to the top of the water slide. They trudged and trudged as the line slowly scaled the artificial mountain, and were only ten or so bodies away from the slide when the announcement came closing the pool. So they had to about-face and follow the crowd back down the steps.

We fought our way through the adults, teenagers and squalling kids all reeking of perspiration and chlorine, retrieved my pants from the locker and headed back to the hotel.

It never did rain.

Back at the hotel we gave the Water Sprites another try. This time Nancy got her own boat and it turned out to be the quickest. She refused to switch with David. As usual, I got a dud and brought it back to the dock after thirty minutes. Nancy and the kids stayed out going round and round the lake for the whole hour.

Today, Monday, our last full day in Orlando, Nancy and the kids went to Sea World to see Shamu the Killer Whale do whatever it is killer whales do. I elected to skip the expedition and write. They just returned at 5:30 P.M. and said they had a great day. David is still looking at the shark picture in the brochure. "The best part of the whole trip," they agreed. Yet I think they are ready for the plane ride home tomorrow morning. The neighbor keeping Lara's dog told them on the phone that it hasn't eaten since they left.

This family vacation was a good one. The memories I will carry with me are of Rachael, Lara and David eating dinner as their mother monitored their manners, their eyes flashing as they told jokes and enjoyed themselves hugely, and their explanations to their stuck-in-the-mud parents of how the world looks to them. I will remember the giggling as ice cream ran down their fingers, the gleeful shouts as they gunned Water Sprites and jet skis with hair flying in the wind, the shrieks and laughter as the roller coaster shot down into the darkness rolling, twisting and bucking on an unknown path through unknown perils toward an unknown destination.

They have courage. They are willing to try and brave enough to pick themselves up when they fall down. They want to see it all, try it all, live it all. Nancy and I have made our share of mistakes, but somehow the children acquired courage. Maybe they had it all along and our mistakes have not diminished or tarnished it. Whichever, all three of them have it, and for that I am truly thankful.

9

FLYING NORTH OUT OF ORLANDO AT 1,200 FEET I AM CLAD IN only a knit shirt and shorts. I am physically comfortable and worried. The air is too hot and too humid and in these climes at this time of year that means thunderstorms. Unfortunately it was 11:25 in the morning before I got the big Lycoming fired off, and nine minutes later before the tail came up as I added power.

I put Nancy and the children on the airliner at Orlando International at 9:15. Then the plane sat on the sun-drenched ramp until 10 while I stared through the window at the puffy clouds probably destined to grow into thunderbumpers and hopped from foot to foot. Finally I asked one of the airline personnel what the delay was. "Nothing mechanical," she told me.

I just nodded. If not mechanical, then what? Air Traffic Control? After they just got their big TCA that took half of central Florida? Apparently she sensed her answer was unsatisfactory, so she went to ask her own questions.

In a moment she was back. "They are emptying the toilet tanks."

I returned to the window where I could look at the Boeing

737 and watch the sky. I began to feel uneasy. Emptying the toilet tanks after a flight is undoubtedly on somebody's checklist, yet it didn't get done. What else didn't get done? All the kids and ex-wives I have in this world are on that plane. I scrutinized the crew in the cockpit. The pilot was middle-aged and had a bigger waistband than I do. He was sitting on the arm of the captain's seat shooting the breeze with the copilot and a flight attendant. Had he checked the fuel load, the oil?

At 10:05 they drove the honey wagon away, closed the hatch, and pushed the plane back. I started for the monorail back to the main terminal. By the time I boarded and it left on its little trip to the terminal, the 737 was taxiing out. He would be above this weather soon and cruising westward into dryer skies. The Disney adventurers should have a good flight home.

Eight miles north at Orlando Executive the *Cannibal Queen* was flashing her yellow skin at me as the line boy drove me across the ramp to where they had her tied down. Her bath had been worth the money.

I borrowed a stepladder and got out my screwdriver. The oil filter for the Lycoming engine does not have a disposable element, but rather has a scraper that needs to be rotated periodically to remove the accumulated crud from the filter element. I have resolved to perform this essential task this morning since I have already postponed it once before. Unfortunately, to get at the oil filter, an accessory on the back of the engine, one must remove the AT-10 nose cowling completely, then open the left engine accessory access panel. I sweated on the hot ramp and managed to get pretty greasy. A fellow came over and helped me reinstall the cowling.

That done, I finished packing the plane, broke down the tie-downs, walked around her once and climbed into the cockpit. There I inspected the charts and looked again at the sky. Puffy clouds. I wiped my face on my shirttail and strapped in. Time to fly.

Still in a hurry, not yet concentrating on the business at hand, I then made a mistake. While working on the cowling I was wishing David were here and wondering what it was going to be like flying without him. When I finished that job, I should have gone inside, washed my hands and had a cup of coffee and a smoke while I shifted gears and thought about flying. I didn't.

With the engine running I flipped open my airport book, found Orlando and dialed in the ATIS frequency. It was scratchy. I resolved to personally rip this radio out with my bare hands and smash it when I got the *Queen* back to Boulder this fall.

Information Yankee. Runway 17. Winds calm. Altimeter 30.07. Okay. I called Clearance Delivery. They were garbled. Someone talking. Finally I found a quiet spot and made my call. No answer. Two calls later I told them who I am, where I wanted to go and got a departure freq and a squawk. Now I called Ground. "Ground, Stearman 58700 wants to taxi with Yankee."

Ground was equally scratchy, practically unreadable. Blast Marconi, anyway. Ground finally gave me permission to taxi, and I rolled the *Queen.* Then they asked just where on the ramp I was.

The light dawned. I stared at the page in the airport book. That airport didn't look like this one. God, I'd been talking to Orlando International! No wonder they couldn't find me on their ramp—I'm not there. I'm at Orlando Executive!

I applied the brakes, stopping the *Queen* dead. Turn the page, begin the exercise in radio departure all over again. Now the radio was clear as a bell.

Coonts, you're a damn fool. You're worrying about an airline pilot flying your kids around and you can't even fly your own piddly little airplane.

During engine runup it occurred to me that Orlando International Ground was probably still looking for that dingaling Stearman pilot who said he was there, somewhere. I asked Executive Ground to give the other airport a call and tell them what happened. But first I had to explain to Executive Ground and everyone listening on the frequency what an idiot I am. I bit the bullet and did it.

I consoled myself with the thought that I was not the first one, nor will I be the last. I am merely the latest.

Floating along over central Florida in my knit short-sleeve shirt, I am finally concentrating on the business at hand. I've been embarrassed before and know that it isn't fatal. Embarrassment doesn't even need stitches. I forget about past mistakes and study the clouds. It's too hot. Too humid. Gonna get bad. And I got a late start.

I want to get the hell out of Florida. Today if possible.

The clouds are covering more and more of the sky. North of De Land I fly through my first little rain shower. On the other side the water clings in beads to the clean fabric of the ailerons and I amuse myself by picking one up, then the other, letting the air push the droplets off the trailing edge.

I fly through another shower just south of the St. Johns River estuary where it turns north and widens out. I follow the rule, Don't enter a shower unless you can see through to the other side. Ignore that rule just once in Florida and you'll think you've flown into a waterfall. In Colorado you're liable to fly into granite.

It looks pretty dark up toward Jacksonville. I give Cecil Tower a call and ask to transit the southern half of their airport traffic area westward in order to remain clear of a restricted area south of Cecil.

"Cecil is IFR," the tower controller says. "Remain clear."

Okay, now I know. That dark stuff is a boomer. But it looks lighter to the west and the ceiling above me is fairly high.

Studying the chart and getting it blown around while I hang on to it for dear life and try to fly the plane with my knees, I see that the restricted area south of Cecil has an 1,800 foot roof. I think I can get over that. I add power and climb.

At 2,200 feet and still almost a thousand feet under the clouds, I head westward with the blue-black wall of clouds over Jacksonville off my right wing. Approaching the Florida state prison, I am tempted to continue west to Lake City. The sky looks good that way. But I remember that grass field at Hilliard. I elect to swing north to hit Interstate 10 at MacClenny, then slightly northeast to St. George, then on to that little grass airstrip at Hilliard—the route David and I took last week on our way to Fernandina Beach—where I will stop for fuel and call Flight Service for a weather update. That's the plan and it works. I pass around the western edge of the storm over Jacksonville and motor northward in fairly decent conditions.

Hilliard doesn't look as inviting as it did the first time I saw it. Water is standing in several places on the runway and I can't see anything that looks like a fuel pump. I need gas. As I make a circuit I look again at the fuel gauge, a float device that sticks down out of the tank in the upper wing. Still a smidgen over a quarter of a tank. I've been airborne for two hours and twenty minutes.

So no fuel at Hilliard. The nearest airfield is Davis, six or seven miles up the road. I swing the plane to the northwest and fly up U.S. 1. Five minutes later I am inspecting the Davis Airport near the little town of Folkston, Georgia. It has a paved runway but no fuel pump.

Now where? Clouds look iffy to the northwest, up toward Waycross, Georgia.

I examine the chart again. St. Marys is nearer than Waycross. It's down the river on the intracoastal waterway. The weather looks iffy that way too. Still black toward Jacksonville. I mull it over for fifteen seconds. St. Marys is darn near at sea level if I have to sneak in. And if it's under a rain shower, I can go across the river to Fernandina Beach.

East it is.

Five minutes later east doesn't look like a very good choice. Fog rises in tendrils from the pine forest, an endless expanse of green broken only by a meandering river. Visibility coming down. I call St. Marys Unicom and get an immediate answer. "Wind out of the northeast at four. No other reported traffic."

I drop to 400 feet over the river as the ceiling comes down, but it is merely a thin wall of cloud that I quickly pass under. On the other side the sky is almost clear, the visibility excellent.

I drop into St. Marys, Georgia, and shut the *Queen* down at the fuel pump with a sigh of relief. Two-point-seven hours in the air and a lucky break on the weather here. I should have gone to Lake City. At least the landing here was decent.

This is the first time I have ever flown an airplane cross-country with no electronic navigation aids. I've done my share of flitting about the nation in a cockpit, but all of it was in airplanes capable of instrument flight—usually on an IFR flight plan—and all of it was done at altitude, not at 1,500 feet above the ground with one eye on a sectional chart and the other on the clouds. So I'm making mistakes. And, I hope, learning, so the mistakes will not be repeated. Over Hilliard I should have called St. Marys and asked about their weather. If it was bad I should have landed right there at Hilliard.

In the future I will try to be more careful, think further ahead and make better use of the radio, but I will have to continue to fly under cloud systems. If I fly only when the weather is perfect this trip will take a couple of years.

Mistakes are inevitable in aviation, especially when one is still learning new things. The trick is to not make the mistake that will kill you.

Experience, the wise man said, is a hard teacher. First comes the test, then the lesson.

Forty-five minutes later I lift off and fly westward five miles to pick up Interstate 95 northward. The wall of cloud that I slipped under coming in has drifted away to the south. I am at 1,000 feet and everything looks fine. Flight Service says the weather improves significantly to the northward, and the fields in South Carolina are reporting 4,000 scattered. The trick will be to get there.

It won't happen today. In minutes I am forced down to 400 feet above the ground. I turn around and head right back to St. Marys.

The lady at the desk gives me a ride into town, where the motel only wants $39 for a room. The room is as nice as the one at Disney World and a whale of a lot cheaper. Within an hour the rain is pelting down. My room is on the second floor, and when the air conditioner is off I can hear the rain pounding on the roof. I lie down and try to relax as I listen to the rain.

Sleep doesn't come. I review the flight again and list my mistakes, analyzing them. The rain continues to fall.

My wake-up call comes at 5:30 A.M. It is still dark outside, but with the curtain back I can see that rain is still falling. An hour later, as the sky lightens, it stops. Clouds up there, but high.

The airport lady picks me up at 7:15. Her name is Stephanie Harmon. Her two young sons are in the car and will spend the day at the airport with her. When her husband, Loren, retired from the Navy several years ago, they fulfilled his lifelong ambition—they bought an FBO. Then Loren got a job flying for Continental and now he's based on Guam, in the Pacific, so guess who gets to run the FBO. That's what I call true love.

Listening to Stephanie, one gets the impression that she can handle anything that comes up at the airport. A couple months ago she returned from a tour in the Persian Gulf with the Naval Reserve. She's a loadmaster on one of their C-9 cargo planes and routinely flies all over the country when she's not running the FBO at St. Marys.

When I taxied out in the *Queen,* Stephanie was getting ready to gas a Piper Aztec that was inbound. She was on top of the above-ground fuel tank, checking gauges and turning valves, and she looked up and waved. I waved back.

The Harmons are dreamers, of course, investing a small life's savings plus sweat, blood and tears in an effort to make a little business go. America was built by dreamers like these, dreamers not afraid of work or big government. I hope the Harmons make it. In a few years I'm going back to St. Marys to see how it worked out.

I watched the Aztec circle the airport as I strapped myself in. The ceiling is obviously well above the 800-foot traffic pattern, maybe at 3,000 or 4,000 feet, which jibes with what the weather briefer at Flight Service told me on the telephone. He was optimistic, full of good news about 4,500-foot ceilings north and east.

Stephanie suggested I fly along the coast taking advantage of the sea breeze that is evident here in St. Marys. The cool air coming in off the ocean will be laden with moisture, but usually it doesn't turn to cloud until it is well inland. That doesn't quite fit with the grand plan, but I mull her suggestion now. If I am going to land in all forty-eight of the contiguous United States, I should strike straight north, then swing over into Tennessee and Kentucky. But the weather guy said the Smokies are gooey and have been like that for three or four days. And I would have to cross them twice.

Flying north at 1,500 feet with the ceiling at least several thousand feet over my head, I decide to follow Stephanie's suggestion. The heck with Tennessee and Kentucky. I'll make my haj to Kill Devil Hill where man got off the ground and visit the Wright Brothers Museum. That'll be more fun than Opryland.

I turn the Queen for St. Andrew Sound. I pick up the town of Brunswick on the north point of the estuary at about seven or eight miles. The smoke from the stack of the Brunswick pulp mill trails off to the southwest at a decent clip. I've got a crisp headwind, maybe 15 knots. To my left are the usual pine forests—to the right a dozen miles or so of salt marshes and then the barrier islands, just visible in the haze. Beyond them, the Atlantic.

I waggle the stick. The Queen shakes herself obediently. We are flying again. If only David Paul were in the front cockpit!

I follow I-95 north from Brunswick. It will run right into Savannah, where I initially plan to land and gas up. I didn't gas up after my weather recce flight last night, so I started today a few gallons short.

Flying north from Brunswick I change the plan. I decide to skirt Savannah along the beach and continue the extra 25 miles or so to Hilton Head. So I turn right, toward the sea, and leave the interstate highway behind.

Along the coast the land becomes water in stages. This low coast is dozens of miles of salt marshes with streams meandering lazily through them. The rare dry land is covered with pines. Only occasionally does one see a road leading down to a shack by the water with a boat dock attached. A few boats are visible all the time, but only a few.

An hour and twenty minutes after takeoff I am abeam Savannah. The headwind is taking its toll. Savannah Beach is the first beach town I have seen, complete with houses and streets and parking lots. Small crowds are visible on the beach but at 1,500 feet I am too high to wave. I wave anyway.

Off to the right sunlight breaks through holes in the clouds and falls upon the sea, making the water glisten and shine.

I fly northeast up Hilton Head Island looking with awe at the houses and golf courses below. Never have I seen so many huge homes or golf courses or yacht basins. I drop down to 1,000 feet to get a better look.

This place is a sea-level Aspen! The whole island is one giant, manicured *estate!* And I thought it was just old-money trendy, like Martha's Vineyard. Ha! Those are *big* houses down there, friends. And this West Virginia hillbilly can fly at 84 knots—less due to the headwind—a thousand feet above all those rich folks' homes in a noisy forty-nine-year-old wood-and-canvas crate with a naked floozie painted on the side and they can't do one blessed thing about it except stand on the seventeenth fairway and shake their fists at me! America is a great country.

At the airport I park the Stearman right beside a shiny turbo-prop twin with the passenger stair open. Waiting for Mrs. Van-derbilt, probably. After gassing up and adding oil, I call Flight Service. Looks good all the way to Hatteras, the man says.

A half hour after leaving Hilton Head I begin to have my doubts. Over the sea the clouds are thickening, leaving no gaps for the sunlight to sneak through and dance on the surface of the ocean. The scattered layer of scud is back at 1,800 feet, and it is also thickening. And the wind—my progress over this chart has slowed to a glacial pace. How slow I am not exactly sure, but it takes me 55 minutes of flying to reach the mouth of Charleston harbor abeam Fort Sumter. (That evening I carefully measure—the distance from Hilton Head to Fort Sumter is 52 nautical miles.)

To the west readily visible in the haze is the city of Charles-ton. Above it airliners circle to land. Just off my right a warship is coming up the channel to enter the bay. To the left a tour boat is tied alongside the fort—probably brought a load of day cruisers down the bay from Charleston. From this altitude I can see the Stars and Stripes over the fort standing stiff in the breeze. No doubt tourists are wandering about the ruins think-ing about that spring evening in 1861 when the Confederates opened fire with cannons upon that fort, sounding the death knell for slavery and starting the American Civil War.

Ten minutes later I decide the weatherman was all wet. The murk ahead makes it obvious that I can't continue to follow the coast to the northeast. But what is going on here? The ATIS at Myrtle Beach Air Force Base says the field is 4,500 broken and seven miles visibility. Either the ATIS is wrong or there is a wall of rain between here and there.

Staring through the prop arc at lowering clouds and worsen-ing visibility, I ponder my karma. Will I ever get to fly from bad weather into good? Not today, at any rate.

Georgetown, South Carolina, is northeast along U.S. 17. I give the airport there a call and ask about the weather. They tell me about the wind, out of the northeast at ten and gusting.

I make a decent landing, considering. The rain starts falling gently as I finish fueling, so I lock the controls and install the waterproof cockpit cover.

Standing in the lobby of the FBO I study their wall chart. Due to the headwind it has taken 1.8 hours to fly the 100 nautical miles from Hilton Head. That works out to about 25 knots of headwind. For the Queen, that's a lot, about 30 percent of her performance. That is the equivalent of a 150-knot headwind for a jet airliner.

The lady at the desk hands me the keys to the courtesy car, but asks that I wait for the two guys from the helicopter just landing and take them to lunch too. I agree readily and watch the chopper settle onto the mat in the gusty wind and rain.

They are ready to go thirty minutes later. By now the rain has become steady, like it is setting in for the day. The helicopter pilot, Dennis Taylor, calls Flight Service, then assures me that this is just a shower.

Sure.

Sharing a table at the Shoney's in Georgetown, the three of us become acquainted. Dennis' passenger is the South Carolina Marine and Wildlife biologist in charge of alligators, Tom Swayngham. He and Dennis have been counting alligator nests all morning and rain or not, they are going to be at it all afternoon.

On the way back to the airport they compare their Hurricane Hugo survival stories from last summer. "I always wanted to go through a hurricane," Tom says with a trace of wonder in his voice, "but I done scratched that itch. Never again."

They ask if I saw the damage the hurricane caused when I was flying up from Charleston. I didn't. The altitude and my concern about the weather caused me to miss any damage I could attribute to last summer's hurricane. I did see visible evidence of the subsiding coast in Georgia and South Carolina south of Charleston—dead trees standing on the beach and lying in the sand, graphic evidence that the beach is eating into the vast pine forest that covers the land to the high-tide mark—

and I tell them about it. Someday Atlanta will be a seaport. Won't the developers love it?

Dennis wants his photo taken by the logo of the *Cannibal Queen;* then he snaps one of me. If I get killed in this airplane this summer, that photo he took will be valuable, worth at least a dollar cash money to any reputable collector.

The rain is still falling when Dennis and Tom fire off their chopper and whop-whop away to look for alligators. I go inside and call Flight Service.

The weather to the north is excellent—well, good might be a better word. If I could only get there! I read the paper, an article about the WPA back in the Great Depression, and examine the fine collection of turn-of-the-century photographs of Georgetown that are displayed upon the wall. I contemplate investing in a candy bar and examine the state of my cash resources, then decide against it.

By 2:30 the rain peters out and I have exhausted my tiny stock of patience. Now or never. I ready the Queen and mount up. At the end of the runway I get an unobstructed view of the low gray sky and the scud fleeing across underneath. I merely turn the Queen around and taxi to a spot where I can tie her down for the night.

Adjacent to my motel in Georgetown is an old cemetery with a large statue of a Confederate soldier. On the pedestal facing Church Street appears the word "Chickamauga." I wander over for a closer look.

The cemetery is old and most of the gravestones are gone. Yet the cemetery was once full: everywhere there are slight depressions in the sandy soil where the graves have subsided. The latest death I can find on the stones that remain is 1888. Burials seem to have started in the 1830s. Among those interred are some preachers and a doctor. Some of the markers are marble slabs that lie flat, covering brick vaults into which the casket was lowered. The flat slabs are covered with vegetation and moss. One is broken and has fallen into the vault.

On one slab I can see extensive writing now mostly illegible, but I can read the words, "Sacred to the memory of . . ." I can't make out the name.

The statue is a memorial to the men of Company A, Georgetown Rifle Guards, 10th South Carolina Regiment of Infantry,
Confederate States of America. The names of four battles appear
on the pedestal: Franklin, Murfreesboro, Chickamauga, and Atlanta. The inscription says the statue was erected in 1891 by
"the women of Georgetown" and is "dedicated to the men who
died, or faced death, in the war that asserted constitutional
liberty and affirmed our manhood." *Our* manhood? The women
of Georgetown? They must have meant that in the larger sense.

1891. *Now* it hits me. That was a *hundred* years ago.

"Asserted constitutional liberty." Now there is a phrase, one
of those slippery little devils that likely some politician thought
up. Sounds like it would be difficult to get a handle on that
one, especially when applied to a war in which the fundamental issue was the South's ability to protect the institution of
human slavery.

Georgetown, South Carolina, is today a beautiful small seaport town, and likely a relatively prosperous one. On the south
end of town are a large steel mill and a pulp mill. A big ocean-
going freighter was tied up next to the steel mill pier. Back
from the waterfront and old Front Street are block after block
of large frame homes beautifully painted and preserved and
shaded by giant trees. The residential neighborhoods look like
models for those idyllic prints of Americana that sell so well
at Christmas.

The population seems to be about half black, half white. I
was eating chicken at a Kentucky Fried that evening when a
three- or four-year-old black boy began to inspect the ashtrays
on every table while his mother's back was turned. When he
saw me watching him he gave me a huge grin.

After the boy was dragged away by his mother, I got to thinking about this multiracial society that those folks buried in that
old cemetery—and those who put up the Confederate memorial
statue—were unwilling to even try to envision. Although civil
rights activists like to look forward and point out the length of
the trail we have still to travel, it seems to me that occasionally
we ought to reflect on how far we have come.

The taste I have gotten of the South this past week or so
makes it seem a far different place from the hotbed of hatred I
entered in the late 1960s. I remember watching a high school

football game in Meridian, Mississippi, in 1968 and listening to the white cheerleader types behind me, the flower of southern womanhood, make bitter, vicious remarks about the "niggers" and "jungle bunnies" who were just then starting to attend *their* high school under court order. If my samplings can be relied upon, that mean spirit seems to have dissipated. Indeed, this afternoon in a Georgetown barber shop some mouthy local yokel was holding forth about this and that, and twice he referred to black folks as "black," not "niggers," although his little audience of three white males would have been, in the past, the perfect forum for derogatory racial references. Those references didn't come.

There are people today who argue that the South has the best racial climate in the country. Perhaps they're right. On Front Street this afternoon a black policeman walking the beat nodded and smiled at me. Black cops don't do that in Denver or Detroit. I returned that smile with my face, and my heart.

10

First light on Thursday morning reveals more low clouds whipping swiftly across the sky from the northeast. At the airport I call Flight Service from a pay phone booth beside the FBO building. Waiting for the electrons to signal a live human that another live human is on the line, I read the notice that informs me that I should call the South Carolina Aviation Commission in the event of an aircraft accident involving death or injury. Presumably if you are butchered on the highway the cops will tell the state, if they are interested.

The briefer is positively jovial. Fayetteville, North Carolina, north of where I stand, is 4,500 scattered—New Bern is 25,000 scattered, Dare County on North Carolina's outer banks is clear, visibility unrestricted. And he informs me this low scud will stop coming in off the sea in a couple of hours. "You're going to have a great day flying."

I thank him and carry my bags out to the Queen. Looking north I can see gaps in the scud with light coming through them. Dark and gloomy to the northwest and west. After the Queen's untied and preflighted and the bags loaded, I light my pipe and watch the clouds.

The gap to the north is growing. Still some wispy dark-gray scud, but there's open sky in that direction. I can see it.

The big round Lycoming engine fires as soon as I switch on the mags. Helmet on, goggles arranged, I taxi out. The ramp is still wet and water thrown from the main tires comes back over the lower wings.

The tail comes up as soon as the engine reaches full power—this is the kick of flying from these sea-level fields. The Queen accelerates readily as the radial roars its song and the prop takes huge bites of the thick, wet air. After a very short run I lift her off the wet runway. It's 7:20 A.M.

I climb to 1,000 feet and fly along just under the scud. My path takes me over Georgetown. I pick up the highway heading north, with the intracoastal waterway on my right. The pine forest that feeds the pulp mills stretches away in three directions, broken only by occasional homes and roads that from this altitude seem to wander aimlessly. To the east is the sea, and I examine the light levels coming through the clouds in that direction. This stuff is breaking up.

Abeam Myrtle Beach I leave the scud behind. Still a ceiling above me, but it's thinning perceptibly. I let the Queen drift up to 1,500 feet. Forty-five minutes after takeoff I leave all the clouds behind. Five or so miles overhead a gauzy thin layer of cirrus admits most of the sunlight, making the Cannibal Queen's wings glow brilliantly for the first time since I left Orlando.

My daughter Rachael has a phrase and gesture for moments like this, and I indulge myself. "All right!" I roar exultantly and jab my fist aloft into the prop blast. "All right!"

After another thirty minutes of painstakingly looking for landmarks amid the North Carolina small farms, it occurs to me that I could go higher. After all, the view will be so much better up there. Why am I crawling across the earth at little more than the height at which robins fly?

Prop to full increase, a little more gas to the engine, then throttle forward to the stop. Up we go into the open sky. I level at 3,500 feet and look around carefully. Oh yes, there's that town fifteen miles to the north, that lake off to the southeast, that large tower that the map says is right there.

But it's cool over North Carolina at 3,500 feet. Clad only in jeans and a long-sleeve shirt, I feel a little chilly. It's a great feeling for the 27th day of June in the South.

After a fuel stop in Kinston, my route takes me northeast toward Albemarle Sound. I need to get around the big restricted area that is the Navy's Dare County bombing range, so I fly eastward on the north side of it, parallel to the southern shore of Albemarle.

At one point I glance off to my right and pick up a jet coming out of the restricted area toward me at my altitude of 3,500 feet. An A-6 Intruder, like I used to fly. This one passes behind me climbing northward toward Elizabeth City, doing maybe 250 knots. His low-visibility paint scheme is quite evident. I look left and watch the Intruder disappear into the vastness of the sky, still climbing. I wonder if he saw this bright yellow biplane?

The FBO at Dare County Airport in Manteo, North Carolina, has the nicest FBO office I have ever visited. The building is wood frame with big windows, obviously not the cheapest shack the proprietor could erect. The ceiling of the interior is two stories up, and everything is painted white. The cheery surroundings and comfortable furniture invite you to give your bottom a treat and linger awhile.

But I have places to go. A six-minute hop across the water is First Flight Airport on the Outer Banks, adjacent to the Wright Brothers Monument and Museum at Kill Devil Hill. The complex is administered by the National Park Service.

The first shock occurs when I get a squint at the airport, a single strip of asphalt in a woodlot of large, mature trees that seemingly come right to the edge of the runway on both sides. Descending on final to runway 2 is like sinking into a canyon.

I make an acceptable landing in front of what I know will be onlookers, then taxi to the parking area just off the south end of the strip. There is no FBO, no fuel available, no snack bar or pop machines, just a ramp full of little airplanes and an entrepreneur giving joyrides to park pilgrims.

I shoot the breeze a little with him, then set off afoot for the monument atop Kill Devil Hill. Another shock. In all the photos and paintings of the Wrights' flight experiments, Kill Devil Hill is as bald as Don Rickles' head. The Wrights went there because the hill and adjacent dunes were devoid of vegetation and the sea wind blew unobstructed. And there were no trees. A wise man who plans to venture skyward in a homemade flying machine should do it in a place without any bothersome trees nearby that would attract his craft like a magnet attracts iron filings. Every person who has ever watched a tree lure and devour kites is familiar with this principle.

Yet today Kill Devil Hill is covered with vegetation that holds the sand in place. The sandy plain to the north of the hill where the Wrights flew the first successful airplane is similarly covered. Huge trees stand to the west on both sides of the asphalt runway, to the north beyond the marker that shows where the Wrights' fourth flight ended that fateful December 17, 1903, and to the east toward the park entrance.

It seems ironic to me—to protect the area from erosion and preserve it for future generations, the Park Service has so altered the place that the Wrights would reject it today if they were looking for a place to fly.

In the little museum you will get the flavor of what the place used to be—a windswept dune by the Atlantic, two brothers toiling with bits of wood and fabric and wire, trying to coax a twelve-horsepower four-cylinder engine to work reliably while the salt wind blew sand into everything. In the old photographs you will see a few of the locals from Manteo. No tourists, of course: the great American vacation at the seashore had not yet become the annual religious pilgrimage that it is today.

The Wrights first came to this place in 1900 to work with a glider. They returned in 1901 and 1902 with other gliders, the last big enough to carry a man. Here they analyzed and solved the problem of control. Here they verified the data from their Dayton experiments on the proper shape of a wing. Here they taught themselves to fly. That was their other great insight, which followed as soon as they understood the realities of control—flying would have to be learned.

When they returned to Kill Devil Hill in 1903 their glider had an engine they had designed and built themselves. Commercial manufacturers had not yet produced a lightweight engine with sufficient power for their purposes. These two dreamers were the eternal Yankee tinkerers—if they couldn't buy what they needed at a reasonable price, they made it themselves. They were always willing to experiment and try until they found something that worked.

102

Finally they were ready. They had learned all that they could from gliders, their engine worked after a fashion, the airplane was as ready as two very careful men could make it.

On December 17 Orville went first. The first flight was a mere 120 feet. Today a white stone painted with a big "1" marks the place where he landed. Wilbur went next, a flight of 175 feet. Orville flew the third one, about 250 feet.

Wilbur made the fourth flight that day, and the "4" stone stands far away with the tall trees behind it. There is no doubt. As you stand beside the commemorative stone at the launch point and stare at that fourth marker 852 feet away, you comprehend the full enormity of the Wrights' achievement. Here man first rose from the earth in a heavier-than-air machine and flew in powered, controlled flight. They had truly flown.

Inside the museum you will find a replica of the Wrights' 1903 Flyer. And you will find a replica of one of their gliders.

Stare at the photographs and paintings: try to get inside the minds of those two bicycle mechanics who were convinced that man could fly and they were the men who could do it. Then go back outside and stand at the launch point and contemplate that fourth stone. That is the yardstick to measure your dreams against.

Back at the airstrip I was smoking my pipe and feasting my eyes upon the *Cannibal Queen* when the joyride entrepreneur asked if I would like to share cookies and potato chips. I begged off. Although it was after 1 o'clock and I hadn't eaten, the thought of all that sugar and carbohydrates killed my appetite.

The man's name is Jay Mankedick, and he and his pilots and airplanes are based at Manteo. They commute to work by air. Jay has a concession from the Park Service to offer rides here. He said he still enjoys the flying and the pilots and seeing the kick people get out of taking their first airplane ride.

"I first came here with five hundred bucks in my pocket and no job. I leased a plane and slept out in the woods for the first month."

We shook hands and I wished him well. As tough as it is to make a living flying planes, Jay seems to have found a niche. And a whole lot of people who go flying with him and his pilots get a taste of real flying, not the airline passenger stuff, which is to flying what masturbation is to sex, merely a pale imitation of the real thing.

I preflight and strap into the *Queen.* "Let's rock and roll," John Weisbart used to say. I used that line once with David, and he used it a couple times after that when we climbed into the plane.

Hearing it from the boy surprised me somehow, and pleased me. Yeah, let's rock and roll.

I take off on runway 2 and climb out over the beach northbound. The *Cannibal Queen* is flying well. If only Orville and Wilbur were here to go flying with me.

I wonder if Orville ever met Lloyd Stearman? Wilbur died young, of course, but Orville lived until 1948. No doubt he saw Stearmans flying.

I don't know much about Lloyd Stearman, but he was a contemporary of Walter Beech and Clyde Cessna, all three of whom worked for the Travel Air Company in the 1920s.

Travel Air is remembered for a magnificent sport biplane of the same name that Lloyd Stearman designed and the company manufactured and sold to wealthy sportsmen in the late 1920s. Travel Air didn't sell many. The plane was expensive and sport aviation was but a dream in a nation that had almost no airports worthy of the name. Anyone traveling took a train. Barnstormers—those itinerant aerial gypsies—were still alighting in cow pastures and buying gasoline by the bucketful from farmers. Anyone with an irresistible urge to aviate could still buy an old Jenny for a few hundred dollars, so the thousands that a new Travel Air commanded meant the company sold very few of them. And of those they sold, still fewer survive today, treasured by their proud owners and only occasionally rolled from their hangars on pristine, perfect mornings to take to the sky.

Stearman, Beech and Cessna all went their own ways and founded their own companies. As was the innocent custom, they all named their new enterprises after themselves.

Stearman's first proprietary design was the 1927 C-1, the first of thirty different models that he produced between 1926 and 1930. After a series of corporate mergers, Lloyd Stearman left the company in 1931. New management decided to try for an Army contract, thinking that there was an opportunity in the

Army's specification for a new biplane trainer. They set engineers Harold Zipp and Jack Clark to modifying Stearman's basic design. Legend has it these two completed the job in sixty days.

Although any knowledgeable observer could see that the future of aviation was in monoplanes that offered less drag and more performance for the same horsepower, the U.S. Army was even more conservative then than it is today. The generals were still insisting on open-cockpit bombers and biplane fighters. And they wanted an open-cockpit, tandem-seat biplane trainer to replace the Jenny.

Stearman's prototype trainer was ready in late 1933 and the military tested it in March 1934. The Army declined to buy any, but the Navy ordered sixty-one of them. Stearman was on its way.

The Army continued to test slightly improved models of Stearman's trainer, but continued to defer purchases. Finally, in 1936, the Army began to buy.

But apparently the coffers of the tiny Stearman company were empty. Boeing took over lock, stock and Stearmans on April 1, 1938. Boeing expanded the Wichita plant during the war, hired thousands of workers and sold every biplane trainer it could produce to the Army and Navy. Some, like mine, went to the Canadians. The British got some too. All the Stearmans were manufactured in Wichita. It's ironic, in a way, that Boeing, the company that was manufacturing B-17s and B-29s as fast as they could crank them out, also made the vast bulk of the 8,584 Stearman biplanes, an obsolete design from a bygone era. Spare parts manufactured raised the equivalent total to 10,346 planes, more than any other biplane produced prior to that time.

The most numerous biplane ever built, the Antonov An-2 Colt, didn't even fly until 1947. The Soviets made 5,000 of them and the Poles made 8,200. With single 1,000-HP radial engines, they were used as ag sprayers, transports, you name it. What does an An-2 look like? A great big Stearman.

Several hundred Stearmans were still on back order in 1945 when the Army canceled production. Skid Henley told me that the Army told Boeing it would pay for the airplanes on the assembly line, but Boeing didn't have to actually assemble them. Boeing didn't work that way—they assembled all the aircraft anyway. Henley said he went to Wichita and paid $600 for

105

one of those brand-new, just-off-the-assembly-line, government-surplus instant antiques. He flew it home.

Today it is easy to see that the Stearman trainer embodied everything aircraft designers had learned about biplanes since the Wright brothers. It had all of the inherent virtues of biplanes—strong, simple to build, cheap and easy to maintain, easy to fly—and the biplane's inevitable vices—slow, thirsty for gasoline, difficult to land in a crosswind. The Army got exactly what the generals wanted—the ultimate biplane with just enough engine to get it off the ground and force the student to learn to fly the wing, not the engine.

To be fair to the generals, the fact that the aircraft was slow didn't matter. As a primary trainer it always took off and landed at the same place. And the generals didn't give a fig about the fuel burn—the government was buying gasoline for a few cents a gallon. The Stearman's crosswind landing characteristics were of equally small concern: in the mid-1930s U.S. Army airfields were huge, mile-square grass fields with a wind sock in the middle and hangars on one side. No less an authority than the visionary Jimmy Doolittle argued in those days that the airfields of the future should all be vast, open meadows without runways. What crosswind?

Norfolk, Virginia, lay spread below the Stearman's nose from Virginia Beach to Portsmouth, clear and pristine in the excellent visibility. Approach let me fly up from the south at 3,500 feet, then begin my descent toward Norfolk International at my leisure. I pulled the throttle back to 20 inches of manifold pressure and pushed the trim lever forward. Soon I was indicating 115 MPH, screaming down from the blue like a big yellow bird. Off to my right I could see an F-14 Tomcat in the pattern at NAS Oceana.

I sat around the FBO executive terminal for two hours trying to reach some people I knew by telephone, but no one was home. The candy machine was out of order. Two business jets came and went, one a Lear that deposited a girl about eight years old and a woman I took to be her mother. Talk about a first-class trip to visit Grandmom!

After three cups of coffee, I gave up on my friends and took off across the Chesapeake for Cape Charles. Below, several ships were passing through the channel outward bound.

What the heck, the *Cannibal Queen* is as first class as you can get. This is how Queen Elizabeth would travel if she only knew how to tweak the rudder in a crosswind.

What was David's comment as we flew south over Kansas bound for McAlester, Oklahoma? "This is the only way to fly." I know that he tired quickly of the wind and noise and vibration, and I suspect he said that only because he thought the comment would please me, which it did. He is a fine fellow— always trying to please his mother and father if he can. As I fly along this afternoon over Cape Charles, with the Atlantic on my right and the Chesapeake on my left, I think again of David and wish his head were sticking up out of the front cockpit. He could even sleep if he wanted to.

Something directly above me catches my eye. I look up. Holy jeepers ... three Hueys in formation, going in my direction, passing a couple hundred feet above me. One by one they cross over my upper wing and go on by.

Helicopters aren't real flying—they're just a crude form of levitation.

I've used that line a hundred times on helicopter pilot friends, and now I feel another twinge of regret that the *Queen* is so slow. Those choppers are levitating faster than I can aviate.

The Hueys spread out into a loose three-ship-abreast formation and alter course to the left. Gradually they disappear into the haze.

The haze is getting worse the farther I go north. Down to ten or twelve miles visibility, I estimate.

Over Salisbury, Maryland, I pick up the road heading north and begin to look for the grass airport at Laurel, Delaware. My airport book says they sell fuel, but even if they don't I'll land just for the heck of it. An all-grass airport! Not many of those still around.

I spot it and swing across the runways to study the wind sock. The Unicom man says the wind is out of the southwest at twelve knots, and he recommends runway 14. That's a 90-degree crosswind perhaps twice as strong as any I have yet

landed the Stearman in. The stick suddenly feels slippery and
I have to wipe my palms on my shorts.

The wind sock is flopping around maybe twenty degrees, first
favoring runway 32, then 14. There's another little runway only
1,400 feet long, just enough, and the crosswind on it will be
only about fifty degrees. I circle again looking the place over
and trying to decide. Twelve knots of crosswind . . . the grass
will help and I've been doing some decent landings these last
few days, although certainly not every time and not with any
degree of predictability. I'm tempted to try the crosswind. If it
was asphalt I would use the short runway, but the twelve-knot
crosswind on sod tempts me like whiskey tempts a drunk. I
swing the Queen out in a left downwind for runway 14.

What was it we said in the Navy? "No guts, no glory." Yeah,
and that Cessna 172 I used to rent in Boulder, ol' November
One Seventy-Seven Charlie Bravo, had a little placard mounted
right in the center of the instrument panel: "Don't do anything
stupid."

John Weisbart's admonishment was equally blunt. "Don't
alter the appearance of the airplane, Steve. Promise me."

Close your eyes, John, and cross your fingers. Here goes
nothing.

Tall trees guard the approach end of the grass strip. And I
am high. I kick right rudder and apply left stick, slipping forward and scrubbing off that excess altitude. Coming down on
the trees, straighten her out, now apply left rudder. . . . I'll hold
her straight with left rudder, use right aileron to keep the right
wing down . . . yeah, and we're floating right over the treetops,
the Queen's nose twitching as the wind swirls about the trees
and has varying effects upon our path through it.

I work that rudder, watching the ground come up, flaring,
right aileron, little less left rudder, now more, nose on up . . .
and the main mounts kiss the grass as I get to full back stick.
Keep on the rudder, holding her, stick more and more right . . .
and we are taxiing.

I add power and exhale. Yeaaaaah!

The young man who helps me gas the Queen has a strange
accent that I can't place. When we are inside he says he is from
the Netherlands. I am tempted to ask if he is Amsterdam Dutch,

Rotterdam Dutch or Goddamn Dutch, but refrain. Instead I ask if he has any food. It is 6:30 P.M. and I haven't had a bite all day. He offers a bag half full of potato chips and I gratefully take a handful. "They took the candy machine out this morning," he tells me—at least that is what I think he says.

The little FBO shack is my kind of place, a nifty place for guys to hang out and tell lies about flying and to play pool when they have exhausted the flying stories. The pool table looks well used.

The proprietor comes in. His tummy pokes out of his pull-over shirt. He wipes his hands on his dirty jeans and asks where I'm from. He looks like he could whip my socks off on that pool table and tell more flying tales than I could count. I wish I had the time to challenge him to a game, but I want to go on to Montgomery County Airpark in Maryland and call my brother. He'll come pick me up. And I have to get there before dark.

The FBO man tells me about the new Terminal Control Areas the feds have inaugurated in the metro Washington area. This is the worst TCA complex in the nation with four of these inverted wedding cakes—Baltimore-Washington International, Andrews Air Force Base, National Airport and Dulles Airport— all running together. They suck up all the airspace from the eastern shore of Maryland to the Blue Ridge Mountains. I spread my chart and he gives me pointers on how to sneak through the VFR corridor that runs between the BWI TCA and the Andrews-National toadstools.

Reluctantly I say good-bye and go outside to study the wind sock. The takeoff will be a little tricky too. I grin. By God, this is fun!

I am aviating at 1,400 feet just to the left of U.S. Route 50 as it crosses the Chesapeake Bay bridges. On my left, near Annapolis, is an impressive array of tall, low-frequency transmission towers that the Navy uses to talk to submarines. The red brick buildings of the Naval Academy are also quite prominent, as is the Maryland capitol. On my right, real but quite invisible, is the Baltimore-Washington International—BWI—TCA.

I have the chart open on the board on my lap, and I make a

tick and note the time as I cross The Generals Highway inter-section. Two minutes later I cross a four-lane running north and south, and I note that. No other airplanes in sight, but they will be hard to see. The sun is only ten or so degrees above the horizon and red in the haze. Visibility down to six or seven miles, a typical summer day in the east—we complain in Colorado if the visibility is less than 90 miles. These poor schnooks.

Three more minutes down U.S. 50 to the road intersection at Bowie where I must turn. Before I know it I am there—I think. There are two four-lane intersections here, and which one is *the* one? Oh well, they are only three-quarters of a mile apart, so it doesn't matter.

At the first one I swing the *Queen* to a heading of 310 de-grees. I carefully measured the chart at Laurel and 315 degrees is the track I need over the ground, but with this southwest wind, I throw in a five-degree drift correction. Now to hold this heading on this sloppy wet compass.

I am sweating. To the right is the BWI TCA and to the left is Andrews. If I make a mistake here and wander off course I will get a flight violation as surely as God made women smarter than men. I think about that now as I kick the rudder to hold course precisely. Maybe for a first offense I'd only get a three-month suspension and a thousand-dollar fine. Maybe I'd lose my license. I'd rather lose a testicle.

But I routinely bet my flying license. Everyone does every time they go up in an airplane sitting in the cockpit. And I can do this—that's why I *have* a license.

I pass over the first of the Washington-to-Baltimore express-ways. I tick it on the chart. Off to the right, up there smack against that 1,500-to-10,000-foot blue TCA circle, I can just make out Suburban Airpark. From there fly a group of aviators who truly bet their tickets every day. A minute later I go over the second superhighway.

I-95 is next . . . there it is, and then Route 29. Yes. I tick it because I have ticked all the others. Now I can turn north and fly over my brother's house in Fulton, a little suburb west of Laurel, Maryland. It's on the other side of that reservoir on the Patuxent River right there, right . . . what if that wasn't Route 29?

Galvanized by doubt, I swing the plane northwest again. That last superhighway had a lot of development around it—I don't remember seeing all that from the ground.

But ... that had to be 29. There aren't any more superhighways heading northeast. Convinced, I swing northeast.

Okay, there's the reservoir, there's the bridge at the west end, and John's house should be in that subdivision right there ... and there it is. Golly, he's out in the driveway. He's waving. And there's Nancy, John's wife, and their daughter, Amy.

I make three circles, waving like a demented fool, then swing the Queen westward for Montgomery County Airpark.

That night I totted up the times. I flew 6.6 hours today, from Georgetown, South Carolina, to Montgomery County, Maryland. And when I got up in Georgetown I thought the weather would be too bad. Just goes to show ...

11

A VISIT WITH MY BROTHER, JOHN, IS ALWAYS A TREAT; HE'S taller than I am, skinnier, smarter, better looking, and fourteen months younger. And he's an extrovert. We fought like dogs when we were teenagers but as the years have passed and we slogged along on separate paths, we have become closer and closer friends. I think part of the reason is that we admire and respect each other.

John and his wife, Nancy, fit each other like a story-book couple. She is even more outgoing than he is, into everything, friends with everyone she meets.

Their eldest son, John Williams Coonts, "Jack," is spending the summer with an uncle who works for the National Park Service in California. But striding down the ramp with John and Nancy this evening came Amy, thirteen years old and all filled out in the womanly places. She wears a retainer on her teeth—the braces came off last year—and she thinks I am a real neat uncle, so I used her as a character in my last two books. Now I can do no wrong as far as she is concerned. This evening I hugged each of them in turn.

They oohed and aahed over the Queen. Amy wanted to go for a ride right then. I begged off. The sun was sinking lower and lower in the thick haze and I was tired and hungry. Flying is like sex—I've never had all I wanted but occasionally I've had all I could stand. This evening I was satiated.

Amy sat in the front cockpit for a moment, then John climbed in. Amy was leaning over looking in the rear one when John pulled the stick back. "Something broke off," she announced. Sure enough, the radio microphone button on top of the rear stick had caught in a tangle of loose threads in the front cockpit shoulder strap knot, and now it was gone.

John was mortified. He got out on the wing and helped me inspect the damage. "God!" he exclaimed, "John arrives, sits down, and breaks something."

"Forget it. I can get it fixed easy enough. I'll bet there's an avionics shop right here on the field."

We spent five minutes trying to get the button off the front stick so we could install it on the rear one while John apologized six more times. No luck. It looked to me like the sticks would have to be taken out to allow the change to be made. John laughed nervously, plainly embarrassed. "Forget it, John. It was an accident that could have happened anywhere."

On the way to John's house we stopped at a McDonald's and I inhaled hamburgers. I started to feel human again. John and Nancy wanted to know all about my trip so far, so the gabfest began in earnest.

Back at John's house I called Steve Hall in Colorado. He confirmed that the original mike button was still in the airplane, Velcroed to a fuselage stringer but still wired up. I could move it to the stick and use it instead on the stick button. Problem solved.

Friday and Saturday were ride days. On Friday my niece Amy Carol was my first passenger while her mother watched apprehensively. She wasn't worried about Amy—just the fact that she was supposed to be next.

As usual, as soon as we were aloft Amy couldn't hear the intercom. I talked to no avail. What the hey, it's a nice hazy day in Maryland and what is there to say?

After fifteen minutes I brought her back. I was unfamiliar with the area and didn't want to venture too far north of the airfield. I went north until it was just about to disappear in the murky haze, shot a landing at Davis Airport, a little strip out in the Maryland countryside—if this expanse of sprawling, manicured estates can properly be called countryside—and then flew back to Montgomery County. Amy was ecstatic.

Nancy was still reluctant. It was an act for my benefit, I suspected, and I played along. Her daughter was not so sure and said, "Oh, Mom," with all the disgust and impatience that teenage girls the world over can inject into that phrase.

At last Nancy seated herself with trepidation and latched onto the side of the cockpit combing with each hand. As we taxied out I told her that we'd do a few stalls and a couple spins, just to let her get a feel for it. Then I gave the engine the gun and we were off.

I didn't get to attend John and Nancy's wedding twenty-two years ago, but I met the bride shortly thereafter. We are all past forty now, our children all teenagers; my eldest just completed her first year of college. In the Stearman with Nancy I thought about the fact that middle age has crept over us, yet we are still healthy, still alive and flying on this hazy summer morning.

Like Amy, Nancy didn't hear a word I said over the intercom system. I talked anyway. Six miles north of the field I did a couple gentle turns, then Nancy found her voice. "Okay, we can go back now."

Back on the ground, I told her that I could see her knuckles turn white. She said, "I can't believe I did that, actually went up in this thing. Do you know that woman who posed for the painting on the side?" She looked at me and grinned widely, signifying her willingness to enjoy a juicy lie.

"Sure," I told her. "I helped with the auditions. The girl that we selected was an exotic dancer who . . ."

As Nancy and Amy were comparing notes on all the things they saw on the ground and I tied the plane down, a young man walked over. He visited with Nancy while he stared at the Queen. Finally he asked her what I did for a living.

Alas, she told him the truth, that I am a scribbler squandering his royalties. Later I told her that in the future she is to tell people that I am a former president of a savings and loan, and since my prison term doesn't start until October 1, I am out flying up all the money I stole.

As I suspected, John and Nancy the extroverts had solicited

114

their friends to see if anyone wanted to commit lift in an open-cockpit biplane when John's vagrant brother turned up, sooner or later. Two women and no men took them up on the invitation, but one of the women backed out. The one who kept her courage was JoAnne Ward. When the time came Friday evening to go to the airport both her daughters and husband decided to go along and watch ol' Mom do something really stupid.

I strapped her in as the spectators snapped pictures and Nancy gave them a running commentary based on her vast experience, acquired that morning. When we got back, Tessa, the eldest daughter, decided she'd give it a try. After Tessa's ride, Randy Ward, the father, pointed to the place where I had tied the Queen down. No more riders tonight.

While helping me install the tiedown straps Randy mentioned that he got airsick in small planes. I assured him that had never happened to anyone in the Queen. There's too much fresh air, the plane is stable, I don't do any sharp maneuvering, and I keep the rides short. Randy listened politely and nodded but he didn't change his mind. He didn't want to chance it.

A lot of people have been sick in small airplanes, including me. I got sick as a hog on my very first ride in a Navy T-34 in Pensacola, Florida. I prayed that I would die right there in the front cockpit, and when I didn't I swore that if I ever got my feet back on the ground, I would never fly again as long as I lived. Like most of my promises, I didn't keep that one. Doped to the gills with Dramamine from the dispensary, I flew again and again and fell in love with it. Yet from then on, whenever I had to ride and watch the instructor do the flying I still got sick. I was okay only as long as I had my hands on the stick.

I'm still like that. Last year the Navy invited me to go for a ride in an A-6 Intruder at NAS Oceana and I took them up on it. Fifteen years had passed since I had last strapped an A-6 to my rear, so I sort of thought this ride would be a big nostalgia trip. Yet after an hour in the right seat watching the pilot flip the plane around I begin to feel queasy. I didn't lose it, but almost.

The admiral invited me to come back and ride in the backseat of an F-14. Thanks, but no thanks—I'll pass unless they put me up front with the stick and throttles. (If you read this, Admiral, believe me, I could handle that Tomcat. Honest!)

115

From the stories I've heard, I think too many pilots giving introductory plane rides intentionally try to make the novices sick. This is worse than stupid—it's grotesque. Aviation today needs every friend it can get, and the only way we're going to get them is one passenger at a time. When I hear some dummy laughing about how he made a passenger sick, I get this powerful urge to kick him in the seat of his pants, where his brains are.

On Saturday John and I set forth to fly the *Queen* to Fallston, Maryland, a little strip near Jarrettsville where Nancy's Aunt Eb and Uncle George Cairnes reside. The fuel pump at Montgomery County wasn't open at 7 A.M., so we decided to fly to Frederick and get gas there. Off we went, John white-knuckling it in the front cockpit. Like his wife, he is a fearful flyer. I know he thinks my passionate affair with aviation is proof that I was really adopted by our parents.

In Frederick we made the discovery that the keys to Nancy's car were in my pocket. And she was supposed to drive to Jarrettsville this morning for a wedding, bringing John's suit and tie. He made a few phone calls while I stood around looking slightly nonplused. So we flew back to Montgomery County and John got out, his wife's keys now in his pocket, and I flew on to Fallston alone.

I beat the Cairnes to Fallston. The FBO proprietor was a man named Fred Mills, with whom I was soon acquainted. He said he was a Cessna dealer for 17 years and frequently ferried new Cessnas from Wichita to Fallston. He got out of it, he said, when the company began making more demands than a small distributor could afford to meet. "There was no way I could put in an avionics shop, not sitting here surrounded by three avionics shops that weren't making a profit." A wise decision. A year later, in 1986, Cessna stopped making light planes and he would have lost the dealership anyway.

"It's the liability," Mills told me glumly as two men sitting on the couch against the far wall talked about who in the area was competent to repair farm tractor magnetos.

"That year Cessna and Piper and Beech lost $300 million in liability suits; Cessna lost $29 million in one suit alone. Hell, somebody just sued Piper claiming that a 1947 Cub had a manufacturing defect. Can you believe it? 1947! Congress ought to do something. If you own a plane five years, the manufacturer ought to be off the hook. How long do you have to own it before it's yours? It's crazy. The Cub was a darn good plane in 1947."

Soon George Cairnes arrived and the rides started. First to go was his granddaughter, Mary. Then George's son, John, then George. Next a nine-year-old boy named J.P. who just happened to be there, and lastly George's grandson, John Jr.

There was a little crosswind and it was gusty, so I had a workout on the landings on that 2,400-foot strip. My first landing in Fallston had been poor, with a moderate bounce to emphasize my ineptitude and the Queen's need for a delicate hand, but no one was watching. Now, performing before an audience, I begin to figure out the winds and set the Queen down with a touch of grace. Fool that I am, I began to feel my chest swell slightly. The last landing deflated me. A mere arrival.

The boy, J.P., was devoid of hero worship. As he was being strapped in he wanted to know if I had enough gas. I assured him I did. He just nodded. A nine-year-old cynic! Yet when he got back he told everyone how terrific it had been. Who knows, maybe he'll become a pilot someday—even an astronaut.

George Cairnes was a B-29 pilot during World War II, but he gave up flying in 1946, when he was discharged. Today he is trim, has most of his hair and all of his teeth and looks ten or fifteen years younger than he has to be.

He took me to lunch before I flew back to Montgomery County. Predictably, we talked about airplanes. He told me about explosive decompression over Chicago, a blown jug over the Pacific that required a month in Hawaii to repair with golf every day, and a night flight through thunderstorms between Kwajalein and Guam with a navigator, one with 35 missions over Germany under his belt, who broke down completely and sobbed that he was lost. This while the other crewmen fought a fire in the radio panel and the giant plane bucked and writhed in vicious turbulence. Flying is like that—some brushes with eternity interwoven with memories of carefree, vagabond adventures with friends back when you and the world were young.

117

I had let George fly the Queen and he did fine, holding altitude nicely even in the turns. I hope that when I'm his age I can do as well.

Mr. Mills helped me gas the Queen before I left. They had been baling hay on the fields around the airport that morning and I could still smell it.

The sweet grass smell mixed with the aroma of gasoline, the soft, hazy sun on my back as I stood on the back of the front cockpit seat and watched the fuel flow into the tank, my shadow on the yellow wings, a gentle breeze stirring my hair—life doesn't get any better. Later you recall that sublime moment and the memory has a wispy texture, like something from a dream, something imagined.

That evening after John, Nancy and Amy returned from the wedding in Jarrettsville, we sat on their back porch and reviewed the day. Here is how John described his morning flight to his wife and daughter:

"When we got to Frederick, Steve parked the plane and killed the engine. He told me I could get out, but one of the earpads on my headset came off as I took off the headset. Uh-oh, I broke the mike button on his stick the last time I was in the plane, now I've broken off this earpad. Everything I touch on his airplane just disintegrates. So I decided to sit there and see if I could stuff the pad back into the retainer ring that holds it in place without mentioning the problem to Steve.

"I'm busy at this little chore when Steve said, 'John, we can't fuel the plane with you in it.' There he stands with the fuel hose in his hand. 'Oh,' I said, and climbed out, feeling a little stupid." Here he rolled his eyes and Amy giggled. She really enjoys his stories, so he hams it up to please her.

"After we called Nan about the keys, I got back into the front cockpit and surreptitiously tried to fix the earpad. Steve got the movie camera going and walked around taking my picture. 'Wave, John.' 'Say something, John.' All this time I'm trying to stuff this earpad back into the retainer ring so Steve won't know I broke it. Finally he asked, 'What're you doing, anyway?'

"So I told him. He flips the retainer ring off, puts the pad in place, then snaps the ring back on. Then he straps himself in and starts the engine.

118

"The plane won't move. So he says, 'We forgot to pull the chocks. John, get out and pull the chocks.' *We* forgot. So I got unstrapped and disconnected the headset so I wouldn't have to take it off and the earpad wouldn't come off again, and got out and pulled the chocks. But as soon as I was back in the plane Steve restarted the engine and taxied. Now I'm trying to get strapped in and the headset plugged in and the plane is bouncing along, and out of the corner of my eye I see this other plane about a thousand feet away coming *right at us*. But my headset isn't plugged in yet."

He pantomimes to show how frantically he was trying to get the plug in properly. "At last I get it in and shout, 'There's a plane taking off right at us!' Anytime I see another airplane I just know it's coming right into the cockpit with us. So I shouted. Steve said, 'Huh?' and slammed on the brakes. Then I saw that the other plane was merely taxiing in our direction."

At this point John shrugged and shook his head slowly. Nancy laughed, Amy giggled hugely and I smiled. I don't remember that our visit to Frederick was this exciting, but John sure can tell a story.

"So we flew back to Montgomery. As we entered the pattern I saw this other airplane ahead of us. Uh-oh! I have to keep my eye on it or we'll hit it. So I kept my eyes glued on that little plane. Then our plane bounced or something, and I lost it. I couldn't find it. I just knew it was going to come right into the cockpit with us. So I searched madly and finally spotted the other plane, just about to land, a mile in front of us." He gave a big sigh of relief. "Saved."

Amy said, "Oh, Daddy!"

John has more adventures than anyone I know.

On Sunday morning, the 30th of June, John and Amy awoke early to take me to the airport and see me off. When we got there I asked Amy if she wanted another ride. She did.

We found her house in the haze and circled it once, then returned to the airport only to find that a bicyclist was riding up and down the runway. The plane in front of me waved off and I made a low pass. As I went down the runway fifteen feet above the ground I made a rude gesture to the man on the bicycle. I was gone before he had time to return it.

I landed long on the next pass. John said he heard a police siren on the other side of the runway before I landed, so presumably the bicycle rider was on his way downtown to be fingerprinted and photographed.

What in the world gets into people and induces them to pull a stunt like that? If that guy had seen my first landing at Fallston yesterday he wouldn't have gotten within a half mile of any place that I was trying to plant the big Stearman.

We said our good-byes and Amy Carol gave me a kiss and a big hug. I think she enjoyed her rides in the *Cannibal Queen*. When I lifted off, she and John were waving. I waved back.

12

A WARM FRONT STRETCHES FROM CAPE COD TO WESTERN PENN-sylvania and I am going to fly under it. Showers and isolated thunderstorms are predicted for midafternoon, but I am getting an early start. Visibility in Maryland is five to seven miles, the broken clouds at 4,000 or 5,000 feet. I level at 2,000 and point the Queen toward York, Pennsylvania. There I pick up a four-lane highway and follow it across Lancaster and on toward Reading as the haze thickens slightly.

Reading sits in a little glade of sunshine and good visibility. On the ground as I fuel the plane the airplane casts a crisp shadow and one can see the hills in every direction. And it is hot, in the upper 80's. As I climb out eastbound the sun disappears and the hazy gloom deepens. My track lies between Allentown-Bethlehem and Philadelphia, both with toadstool-shaped controlled airspace sectors that I intend to avoid.

I cross Green Lane Reservoir, Quakertown, and Lake Nocka-mixon, then alter course more to the north. Still flying at 2,000 feet—about 1,700 feet above the ground—the limited visibility means that I can see no more than three miles in any direction. The plane passes under dark gray areas, then back into lighter areas, but no rain. My finger rests on the chart marking our position, and at every little landmark I make an X and jot the time. These time ticks look like beetle tracks. I feel like a beetle, crawling along in marginal visibility, working hard to stay unlost.

I plan to stop in Newton, New Jersey, for fuel, so I dial in the Unicom frequency, 122.9. Someone else aloft in this goo is lost—he and another airplane are talking back and forth, trying to find a familiar landmark.

Listening now to the rising pitch in the voice of the pilot who is lost, I feel sympathy for him. There is nothing I can do to help. I know where I am but not where he is. The most important thing he can do is keep his wits about him and not panic. He can use electronic navigation aids to get a fix, if he has them and knows how to use them. Even if he doesn't, he can ask one of the many approach controllers in this area for a steer.

Apparently that is what he decides to do. He tells the other pilot he is leaving the frequency.

In this soup my mere 84 knots is a blessing—I have time enough to study the roads and lakes, consult the chart, then recheck. That little village is on the south end of that lake, by the dam, and the highway runs off to the northwest. Hmmm. Yes, that makes it this little lake right here. Confident in my decision, I uncap my pen and X the chart. A glance at my watch for the time, which I scribble beside the X.

Studying the chart requires that I look down into my lap, with my head bent, so I momentarily lose sight of the outside world. This is slightly disorienting, but I still have my right hand upon the stick and that keeps me in touch with how she's flying. Writing on the chart with my right hand requires that I release the stick, and this is more disorienting. In that moment, with my head bent, my eyes focused on the chart, and the Queen flying as the trim and the wind currents dictate, I experience a touch of vertigo, or spatial disorientation. The sides of the cockpit completely block any glimpse of the outside world from my peripheral vision. For these seconds my entire universe consists of the chart in my lap, the sides of the cockpit, and the sensations of motion unrelated to this tiny visual world.

Sometimes after I get my little X in precisely the right spot upon the chart, I must look up for a few seconds and put my hand back on the stick until I assure myself that all is well—until my body's sense of balance stabilizes—before I can again devote myself to the chore of marking the time beside the X. Turbulence, or chop, worsens the vertigo.

An artificial horizon on the instrument panel that I could keep within my visual scan would prevent the sensation of spatial disorientation since I have spent many hours flying instruments and am quite comfortable in that environment. But if I do this enough in the *Cannibal Queen*, I should become used to the sensations and will stop feeling that jolt of anxiety—twinge of panic?—that accompanies vertigo.

The strip at Newton, New Jersey, is south of a small lake. I eye the wind sock, make an unanswered call on Unicom, then land to the south.

The fuel pump is in a grassy area off the northern end of the runway. Several small airplanes are tied down nearby. There is no office, just a shed and two houses. I kill the engine and unstrap. When I am out of the plane and lighting my pipe, a man walks over from one of the houses.

His name is Richard Jump. After I fuel and pay him, I learn that he is a financial printer by trade and is merely here for a week of business on Wall Street. This Sunday he is visiting his parents. Where's home? Littleton, Colorado, a suburb of Denver. We visit awhile, look at the sky, then I get back in the *Queen* and am on my way.

Going east toward the Hudson River, I fly out from under the front. The temperature at 2,000 feet cools markedly. Now I am on the cold side of this rascal and the visibility gets better quickly, a lot better, as I chill in the cockpit.

With the wide river of Henry Hudson spreading under me, I turn north to fly up the river. Everything is green, luxuriant, and the scale of the river and valley is such that all the man-made items below appear miniaturized. I cross above model bridges and pass tiny cities and towns. The Military Academy at West Point goes by under the left wing.

The guy in the control tower at Dutchess County Airport cheerfully allows me to fly through his airspace. I pass Poughkeepsie and boresight Rhinebeck, New York, where I know the Old Rhinebeck Aerodrome is located. It is not on any chart, but

I have read of Cole Palen's flying circus of World War I airplanes for years and intend to stop. I'll land at a public strip near Rhinebeck, Sky Park, if I can get there before I freeze to death.

While I am scanning for the Sky Park airport, I spot a red biplane down low, just above the trees.

This is the place! Aha! Two or three brightly colored biplanes, a grass strip amid tall trees, a grandstand full of people. Luckily I am still at 2,000 feet, so I am no hazard to the performing pilots. I fly over them just the one time and enter the Sky Park traffic pattern.

The strip is narrow, bumpy, and the asphalt is coming apart. I manage to keep the Queen on it and pull up to the parking area.

An elderly man comes over to stare at the royal persona on the fuselage and examine me. As soon as my feet hit the ground I open the baggage compartment and grab a sweatshirt. Over that I don my leather jacket. Beginning to warm up, I look around. The place is untidy, in disrepair.

Soon a man comes out of the small hangar wiping his hands on a rag. I ask about renting a car. "We don't rent cars. You want gas?" No. He nods once, glances at the yellow Stearman, then turns and walks back into the hangar.

I resolve to fly back south to Dutchess County. That is a large airport with two big runways and a control tower. Maybe I can rent a car there and find a motel. Tomorrow I can drive back to the Old Rhinebeck Aerodrome.

But at Dutchess County my priorities change. The car rental places are only open Monday through Friday, and this is Sunday. There is a motel just a block from the FBO building. I taxi the Queen into the grass and tie her down. As I wipe the oil off her I find a broken piece on one of the two forward latches on the nose cowling.

The cowling around the engine was a Skid Henley touch—it came with the engine when he bought the 300-HP Lycoming in Indianapolis and he installed it since he liked the look. It's a clamshell affair, in two pieces, a top and a bottom. There are two leading-edge latches, one on each side. The left one is broken. Two other latches on each side. Obviously the latch with the broken piece is still holding and the cowling is still on the plane, but for how long?

I stand there staring at the broken piece and wondering what would happen if that left front latch failed completely in flight. The strain on the forwardmost left side latch would increase dramatically, and it might fail. If that latch were to go, the remaining latch would probably fail instantly. At this point the pressure of the air entering the engine would force the cowling away from the engine and the prop blast would force it aft.

If the bottom half went under the plane, that would be no big deal. But the top half . . . it might try to go between the top of the fuselage and the upper wing. Pounded and ripped by the prop blast, the cowling or a piece of it might tear off the fuel sight gauge, that glass pipe that sticks down below the fuel tank. If that happened fuel would pour out of the tank and soak me in the rear cockpit. Very shortly thereafter the engine would die of fuel starvation, if the plane hadn't already caught fire and incinerated me.

So I would have to make a quick dead-stick landing if I were lucky enough to avoid immolation. Slightly nauseated by my speculations, I resolve to get that latch fixed before I get very much older.

Only two cars were parked in front of the motel, but it was indeed open. Two Chinese women sat in the lobby watching a Chinese movie on television. I registered as the singsong sounds of Chinese speech and the twanging of Chinese music poured from the boob tube. Only in America . . .

The motel used to be a Quality Inn before it fell on hard times. Now it was merely the Dutchess County Airport Motel. There was a restaurant—beer joint next door and they fixed me a great sandwich, which I ate while watching the Mets lose one to the Philadelphia Phillies.

After dinner I walked back to the airport and examined the Queen and her bad cowl latch again, then inspected every nut and wire and bolt that I could see.

She looked to be in good shape except for that latch. The Lycoming engine's leaking more oil these days, maybe a quart and a quarter an hour, blowing it back all over the plane. I've been swabbing oil from the floor of the front cockpit that comes in through the gaps in the nose panels. Those panels don't fit tightly—Stearmans were working planes, with little attention to cosmetics. I wonder if oil is shorting out the IFF antenna that protrudes through the bottom of the plane in the front cockpit floor area. Perhaps.

I wander back to the motel and stand staring at the pool, which has been drained. Now it is just a concrete-lined hole in the ground without a diving board. No motel I have stayed at since leaving Boulder has had a diving board. All have had NO DIVING signs prominently posted. David was always disappointed. Too risky to allow the public to enter the water headfirst. Because the possibility of a freak accident cannot be absolutely eliminated, no one gets to dive. So no one can sue.

It's as if today's Americans have collectively decided that safety is the highest social good. Even sex, the riskiest activity known to man and therefore one of the most rewarding, must be "safe."

Ultimately the question boils down to a judgment about how much risk makes life worth living. Success at a risk-free endeavor is impossible. Without some level of risk life has no meaning. Americans have traditionally believed that each person should be allowed to make the risk judgment for himself. Perhaps they sensed that such judgments were intimately related to that "pursuit of happiness" clause in the Declaration of Independence.

Today more and more Americans seem willing to allow bureaucrats in some hermetically sealed office somewhere, usually Washington or its environs, to decide that the social cost of a certain activity is too high, so the risk must be lowered or the activity eliminated. And some political hack who believes government is Big Mother will be delighted to introduce the legislation.

Rock climbing, motorcycle riding, sport aviation, skydiving, all the shooting sports, hunting, bicycle riding, sunbathing, nudism, and swimming in creeks and lakes are all activities that will attract more unwanted attention in the future. Sunbathing and nudism? Yeah, skin cancer.

Although we all know that nobody gets out of life alive, we strive to avoid any possibility of a fatal or debilitating accident or dread disease so that we may spend our final—"golden"—

years in a nursing home, senile, hugging a teddy bear, wearing soggy diapers, spoon fed by nurses and kept alive by machines, as long as technology allows and the insurance company can be forced to pay. Only then, stripped of all human dignity and too goddamn old to care, will we be willing to cross that threshold beyond life to find out if the preachers were lying.

When I was a young man during the Vietnam War I thought it a good bet that a cockpit would be my coffin. Now, at middle age, I have raised my sights. I want to die at the age of ninety-five in bed with a twenty-three-year-old nymphomaniac, shot to death by her jealous husband. Alas, a more likely scenario is that I'll be driven mad by an incurable case of diaper rash and be shot to death by a police officer trying to prevent me from strangling my teddy bear.

Whatever, before I go I hope I don't drool too much. I want to cry when I see old folks drool.

Tom Cawley is a few years older than I am, but only a few. He eyes the *Queen's* busted latch with a practiced eye and heads back into the hangar for his drill. The broken part is riveted on and the rivets will have to be drilled.

No one at Dutchess County Airport could do the work on Monday morning, but one mechanic telephoned Tom Cawley at Sky Acres, an airport eight miles to the northeast, so I have flown over. The airport is a hilltop affair. To reach Cawley's maintenance hangar I taxied to the north end of the runway, then up a paved ramp with a precipitous drop-off on the north side. He has the only aircraft maintenance facility with a view that I have ever found in my travels. Most airports are vast flat places, usually in valleys, and if they have a view it is upward at surrounding hills. From my position beside the *Queen* I can look across the hills of the Hudson River Valley and see the low mountains beyond. The Catskills are quite prominent to the northwest.

I tell him I was worried about the latch failing and the cowling coming off.

"Thousands of twin Beeches flying around with busted latches," he says.

"Does the cowling ever come off?"

"Occasionally."

I tell him my fear of the top cowling breaking off the fuel gauge under the fuel tank.

"If the cowling comes off, it'll go forward," Cawley says, "into the prop. It's an airfoil."

I can visualize what happens next. In seconds the cowling will be chewed apart by the propeller. Inevitably some of the pieces will come aft instead of being flung outward. Even if there is no other damage to the plane, the prop will be trashed. I decide that I could leave the cowling here with Cawley for a week if necessary and come back and get it when it is fixed. The plane will fly five or six MPH slower without it since the engine is baffled, but what the hey—that's a small price. I explain to Cawley that I can leave the cowling and he just nods. He's busy.

He soon gives up on drilling the rivets with the cowling still on the airplane, so we drop it off. He takes the lower half into the hangar to work on it, and I borrow a grease gun and set about greasing the knuckle-joint fittings on the landing gear. Some of the zirks won't take grease, so I get my wrench and change zirks. In minutes I am filthy.

Soon Cawley has the broken latch part off the cowling. I am still unsure if it can be repaired today, but he says yes. "Let's ride into town and let Siggy weld this."

The trip is eight or nine miles, and soon Cawley and I are getting acquainted. He is a shy individual who doesn't want to tell me much about himself until he hears about me. Finally he opens up. He has spent most of his adult life in civil aviation—hauled freight in Beech 18s, Aztecs, currently a twin Navajo, flies for an outfit that does infrared mapping, runs his own maintenance facility—basically done anything and everything that a person can do to earn a living around airplanes. And for recreation he has restored and flown old aircraft—he owned a Stearman for thirteen years—and skydives. He has over 800 jumps and likes to compete.

And he has opinions. On Saddam Hussein: "I know that there were political complications, but we should have run a pipe into that bunker and pumped in crude oil until the scratching on the door stopped, then sent in the historians." On New York City natives: "They think upstate starts at the George Washington Bridge." On me flying over the Adirondacks: "Follow the

128

roads. If the engine quits up there you won't have an antique airplane anymore."

True, but . . . engine failure and the resultant emergency landing was one of the risks I decided to assume when I was contemplating this trip. If it happens, it happens. I wonder what Tom would have said if he had seen me this spring at 14,500 feet over the Rockies in the *Cannibal Queen*. I don't say that, of course, but let him do the talking. He's the guy fixing the *Queen*.

Siggy has a large, well-equipped metal fabrication and repair shop, and he turns the broken aluminum part over in his hands and studies it carefully. In minutes he has the part braced down and his welding equipment rigged. I wander outside so I won't be tempted to look at the arc.

Ten minutes after he saw the part, Siggy is finished. The metal is still too hot to hold so he rigs a wire for me to carry it on. After I pay him I thank him. He follows me to the door, and I thank him again.

"No need to thank me twice," he says. "You paid me."

"Ah, but the money was just for doing the job," I tell him. "I'm thanking you for doing it while I waited and for not telling me to come back and pick up my part a week from Thursday."

Outside in the car, Tom says that Siggy used to have a hundred men working in that shop. This morning there was just one other machinist there. It is a sign of the times. The deindustrialization of America and the rise of the information age cease to be academic trends in Siggy's shop—the helper had a stack of aluminum equipment tops arranged around him that he had fashioned for IBM, which has a big plant in Poughkeepsie. "For their equipment," he told me. "Special order." Enough work for one or two men, but not a hundred.

Two hours after I arrived at Cawley's shop, the cowling latch is repaired, the cowling back on the plane, and I am ready to fly. I ask him what I owe him. $60, he decides, then studies his watch. "It was less than two hours, so let's say forty."

The people in aviation are like that. Aircraft parts are expensive, fuel is expensive, the government mandates that inspections be done, hours be flown, training be done periodically—it all adds up to money, usually a lot. So many people in aviation cut their profits, and consequently their wages, to the bone

129

in order to stay in business that occasionally one wonders how they manage to survive. Many don't. Yet they see so much pain in their customers' faces that when it comes time to settle up, they usually approach the subject of money apologetically.

I telephone my editor at Pocket Books in New York and ask him if he wants to go for a Stearman ride that afternoon. *Yes!* He and his wife will meet me at the Westchester County Airport in White Plains about 3 P.M.

As I leave Tom's office, he hands me a T-shirt. The legend reads, "Cawley's Aviation Service, formerly the largest aerospace employer in the town of Shawangunk."

Tom and his men help turn the Queen around so her prop blast won't go into the hangar. I ask if anyone has ever rolled a plane over this hill. No. I don't want to be the first. Taxiing a plane down a sloping ramp with a steep drop-off on the right will be another new experience. After handshakes all around, I climb into the Queen and give it a try.

Much to my surprise, I make it safely to the runway.

While I am waiting for my joyriders at Westchester County, I call the Old Rhinebeck Aerodrome at the phone number that is listed on the brochure that Tom Cawley gave me. A personable young woman answers. I ask if I may fly a Stearman into their aerodrome tomorrow morning to visit and she says yes, as if this request is quite common. The strip is only 2,000 feet long, she informs me; there is no Unicom but there is a wind sock, and I use the strip at my own risk.

I have taken so many risks to get this far that the burden of one more won't be noticeable. I assure her that she will see me on the morrow.

My joyriders are Paul and Chicquita McCarthy, residents of Roosevelt Island in the East River in the heart of the naked city, and they don't own a car. They are venturing into the wilds of Westchester County by bus, aerial tram, taxi, train, and taxi again. Sitting in the cafe of the tiny Westchester airport terminal sipping coffee served by a surly waitress, I decide to rent a car and drive them home. No doubt they will arrive exhausted by their public transport ordeal.

That is the way it goes. Paul and Chicquita emerge from the

taxi and stand blinking in awe at the wide-open spaces of Westchester County, the uncharted wilderness north of the Bronx. New Yorkers tend to forget how nice the sky looks without buildings poking holes in it.

Their rides go okay except for the fact that I make two truly terrible landings. I flare too high, then await that sickening moment when forward motion stops and the plane starts to fall . . . straight down. This is a religious experience. If I have not sinned too wickedly the moment of truth is swiftly over as the tail wheel touches, then the main mounts. If I have committed serious transgressions since my last conversation with the Almighty the moment lasts and lasts, then ends with a terrific thump.

Dear God, we must stop meeting like this!

After dinner in an Italian restaurant on the outskirts of White Plains, we venture forth southbound on the freeway with me at the wheel. The trip is a revelation. These New Yorkers have absolutely no idea which highway leads where. Even Ed Koch would be appalled.

"Queens, go to Queens," Chicquita says, which would probably be sound advice if I knew how to get to Queens.

"The George Washington Bridge," Paul suggests when he sees a sign with an arrow.

For some reason I have gathered the impression that day that the George Washington Bridge spans the Hudson River and would take us to New Jersey, and I voice that suspicion now.

"The Triborough Bridge," Paul says shamelessly, without a trace of embarrassment.

"No," his wife insists, "FDR Drive."

My guides to the Bad Apple are two country cousins just in from the Great Bend of the Yukon.

They finally agree on the Triborough, which does indeed lead to Queens. Soon we are cruising slowly through the true heart of the city of New York, the neighborhoods with people lounging on stoops on a hot summer's evening, kids playing on the sidewalk, teenagers committing romance at corners, every street lined with cars as far as the eye can see.

Even I can see the character of the neighborhoods change, almost from block to block. Traffic is heavy, mostly young men cruising in loud old cars and spending more time looking out the windows at the girls on the corners than at other traffic. Manhattan is the New York of my experience—this is another world altogether.

My passengers know to go south to 31st Avenue and to follow it west to the bridge to Roosevelt Island. There are actually *empty* parking places on the island and I whip the rental into one. In all the years I've been visiting New York, these are the first empty parking places I've ever seen. On the sidewalks are hordes of awestruck natives who have traveled for miles to gaze at these rarities. We fight our way through into the courtyard of the McCarthys' building, where we stand looking at the lights of Manhattan across the East River as the sky turns black.

"How are you ever going to get back to White Plains?" they ask.

I strut, I posture, I play the role. I can retrace my path, I hope.

I only make two wrong turns on my journey. Eventually I do arrive in White Plains, and even more amazing, I actually find a hotel. Hotels north of midtown Manhattan are devilishly difficult to find—apparently tourists never venture here.

That night getting ready for bed, I fret about my landings with the McCarthys and the upcoming landing on the 2,000-foot grass strip at Rhinebeck.

"It has a dip in it," Tom Cawley told me. "You'll come floating down with the ground dropping away at about the speed you're descending. Hold everything. The ground will start coming the other way."

That would be a hell of a place to flare too high. I can see myself running out of airspeed and ideas and having a religious experience at the place where the ground starts to rise. Ouch!

I decide that the problem is that I have been too concerned about nose movement and crosswind drift and relying too much on my peripheral vision to pick up my height above the ground. I resolve to consciously look down to the left, then the right, before I start my landing flare.

I crawl into bed and lie there thinking about how it will be tomorrow on that little grass strip with a dip in it nestled amid the trees, how it will look, how I'll handle it, how the *Queen* will feel. Come in slow and not too steeply, that is the key. I am still thinking about it when I drift off to sleep.

13

THERE IS A HIGH THIN OVERCAST THIS MORNING, WAY UP AT 25,000 feet, the Flight Service briefer said. The front that is stalled over New Jersey is supposed to start tracking northward. Visibility is excellent as I fly north from Westchester County headed for the Old Rhinebeck Aerodrome.

At last it comes into view. There are no other planes aloft—I look very carefully indeed. Since they don't have a Unicom frequency here, I cross over the runway at a thousand feet and stare downward, trying to find the wind sock that the woman on the phone said would be there. Blast, I can't find it. I make another circuit, still looking. Well, at Westchester County the winds were out of the north. This strip is oriented north and south, so I'll come in from the south and if I feel the plane floating on me, I'll wave off.

When you're landing with the wind behind you, the plane actually passes over the ground faster than it usually does, so it doesn't appear to descend at its normal angle. I call this sensation floating. Two thousand feet is plenty of runway for a Stearman, but tailwinds cause the plane to cover ground quickly.

I set up a circling descent at 15 inches of manifold pressure, airspeed at 75, five MPH slower than usual. Trim set, mixture up, prop forward to full increase, everything is set. I straighten her out and let her descend. Looking very nice, coming down between the trees, with no apparent tailwind or crosswind, I elect to continue the approach.

In seconds I am there. Consciously looking down to judge my height, I flare. And float a tad, that must be the dip . . . now the Queen touches on all three wheels and stays planted. I apply the brakes and slow to taxi speed.

This is better than sex!

I park the *Cannibal Queen* as far off the runway as I can, right near the grandstand, then kill the engine.

As the silence engulfs me I take off the goggles and headset and look around. Not a soul in sight. The empty grandstand, a gorgeous red high-wing monoplane tail-dragger parked down at the bottom of the gorge—yes, that dip in the runway is really a gorge. Calling it a dip is serious understatement. Looking at the runway now, it does indeed descend into the gorge, then there is a long gentle hill leading northward—I landed on this slope—and it crests way up there somewhere to the north amid the forest.

I lucked out. This strip is safe only when coming in from the south. And all takeoffs should be to the south, down this long slope, regardless of the wind. The wind should be of little concern here amid these trees, which pretty much guarantee that there will never be a crosswind at ground level. Maybe at a hundred feet, treetop level, but not on final or touchdown, where it counts.

Actually, I conclude, this is a perfect strip for antique bi-planes. A little downhill run to help them accelerate, no crosswind, a little uphill run on landing to help planes without brakes get stopped.

Two men come wandering up the hill toward the Queen. The one in torn, oil-soaked jeans and faded pullover is Gene De-Marco. The other introduces himself as Jim. They invite me to look the place over. The girl at the gate won't be in until 10 o'clock and I can pay her when I get around to it.

"Be sure to go up the hill"—they gesture to the west—"to see the museums after you look around here. You won't want to miss that."

And I am on my own. I cross the runway to the eastern side and climb a gentle grade into the trees. Here are some open-sided hangars that resemble a farmer's tractor sheds—and there are a couple antique tractors in them—packed with airplanes. I try to photograph them but the light inside is terrible.

Here I find a 1927 New Standard biplane. The span of the upper wing is much longer than the lower one. The landing gear is a system of trusses to support the craft's weight. The shock absorber system consists of bungee cords. There are only a half dozen or so New Standards still extant, and here I stand looking at one. This one has a black fuselage and red wings and has lettering on the side that invites you to "See the Hudson River Valley by air."

This is the same type of airplane that Noel Wein took to Alaska in the '20s when he became the first bush pilot in that state. He flew it in the summer on wheels and for several Alaskan winters on skis. The New Standard only cruised at 75 miles per hour, but it held four passengers in the front cockpit, so a man could haul enough people or freight to make it pay, even in Alaska.

I try to imagine myself hunkered in the rear cockpit of this plane, flying four sourdoughs and all their equipment in the forty-below-zero still air over a frozen white Alaskan wilderness, with nothing but a wet compass for a nav aid, one that often reads forty degrees off that close to the pole. Of course there are mountains all over that you can't top, but if you can see and recognize them, you can't get too lost. Wein drained the engine oil after every flight while it was still warm, then the following morning used a blowtorch to warm the cylinders before pouring in the oil that he had just cooked on a potbellied stove. And I think a summer jaunt around the lower forty-eight in a Stearman is an adventure! Ha!

An hour later in one of the three large Quonset huts that house Cole Palen's collection, I find another New Standard, a twin of the first one. There are only six or seven left in the world and Palen owns *two*.

Crossing the runway to the western side I stop to look at the gorgeous red fabric monoplane parked there. Gene DeMarco sees me examining it and comes over. It's his plane, a 1940 Howard wearing a 450-HP Pratt & Whitney engine. The interior is exquisite, reminding me of a 1950 DeSoto that I once saw displayed at a car show. Gene restored this aircraft himself and won the 1979 Grand Champion Award at Oshkosh. Looking at it, I can see that the award was richly deserved.

Later I find Gene working on the original rotary engine of the Sopwith Camel replica, preparing it for flight. He takes the time to explain the workings of the engine to me. As I listen that doggerel from World War I keeps running through my head: "A Fokker, a Snipe, and a Bentley Camel, met for a scrap over Beaumont Hamel . . ."

Gene's hands are the hands of a workingman—short nails, thick fingers, with ground-in dirt. It is obvious that working on airplanes is a passion with him. We should all be this lucky, to have a trade that fulfills us so completely.

I wander on in awe, trying to take everything in. There are treasures everywhere. Near the runway on the western side are a half dozen hangars that house the airplanes currently starring in the Old Rhinebeck airshow that is performed every Saturday and Sunday, two shows a day, from June 15 to October 15, weather permitting. The place is open for tours Monday through Friday from 10 A.M. until 5 P.M. from May 15 through October. The aircraft used in the show are original World War I fighter planes or replica aircraft with original engines.

Here you can watch the replica Sopwith Camel with an original rotary engine take to the skies. You can see a 1914 Avro 504-K, a 1918 Spade XIII, a 1915 Nieuport 10, a Fokker DR-1 Triplane, a 1911 Blériot XI, a 1917 Morane-Saulnier A-1, a 1918 Curtiss Jenny—*and they all fly on weekends.*

The place resembles nothing so much as the ultimate farmer's fantasy storage shed out behind the barn. Treasures from yesteryear sit in the shadows gathering dust, dripping oil into delicate little puddles in the dirt while cats wander about on their eternal quest for mice. Antique planes, cars, motorcycles and aircraft engines are crammed in everywhere.

Up in the museum—the three Quonset huts—you will find not only the second New Standard, but a 1929 Pitcairn Mailwing wearing a 220-HP Continental radial engine, a 1931 Bird Model K with a 125-HP Kinner B-5 radial, a 1929 American Eagle with a 100-HP Kinner, a Waco Model 9 dating from around 1925 to 1927, and a Waco Model 10 from 1927 to 1930. These are just a few of the treasures.

None of these planes are in museum display condition, and that somehow seems appropriate. They are working aircraft flying every weekend, or retired working aircraft awaiting rebuild or refurbishment so that they may fly again. To the best of my knowledge, this is the only place in the world where you can see aircraft of this vintage fly every weekend, all summer long.

You lean over and blow a layer of dust off a fabric-covered wing, study the oily engine, and a little voice whispers that you could climb into the cockpit and fly this thing if only someone would swing the prop for you. You couldn't, of course. I couldn't.

These planes need the hand of a highly skilled pilot thoroughly schooled in their quirks. These machines with rotary engines built their reputations in World War I killing the fledglings who tried to fly them. As many as thirty percent of the British pilots on their first solo in the Sopwith Camel crashed, and most of those crashes were fatal. Those were the statistics bandied about in Parliament at the time, although the Royal Flying Corps denied that the casualty rate was that high.

These airplanes became obsolete because better, safer aircraft with larger performance envelopes and more reliable engines came along. The pilots who flew them switched willingly and thankfully to machines that were better in every way imaginable. Only now, when the world of aviation includes spaceships that can go to the moon, do we look back so nostalgically at the early days.

Cole Palen started looking back as a very young man. The Old Rhinebeck Aerodrome and collection is his. He bought the airplanes one by one wherever he could find them, sometimes literally in farmer's barns. He restored the originals to flying condition, gave people rides, finally started airshows at the Old Rhinebeck Aerodrome.

Palen wasn't there the day I visited. I would like to meet him. Here was a man trying to make a living who attended auctions, hunted through barns, attics, tee-hangars and the pages of *Trade-A-Plane*. He paid hard-earned money for trashed-out old planes and engines that no one else wanted, convinced that somehow, some way, he could make them pay.

137

He has. He's even built replicas of planes that no longer exist from original drawings.

I doubt if Palen is getting rich on the Old Rhinebeck Aerodrome, but he's making it. And the world is a richer place.

I ended my visit to Rhinebeck watching Mike Lockhart and his three children wash the original 1918 Curtiss Jenny. They pulled her from her shed into the weak sunlight and went after the winter's accumulation of dust and dirt with rags, buckets and a hose. Mike is a professional aircraft restoration expert who works for Buehler Aviation Research in Florida. On his vacations he returns to Rhinebeck, where he grew up, and washes aircraft and helps with the mechanical chores.

As I watched the Lockhart children, all under ten years, scrub the Jenny and get filthy, I couldn't help wondering how many kids in America today have even touched a Jenny, let alone scrubbed and poked and prodded and examined every nook and cranny. To the best of my knowledge, there are only four or five Jennys still flying in the world. The bath, Mike explained, is preparatory to the Jenny's annual mechanical inspection so she can be used this summer in the airshow. Maybe this coming winter she will be overhauled.

The *Cannibal Queen* accelerated readily on the hilltop—she was off before she got to the downslope. I climbed above the treetops feeling like Eddie Rickenbacker and headed east looking for Huns.

The FBO in Meriden, Connecticut, Robert Carlson, had the naked fuselage of a Stearman parked beside his office building. Carlson and his partner are going to restore her. She was a sprayer—the spray tank that filled the place that the front cockpit occupies in mine sat beside the fuselage on the ground. The 450-HP Pratt & Whitney was off for overhaul. The wings were in the hangar being inspected.

I carefully examined the bare fuselage structure. This is the way the *Cannibal Queen* looked after Skid Henley finished welding on a new tail section. For the first time I began to appreciate the true magnitude of the job Henley, and these fellows, faced.

Carlson took photos of my Stearman to send to his partner, who is away for the summer. He told me the caption will read,

"Finished the Stearman and she's flying great. Wish you were here."

Carlson drove me to a Taco Bell and bought me a burrito. Three years ago he and his partner quit well-paying corporate jobs, he said, sold their toys—among them a North American AT-6 Texan—and got the city lease on this FBO business. So far they're loving the work and making a living, although at times it's a tight squeak.

I admire the courage of these optimists who believe in aviation in spite of everything. Like me, they love flying and all that goes with it. And like Gene DeMarco and Cole Palen, they are working like hell to create the niche that they want to be in.

Somewhere over New Hampshire I fly out from under the clouds. All that remains between me and the sun is an extremely thin cirrus layer up high where the angels sing. The sun feels good.

I have the *Cannibal Queen* flying high in the crisp, clean air at 5,500 feet. Visibility is 40 miles or so. I saw the tall buildings of downtown Boston off my right wing 30 miles away all the way across Massachusetts. In fact I saw them on the horizon as I climbed away from the Providence, Rhode Island, airport, a visible reminder that New England is small, like its namesake across the Atlantic.

Passing over Concord, New Hampshire, I swing the *Queen* to 060 degrees, aiming to overfly Lewiston, Maine. My destination is Knox County Airport at Rockland, on the coast by Penobscot Bay. I called ahead from Fitchburg, Massachusetts, and the hotel has a room waiting. Normally I take potluck, but that seemed unwise with the Fourth of July just two days away. I like showers and clean sheets too much to relish the prospect of trying to sleep under a wing while swatting mosquitoes all night.

Below me is a forested, hilly land dotted with lakes. I have never before been to Maine, so this will be fun. In fact, the only states that I had never visited before I started this trip were Maine, Vermont, and Alaska. Alaska won't be graced with my presence this year, but Maine and Vermont soon will. Somehow

I doubt that the governors of those states will be waiting at the airports to shake my hand.

The big Lycoming drones steadily as the *Queen* flies through still, cool air. My leather flight jacket and jeans feel good today. From this height, with this visibility, navigation ceases to require much attention and I can relax and look at the sights.

"Don't you ever get bored up there?" someone once asked. No, I don't. As the miles slowly pass I think of many things, of things I have done, of things I wish to do, of my children and my parents and people I have known. Over a mile above gorgeous country on a gorgeous day, my mind wanders freely.

Up here life takes on its proper perspective. You are a mere gnat afloat in this endless sea of air, above this huge, sprawling land. You and your earthly concerns shrink to their true significance. Ambition, love, lust, acquisitiveness, pride, envy—all of these components of the human condition lose their attraction and their sting up here in the vastness of the sky.

Today is my day to fly and get a glimpse of eternity. This is my day in the sun. Yet like all living things, I will grow old and my eyes will dim and someday soon I will again be a part of that earth below. Then it will be someone else's turn to fly up here, breathe this pure air, feel the sun's warmth on his arms and hands, look with mortal eyes toward that horizon that stretches into forever. Perhaps, just perhaps, he will do it in the *Cannibal Queen* or one of her sisters. With proper care this mechanical contrivance of Lloyd Stearman's brain and the hands of Boeing craftsmen will still be flying long after I have joined Stearman in the grave. Stearman, the Wrights, my grandparents, my parents—all of those who went before.

But that still lies ahead for me in this great adventure we call life. Today I am here, aloft. Today is my day. Today is my day to fly.

14

———————

ROCKLAND, MAINE, JULY 4. THE RAIN PREDICTED FOR TODAY hasn't arrived. Maybe tomorrow, when I'll be trying to fly west. The morning dawned dead calm, the flags hanging lifeless from their poles.

I studied the limp flags with mixed emotions. Flying the *Cannibal Queen* this past year I've become a fervid petitioner of Mother Nature and the Almighty—I'm unsure of just which is in charge of wind, theology being the arcane art that it is—to keep the air still, quiet. But this afternoon I am scheduled to go sailing on a small schooner in Penobscot Bay, and we won't sail very far without wind. So today, Mom or Dad, as the case might be, please send a nice stiff ocean breeze. I don't ask often for wind and I won't make a habit of it, but today please favor your petitioner with a canvas-bellying breeze laden with salt and the smell of the sea.

Sailing seems to me to be to boating what flying the *Queen* is to aviation. Biplanes and sailboats are craft from a time now past, short on the modern conveniences and technical advances that are supposed to improve our lives and somehow us. Both make light of the value of time, assuming in some Zen-like way that those who choose these forms of transport have plenty of it. More fundamental, in biplanes and sailing vessels the journey is more important than the destination. Modern forms of transportation reverse this priority—you board an airliner to go somewhere: the journey is merely an experience to be endured.

By noon it was obvious that my petition had been received favorably in whatever headquarters it was routed to. The wind was a good ten knots out of the southeast.

As 12:45 P.M. I was standing on the public pier in Rockland with my camera, a sweatshirt and a couple cans of grape soda pop in a bag. At five minutes before the hour a bewhiskered gent in a dark-blue cap came rowing through the anchorage in a double-ended wooden boat. He maneuvered expertly to the pier and slipped a rope over a thingy that had been provided. As he walked toward me I could see he was barefoot and had a modest tummy under the disheveled long-sleeved shirt and faded khaki trousers that hadn't had a crease in years. No designer duds for this salt.

"Mr. Coonts?"

"Yes. You're Captain Yossarian?"

He smiled and led me back toward his boat. I studied this barefooted sailor as he rowed us through the anchorage. I confess, looking him over and feeling the motion of the little boat and the sea breeze on my face, I felt like Jim being rowed out to the ship that was to take him to Treasure Island. If only this barefoot sailor had had one peg leg and called me "Matey" . . .

Captain Yossarian's trim little schooner lay at the outer edge of the anchorage, which was why I hadn't spotted her from the pier. With a green hull and black trim *Annie McGee* looked like the object of a man's passion. She was a wooden ship—"boat" is a word that somehow implies one of those fiberglass things—and her deck was about half resanded. Yossarian later told me that he did all the sanding by hand. He didn't trust a belt sander on those soft cedar planks.

Captain Yossarian had one other passenger, a woman he introduced as Patty. She stepped very lively when Yossarian started issuing orders, which he did about sixty seconds after we were aboard. She obviously knew which rope was which and a lot of other nautical stuff. I watched as he and Patty untied this rope, pulled on that one, hooked up this and unhooked that.

142

The triangular sail on the bowsprit went up first, then the funny rectangular one on the forward mast, then the mooring rope was let go. As the main sail on the aft mast went up, without fanfare or noise the sails filled out and *Annie McGee* began to move through the water with Patty at the tiller.

"I never cease to be fascinated," Yossarian remarked, "with the subtle way that sailing vessels just go in motion."

In moments we were clipping along to the northeast, out of the harbor into the huge open bay. Yossarian and Patty arranged themselves in the cockpit, so I did too. Yossarian adjusted a couple of ropes that trimmed the sails, then sat there looking all around.

I like this aspect of sailing—apparently when you aren't changing course, there is a lot of sitting around contemplating things.

We got acquainted and they answered a good many simple questions from their passenger. Pretty soon we were discussing the breeze and the sea and other boats and having a fine time. Captain Yossarian and Patty were an excellent pair to go sailing with.

You can hear a sailing vessel go through the water. Without engine noise or vibration, you can hear the water lapping at the hull. It's a nervous sound, but very pleasant.

The boat moves in response to the wind's pressure on the sails and the action of the swells against the hull. The water was relatively calm and I didn't feel even a touch of queasiness, which I feared I would. The wind blowing, the sails taut against the sky, the sun on the water, the motion of the boat—it was fascinating. I can see how a man could fall in love with it.

"How fast are we going?" I asked.

Yossarian studied the water flowing by, the angle of the sails and our heel, the strength of the wind, then said, "Oh, maybe three and a half or four knots."

He owned a house in Rockland, he said, and did some graphic art. But his love was taking passengers sailing on *Annie McGee*. He had been sailing since he was "this high," and made a gesture indicating a small boy. He had only flown once, he remarked, and the pilot let him fly the plane for twenty minutes, so if he ever decided to take lessons he had twenty minutes to put in the logbook. He had owned *Annie McGee* for four years. Her keel was laid in 1950 in Brunswick, Maine, by a builder who had a real day job. So working nights and weekends he took seven years to finish her. When Yossarian acquired her she had been neglected. He was fixing her up board by board as time and finances allowed.

Patty had been a cook last summer on a cruise schooner and now was pushing paper ashore. She was learning to sail and tried to go out with somebody every time she had a day off. After we had been sailing for about an hour, she went forward and stretched out on the cedar deck for a nap. The boards were warm in the diffused sunlight and the motion of the schooner quite pleasant. If I had been an older hand at this, I would have enjoyed a nap too.

All in all, it was the most delightful Fourth of July I have spent in many a year. Watching other boats pass by, waving, steering with the tiller and feeling the sea's pressure on the rudder as I listened to Yossarian tell me about his ship, I felt completely relaxed. Normally I get this feeling only when flying way up high on a beautiful day. I decided that if I ever get tired of flying—fat chance!—or lose my medical certificate, I'm going to learn to sail. I know there are schools here and there that teach lawyers, lottery winners and heiresses how to do it, so I'll find one and sign up.

That evening I dropped into bed while the fireworks were booming over Rockland and promptly went to sleep. Sailing apparently has that effect.

The day before the Fourth, I drove around Rockland and Rockport and Owls Head, the peninsula where the airport is located. I was impressed. The weather was warm, almost eighty degrees, the breeze just a zephyr, the white houses hard to look at in the sun. The lawns were neatly trimmed and the streets free of potholes. All in all, a person looking for a place in the United States to drop anchor could do a whole lot worse. They even had a McDonald's.

The next day I asked Captain Yossarian about the winters, and he told me they are usually long, cold and snowy. But this past winter, he said, it didn't snow after January so the rain just made mud. He didn't like mud.

On the fifth of July I drove slowly through town at 7 A.M. on my way to the airport and looked again. I could live in a town like this on the coast of Maine. I can personally attest that the summers are fantastic, although Yossarian said fog often rolls in off the sea. One can see why this coast inspired artists like Winslow Homer and the Wyeths and politicians like James G. Blaine and George Bush.

What the Maine coast doesn't have are beaches with golden sand and warm water. Yossarian referred to the water as liquid ice. I dipped a hand in and quickly withdrew it. This ocean is the North Atlantic, folks, and it's cold and gray all year long. The surf breaks on limestone and granite rocks. Still, if you can do without sand in your swimming trunks and the occasional frolic in the surf, I highly recommend the Maine coast. I'm coming back someday soon.

I'm flying under the leading edge of a warm front, only this time I'm approaching from the cold side. This is the same front I flew under coming north through western Pennsylvania and New Jersey. It stalled there for three or four days, then gradually resumed its track to the northeast.

The clouds are well above me—I'm flying at 2,000 feet—and thickening. I can no longer see shadows. The weather briefer at Flight Service predicted showers and low ceilings today over northern New Hampshire and Vermont, and isolated thunderstorms this afternoon. I hope to be through here before the thunderbumpers start cooking.

Showers I can handle. Low ceilings I can handle. What I can't handle are mountains obscured by clouds and mist. These old, eroded mountains are pale imitations of the Rockies, but a little mountain will kill you just as dead as a big one if you fly into it.

From Rockland I flew north up the coast of Penobscot Bay. I hadn't yet had enough of picturesque little villages huddled around harbors filled with boats. At Belfast I turned inland. Over Waterville I saw the low clouds over the mountains to the west. The mountains looked blue and indistinct in this moist air.

Now west of Waterville, I let the Queen drift up to 2,300 feet and alter course twenty degrees or so to the left to hit Livermore

Falls. I am paying close attention to the compass and meticulously time-ticking my chart, noting my position at least every five minutes. I have absolutely no intention of wandering through mountain valleys with no idea which valley I am in.

Livermore Falls comes up right on the nose. Off to the right a big pulp mill in Wilton is belching smoke, which the wind is trailing off to the north, maybe slightly northwest. That's about the same wind I have here at my altitude. I've got a ten degree left correction set and I'm making a good ground speed, so the wind is probably right from the south or slightly southeast.

I cross Livermore Falls 55 minutes after I took off from Rockland. Another heading change, this time fifteen degrees left. In three minutes I cross over Canton Point and pick up the valley headed west. The valley has a river—the Androscoggin—and a road in it, and they are easy to follow. Off to my right are mountains higher than I am covered with trees. I can see a cloud coming up off the slope of one of them. That's the goo that you can't go under.

Visibility is down to six or seven miles as I pass Mexico and Rumford and continue west up the valley. The *Queen's* engine has been balky to start of late, almost as if the mixture is too rich. She catches only as I pull the mixture knob back from full rich. Maybe it's the low altitude, but funny I didn't notice that in Louisiana and Florida. Flying now up this New England mountain valley, this thought nags at me and I listen carefully to the engine while I check the oil pressure and temperature and cylinder head temp, then scan the earth below for likely looking emergency fields.

You get in the habit of looking for places to land if the engine should quit. I have never lost an engine in 2,700 hours of flying, but there is always a first time. I imagine the engine will start running rough and coughing before it stops completely, if the problem is a thrown rod or plugged-up carburetor or busted valve. If something catastrophic happens, like the crankshaft breaking or seizing, then it will just quit dead without warning.

That would be a once-in-a-lifetime thrill, I imagine. There's a terrific scene in the movie *Spirit of St. Louis* in which Jimmy Stewart's engine dies abruptly—he runs a fuel tank dry. Only a great actor could make that look of stupefied amazement so real that you know that is exactly how you would feel if it happened to you.

In the Navy we referred to a moment like that as a lummer, a shot of cold urine to the heart. Actually the drug is adrenaline and the quantity is about a quart.

Thank heavens the *Cannibal Queen*'s big Lycoming is humming like a champ. There are few places below that I would want to try to set her down and the clouds above prevent me from climbing higher to increase my options. I am in a valley now with mountains on both sides that are higher than I am.

Passing Bethel I fly through my first spattering of rain. In a moment we are out of it. Visibility improves somewhat, up to ten miles or a little more. I can see the bulk of Mt. Washington rising ahead to my left, and I can make out the peak. So here, anyway, the clouds are above 6,288 feet, which is how high that monster is. From 2,300 feet it looks like an Alp. If the weather were better I would climb up and fly around the peak, just to say I did it.

Abeam of it I catch my first glimpse of the runway at Mt. Washington Regional Airport. I'm ten or eleven miles from there but I give them a call. In less than thirty seconds I get an answer on Unicom: "Winds nil, landing runway 28, right-hand pattern, altimeter 30.07."

I announce that I will land straight in. The airport sits in a large, relatively flat, forested valley, three or four miles east of the town of Whitefield, New Hampshire. The runway is wet.

I make a fairly decent landing. This conscious look right, then left just before the flare is proving itself very well. Every landing I have made since I began using this technique has been satisfactory or better. Maybe I'm getting the hang of this tail-wheel stuff!

Rain is misting down as I park. I take a squint back toward Mt. Washington but I can't see it. First one, then three men come out to watch me fuel. They don't have any Aeroshell 50-weight ashless dispersant oil, but after rejecting two quarts of mineral oil, I find some multiweight ashless dispersant in the FBO office. I buy it and pour it into the *Queen*.

By now Her Royal Highness has a half-dozen admirers. I'm not jealous. The gorgeous old gal deserves every flirtatious glance sent her way. I'm well aware of the fact that all this

attention is a tribute to Skid Henley and his craftsmanship, not
to me.

I use the phone to call Flight Service. The weather has not
improved. Nor has it gotten worse. Yet for the first time the
briefer talks about mountain obscuration. "Patchy," he says.

The rain is falling gently and steadily. The *Queen's* admirers
have retreated to cover. I walk around her, looking her over as
I meditate on the situation for a minute or two. Then I plunk
my bottom in the wet seat and strap in.

The seal on the engine primer is apparently going. Since Florida it has been leaking fuel onto my fingers when I pump it.
Now it squirts some. Great!

I leave the mixture knob half open and crank the engine. She
doesn't fire. I prime another couple of squirts, open the mixture
full rich, then retard it as I crank. The Lyc fires and belches a
cloud of white smoke and settles into a steady idle. I think at
this altitude you must just retard the mixture knob quickly—
that's the hot engine start technique.

With the wind sock hanging limp, I elect not to taxi the
length of the runway to take off to the west. I add power and
lift the tail and take off eastward and make a climbing turn.
I will follow the highways through the valleys to Burlington,
Vermont, on Lake Champlain, then call it a day. This would
be the most scenic terrain in the East if I could just climb high
enough to see it properly. Maybe tomorrow. Or the next day.
It's not like I'm really going somewhere.

At Littleton, New Hampshire, I pick up the four-lane headed
northwest. This quickly peters out at St. Johnsbury, Vermont,
and I am left with a two-lane ribbon of asphalt going the way
I want to go, southwest toward Barre and Montpelier. Occasionally I have to weave my way around wisps of cloud. Off to my
right the mountains are wreathed in mist and heavy clouds.
Same on the left.

Darn! These would be great mountains if I could just see
them. These are the Green Mountains of Vermont, where Ethan
Allen and the Green Mountain Boys hailed from. I read Allen's
biography in the fourth grade, that winter during arithmetic
class. Ever since I have had an itch to own a flintlock rifle.

When the Knapp State Airport on top of a hill between Barre
and Montpelier comes into view, I am tempted. I am flying in

rain, not seeing all the nifty things I wanted to see, the mountains are topped with crud. I call Unicom and land.

Ta da! I have now been to every state in the union except Alaska! I'm sorry, but I don't want to go anyplace where you have to eat your whiskey and cook your motor oil. Noel Wein was a better man than I. I admit it.

The FBO offered me a spot in his hangar to get the Queen out of the rain. I took him up on it. I taxied her straight in. He helped me fuel her there, but he didn't have any 50-weight oil either. Luckily I had two quarts in the baggage bin that I'd been saving for a rainy day, like this one turned out to be.

Later I visited the National Weather Service meteorological observer in his little office in the terminal. His name was Roger Hill and he looked genuinely glad that I stopped by. In addition to all his weather gear, he had the Unicom radio—this was why the answers to my transmissions were so prompt—and a large black mongrel dog that was asleep on his couch.

I asked Roger when this front was going to be out of here. He said it should be clearing nicely by noon tomorrow. I told him I wanted to go west through the Adirondacks and then southwest along the southern shore of Lake Erie.

"Shouldn't be a problem tomorrow afternoon," he said. "But there is another front over Wisconsin and Lake Michigan and it'll be slowly moving this way. Tomorrow afternoon and maybe the next day you'll be between fronts. It'll be hazier on the back side of this front than it's been here the last few days."

Roger grew up in Los Angeles, he told me, but married a Vermont girl and came out here. It's for the best, he thought. "Being a meteorologist in L.A. is like drinking only milk—they don't have weather there." He said he likes places with four seasons and he can tolerate snow. Several times as we talked he glanced out the window at the sky.

I like weathermen who look out the window. More of them should.

I thanked him and thought about patting the sleeping dog, but decided against it. Let sleeping dogs lie, the wise man once said, though I've forgotten which wise man that was. Either Confucius or W. C. Fields.

That evening I went down to Montpelier for dinner and a

look around. The state capitol is a building in the tradition of American state capitols, but it is modest in size and the lines are clean. It has a shiny golden dome on it that I saw from the air just before I landed. I've seen a couple dozen capitol buildings, and this is far and away the nicest. Across State Street from the capitol are some four-or-five-story turn-of-the-century brick and stone buildings that are used by state government. The scale is a human one.

Wonder of wonders, downtown Montpelier is a thriving place, full of people and stores that are still open on a Friday night. How these Vermonters avoided the mall plague that devastated most American downtowns is a secret they should share.

But Montpelier is just a small town, maybe twelve thousand people. Fifteen at the outside. I suspect it's the smallest capital city of any state. Of course that means the politician per capita ratio is extraordinarily high. The politician density in Denver is much, much less. In Denver you can go weeks without running into a politician if you stay out of the cheap saloons.

I had a pizza at Angelo's, which offered peanut butter as a topping for real gourmets. I elected to go with more traditional fare, then drove over to Barre for ice cream. Barre is smaller than Montpelier—people make U-turns in the streets on a regular basis. The residential districts I drove through are filled with trim, well-maintained frame houses on quiet, tree-lined streets.

Still trying to imagine what a peanut butter pizza would taste like, I ordered a peanut butter sundae topped with whipped cream and a cherry at a trailer-emporium on the north end of town. It was delicious.

On the way back to my motel I found myself thinking about tomorrow's flight. The rain had stopped. I hoped the transplanted L.A. meteorologist's prediction would come true.

Yesterday morning, the Fourth of July, I saw an article in the Portland, Maine, paper on patriotism. The gist of the article was that a lot of folks think patriotism's bad. That's okay with me—I don't really care what they think.

The reason I'm still thinking about the article is because it contained a quote from a professor of political science at some little college here in New England. It went like this: "As an

150

intellectual, I believe that American imperialism is a knife at the world's throat."

Now I ask you, do you ever start sentences with the phrase, "As an intellectual . . ."? Nor do I. And I know why. Most people automatically translate this phrase as they hear it into something like this: "As an overeducated, impractical fathead, I believe blah blah blah."

But I have been thinking about this off and on all day yesterday and today, maybe fifteen minutes total, and I'd like to give it a whirl. So here goes:

As an intellectual, I think that skinny girls are cuter than fat ones.

That phrase makes any sentence a grabber, doesn't it? So far so good. I'll try it a few more times.

As an intellectual, I believe that masturbation is the leading cause of acne.

As an intellectual who has done a lot of pondering on the state of the universe and mankind's position in it, I have come to firmly believe that the world will end tomorrow.

As an intellectual, I am convinced that people who like anchovies on their pizza shouldn't order peanut butter too.

As an intellectual, I have found that thick books cost more than thin ones and take longer to read.

I think I'm getting the hang of this. You should consider adding this phrase to your lexicon—you'll really impress your friends. One more, then as an intellectual, I'll call it a night.

As an intellectual, I think patriotism is like beer—a judicious quantity is great and too much isn't good for you.

15

The rain was showering down in Montpelier, Vermont, on Saturday morning at 8:30 A.M. The window of my motel room actually opened and I rested my elbows on the sill and watched the rain pound the cars in the parking lot and make little rivulets where it ran along the asphalt. The rain came down hard for a while, then slacked off, then came hard again.

As usual, this morning there were deadlines. I had to be out of the motel by 11 A.M. or pay for another night. The car was from a dealership across the street, and it had to be back by 5 P.M. today, regardless. The dealership was closed on Sundays. So if the weather stayed yucky, I was going to be afoot in a motel two miles from the airport, five miles from Barre, and eight miles from downtown Montpelier. And the motel didn't have a restaurant. If I could get a room for another night.

I watched the rain fall and pondered my luck. Everyone has luck most of the time. The only time they think about it is when their luck takes a day off; then they think they are unlucky. Take yourself, for instance—how often do you get run over by a car while you are crossing a street? But the day you do you will curse your luck, if you are conscious at the hospital. I know that I am one of the luckiest men alive, but apparently my charm lady was temporarily indisposed today.

Stephen Coonts, the flying fool, in the rear cockpit—the captain's seat—of the *Cannibal Queen*.

The *Cannibal Queen* flying free over Boulder, Colorado, with the cloud-shrouded peaks of the Continental Divide in the background.

With his son, David, in the front cockpit, the author practices wheel landings for the photographer at Billard Field, Topeka, Kansas. This method of touching down on the main wheels and holding the tail off as the aircraft slows is fun to practice, but it is not the recommended method for getting a taildragger safely down on strange airports in gusty winds.

The *Cannibal Queen* as drawn by the author's daughter, Rachael. This surrealistic interpretation of the aircraft in flight without people seems somehow symbolic of the dream—you put yourself into the cockpit surrounded by yellow wings, above endless vistas of summer landscape, flying in an infinite summer sky.

(OVERLEAF)
Newspaper photographer David P. Gilkey rigged a camera on the left wing strut of the *Cannibal Queen* to capture this view as she soars around the Flatirons, a rock formation near Boulder, Colorado. That's Gilkey in the front seat, triggering the camera with a remote control. He chose to shoot the left side of the plane so that the feminist editors of his newspaper would not see and be offended by the nose art on the other side.

Skid Henley, the artist in steel, wood, and fabric who totally rebuilt the *Cannibal Queen,* poses with the author. Skid logged over 15,000 hours in Stearmans, spraying from New Brunswick to Nicaragua. His restoration of the *Queen* took thirteen months of intense effort.

The *Cannibal Queen* on the ramp at NAS Whidbey Island, Washington. She started her flying career as a military primary flight trainer during World War II, so this is not the first military ramp graced by her presence.

The Canadian side of Niagara Falls as seen from the *Cannibal Queen* on a hazy summer day. What can't be seen in this photo are the suds caused by industrial chemicals that coat the river below the falls.

Mount Shasta as viewed from the rear cockpit of the *Cannibal Queen*. This monstrous old volcano dominates the northern California landscape.

The author and son, David, pose for the camera. This shot captured David's infectious grin and the zest with which he approaches life.

The author and the Cannibal Queen, nose art created by photographer/artist David Zlotky, a man of many talents. He refused to reveal the identity of his model.

At 9 A.M. I checked out of the hotel. I had to do it sooner or later, so why not now? I drove down to Barre and found a laundromat. The rain quit while I was loading the washer.

At 11 I went out to the airport, which is on a hilltop, and looked in all directions. The mountains to the south and west were obscured, but the view northward was pretty good. East was only fair. Ceiling maybe 800 or a thousand feet, five miles visibility in haze, wind out of the south at about twelve knots. I went in to see Roger Hill, the L.A. meteorologist.

"It'll get better," he said, laughing. "You wait and see."

I ate lunch in the airport restaurant, which is pretty nice, and tried to nap in the front seat of the car. At 12:45 the glare of sun on my face brought me alert.

It was breaking up. I could see the tops of the mountains! Sunshine! Bless you, Roger, you bald-headed weather guesser!

By 1:30 I had taken the car back to the dealer and hitched a ride back to the airport with one of the salesmen. When I saw the Queen in the hangar I got a jolt. Fuel was leaking from the gas sight-gauge, the glass pipe that sticks down below the fuel tank in the center of the top wing. The blue coloring in the fuel had smeared the left side of the aircraft. It was leaking even as the FBO man and I stood there watching.

I got out my wrench and climbed up on the wing to lean in and tighten the nut that holds the thing on. The FBO man beat me to it. "It's coming out around the glass here. Let's see if we can tighten it."

Using both hands and being careful not to break it, he twisted the tube half a turn. The leak slowed to a drip. Now I tried it. After one and a half turns, the leak stopped completely.

"What happens," my host asked, "if that thing breaks off in flight?"

"I'll have a major problem," I said irritably. I didn't need him telling me about getting burned alive in a flaming airplane. I went through all that last week.

My host didn't want to drop the subject. "Knew it to happen once on a biplane, not a Stearman, but a Great Lakes. Luckily the guy had eight gallons left in the fuselage tank or he wouldn't have made it. You have a fuselage tank?"

"Nope. But I can land this thing about anyplace." That's a

153

lie. Exasperated, I made it a whopper. "I could put it in a tree if I have to."

He went back to his office while I diddled with the manual fuel primer. When we parked the plane in the hangar we unscrewed the push rod and examined the rubber gasket. It looked fine and the FBO didn't have another anyway. So this morning I carefully inserted it back in its hole and tightened the nut as tight as I could get it with my fingers. Then I opened the fuel valve, shoved the mixture knob to full rich, and gave the primer handle a pull, then a push. No leak. Dry as a bone. It just needed to be tightened up.

It seems like all this stuff is getting shook loose by the vibration. The engine seems to be leaking more oil, the primer, the fuel gauge tube . . .

At 2:10 I cranked the engine. Roger wished me a good flight on the Unicom, and I thanked him. At 2:17 I was airborne.

As usual, the weather looks worse from the air than it does on the ground. From 2,000 feet some of the ridge tops are invisible in this haze, which limits visibility to about seven miles.

I fly northwest down the valley toward Burlington on Lake Champlain. The interstate runs from Montpelier to Burlington, so I check it occasionally and watch the mountains and clouds float by on either side. Short of Burlington I turn southwest to avoid the controlled airspace of the Burlington Airport Radar Service Area.

I fly under the clouds and over the ridges comfortably, but off to the right a dark cloud is giving Burlington a bath. On Burlington Approach frequency the pilots and controllers are talking about turbulence and reduced visibility. Approach is trying to get some guy in a Cessna to climb to 3,500 feet and maintain VFR. Needless to say, the pilot is telling Approach that maintaining VFR at those altitudes today is just not in the cards.

Twenty minutes after takeoff I am over the shore of Lake Champlain. It is a long, narrow, big lake, maybe a couple miles wide on the average. Today it is full of power boats and a few sailboats. From 2,000 feet the wakes in the dark water are very prominent as I fly south.

Another dark cloud pouring rain looms on the right. I swing

154

east slightly and drop to 1,700 feet, but rain starts to spatter on the windscreens and run over the wings. To my right the Adirondack Mountains are completely shrouded in cloud and rain, so thick that I can only catch an occasional glimpse of a high ridge up in there. This front is coming up from the southwest, and all this black rainy stuff results from the warm air being pushed up the slopes of those mountains. Lake Champlain and Lake George, to the south, are in the rain shadow of those mountains. I wish the weather were better!

The shower is behind as I reach Chimney Point at 2:56 P.M., 39 minutes after takeoff from Montpelier. Crown Point goes by the left wing, then the Ticonderoga Airport at 3:04. I swing over the town and head south on Lake George. Below on my right I can see a sheer wall of granite rising at least five hundred feet above the lake. Forested ridges on both sides as high as the Queen, boats charging about the water at random—this country must be as spectacular from the ground as it is from this altitude. The show has a dark side, however—if the engine quits there is absolutely no place to put the Queen down except in the lake.

Another storm is coming off the hills to the west as I approach the southern end of the lake. More raindrops slide across the skin of the Queen.

I make a straight-in approach to runway 19 at Glens Falls, New York. The wind is out of the south at twelve knots. My look-look technique is working well and I make a nice landing, which helps loosen the tension. The landings are getting consistent. Something is going right, anyway.

I really don't like to fly in this marginal weather. Flying should be relaxing and this flying isn't. I'm tense as a spring.

I shut the engine down an hour and a half after takeoff from Montpelier.

"I want to go west, maybe Ithaca," I tell the Flight Service briefer. He is cautious. "Marginal VFR," he says in one breath; then after reviewing his reports, he changes it to "VFR not recommended."

Out in the parking lot I smoke my pipe and look at the sky. Ithaca, the briefer said, is 4,000 feet scattered, 8,000 feet scattered, with ten miles visibility, wind 310 at eight knots. Between here and there something good happens.

I decide to give it a try. I tell myself that I can always return here if I run into clouds I can't or don't want to go under. If only that were always true!

The sky to the north, the direction I flew in from, is a dark purple as I taxi out. Westward it just looks gray.

After takeoff I climb to 1,500 feet and pull the throttle and prop back to cruise and lean the mixture. The ridge west of Glens Falls has a dark roll cloud about eight hundred feet above it. Visibility no more than five miles. Why me, Lord?

I squirt between the cloud and the ridge and keep flying west, feeling my way, my finger tracing my progress on the chart, my pen uncapped and ready for time notations over landmarks. I pick up the northern finger of Great Sacandaga Lake and follow it. Wonder of wonder, the clouds lift and visibility starts to improve. The wind is still out of the south and I'm bucking it, so I don't want to go too high or the *Queen's* progress over the ground will be arrested by stronger winds. Still, I want to get high enough to see. I let her float upward to 2,500 feet. I fly over the city of Gloversville (Yuck, what a name! It has no style! Say London, Paris, Rome and Gloversville and you'll see what I mean) and point the *Queen* toward Fort Plain on the Mohawk River.

The Mohawk! *Drums Along the Mohawk* with Henry Fonda was on late-night TV a couple months ago, but I didn't watch it. I should have.

Crossing the Mohawk Valley the clouds open up extensively, except for one little rain squall just off to my right. The *Queen* gets another bath.

Higher still, up to 3,000 feet. Ahead, south of the Mohawk, likes Lake Otsego, or the Glimmerglass as James Fenimore Cooper called it in his book *The Deerslayer*. That's a book that kids don't want to read anymore because of the archaic, tedious style, and adults don't want to read anymore because Mark Twain slammed it hard and said, truthfully, that Cooper wasn't much of a writer. But I like it. It's still a good tale.

What Twain forgot to mention is that Cooper told a whale of a story. Cooper was one of the first novelists to write action-adventure plots as we know them today. It would be nice if every published work by every author was a masterpiece, but this is the real world. I think a book should be enjoyed for what the author *did* put in, not discarded because of what he *didn't*. But nobody is ever going to hire me to do literary criticism.

Otsego is not large in comparison with other lakes in this part of the world. Rather modest. Staring down from 3,500 feet, I see the roughness of surface chop and speedboats plowing wakes. Still, with only a little stretch I can imagine Deerslayer and his Indian pal gliding across the glassy-smooth surface in a birchbark canoe. That's really a personality defect—I've a hyperactive imagination and I'm a hopeless romantic. Maybe a good shrink could help me.

At the lower end of Lake Otsego is the town named after the Cooper family, Cooperstown. In this municipal memorial to the writer that couldn't write, the power that rules the universe has placed the Baseball Hall of Fame. I've never been there but I'm going someday. I want to see the bat that Babe Ruth used to hit his 60th home run on September 30, 1927, and the ball that went soaring out over the fence as those fans chosen by fate to witness that blow screamed themselves hoarse.

Leaving Cooperstown I point the *Queen* 260 degrees, then fudge a little to the south to allow for the prevailing southerly wind. The country west of here is small farms and woodlots in gently rolling terrain with few prominent features. There are a few crossroads villages, but I can't tell one from the other. To my weary eye they all look alike with their few dozen houses clustered around a pointy church steeple. The weather is getting better and better. The sunlight makes the *Queen*'s yellow wings too bright to look at without squinting.

I'm flying at 3,500 feet now, my visibility limited only by the haze. As the minutes tick by I begin to fidget. Let's see, we left Cooperstown at 5:21 P.M. on a course for Norwich, thirty miles away. That town on the right should be New Berlin, but where the heck is the sawmill south of town? And that race track to the east, that's not on the chart. Well, it's got to be New Berlin, that's the only place it could be, so I'll mark us here at 5:34.

More minutes pass. Where is Norwich? Well, it's a cinch it should be around here someplace. The wind must be drifting me north.

I scan southward and see a town. The town's in a valley,

157

that's right. . . . I fly south. Boy, I sure got pushed off course. That's a good breeze from the south.

But that isn't Norwich! Norwich has an airport north of town. That town has an airport . . . is that the airport? Yes, the airport is on the western edge of town. That's *Sidney!*

Oops!

I swing the plane northwest and study the chart. Ah ha, that town I thought was New Berlin was really this little village of Morris, which has a racetrack. So the wind is out of the *north,* and I compounded the error by turning south. You should have noticed that, Steve! You should have noticed the drift on the last leg, down the lake toward Cooperstown. You should have been examining the chop to see which way the wind was blowing, but you were thinking about guys with flintlock rifles in birchbark canoes.

Feeling rather asinine, I ponder how devilishly easy it is to make a mistake like this even when I am flying at 3,500 feet with eight or ten miles visibility.

Just then the engine stumbles. Just a hiccup, a half second of dead sound.

The adrenaline whacks me in the heart; the heart and respiration rate instantly double.

With a shaky hand I shove the mixture knob forward a half inch and study my three little engine gauges. Oil temperature 160 degrees, oil pressure 55 PSI, and cylinder head temp 190 degrees. All normal.

I listen like an old maid trying to hear a cat burglar at three in the morning. *Now* the Lyc runs smooth as sipping whiskey. The RPM and manifold pressure needles look like they're glued in place. The sound is a steady, throbbing hum.

The mind races. This happened to me once before, so I'm not as scared as I got the first time. I talked to Steve Hall about it and he assured me that there was nothing wrong mechanically.

"Nothing mechanical," I chant to myself.

Steve thought that maybe a slug of water or dirt went through the carb. But he could find absolutely nothing wrong with the aircraft.

The *Cannibal Queen* is going to age me before she eats me. That little hiccup cost me two years off the top end.

As I fly I meditate on the evil perversity that all mechanical

158

devices possess, and decide that I probably had the mixture just a touch too lean. That must have been it.

Relief floods me when I sight Ithaca in the haze and pull the power back for a descent. The tower gives the altimeter setting as 29.78 inches of mercury. The barometer is dropping. Another front is on the way!

I don't care. I've had enough excitement for one day.

At 7 A.M. on Sunday morning at a Sheraton in Ithaca I stare glumly at the rain pouring down, watch the lightning flashes, listen to the booming of the thunder. I haven't seen a storm like this since Florida, and it's only seven o'clock in the morning! The front is no longer west of here someplace; it's right over my head!

Out at the airport the *Cannibal Queen* is getting another bath. She'll be the cleanest dirty airplane in six states when this is over. Unfortunately rainwater will not take off the oily grime. Dirt and dust yes, but not the real crud.

Grounded in Ithaca without a car. Sounds like the title of a soap opera. If only David were here, with his cowlicks and braces and impish grin; he'd liven things up.

16

At 9 a.m. that Sunday the rain stopped. At 11:20 I was airborne and headed northwest for blue skies and Niagara Falls. The plan was to get fuel at the Niagara Falls airport, fly over the falls and photograph it, then head southwest for Ohio. Alas, my schemes rarely go as planned and this one was no exception. The weather was fine, about 4,500 scattered, visibility about 30 miles near Rochester but deteriorating as I neared Buffalo. I bucked fifteen knots of headwind from Rochester westward as the engine hummed merrily, no stumble or burble or hiccups. Lord, what do *you* think?

The Flight Service briefer thought I was trying to be funny when I called from the Niagara Falls airport and told her I wanted to go southwest VFR in the general direction of Cleveland. Intense thunderstorms covered half the sky in Detroit and Cleveland, Erie was IFR, and I should keep my antique flying machine firmly on the ground.

"But tomorrow will be better," she told me, trying to soften the message. "The front will have passed by then. The prog (forecast, or prognosis, charts) shows patchy ground fog in the morning across your route, but it will burn off by ten or eleven o'clock."

I thanked her and tied the *Queen* down in the grass beside the fueling mat. Yeah, tomorrow will be better. I've heard that song before. I can even hum it and sing a few stanzas.

The fuel attendant was a guy named Chuck who looked at the big yellow Stearman with affection. "Haven't seen one of those since the Red Baron Pizza Team was here." He told me the team gives pricey rides in Niagara Falls every year and donates the proceeds to Children's Hospital. "And they sell a lot of pizza," he added.

I'm familiar with Red Baron Pizza's red-and-white Stearmans. They were out in Colorado this spring giving rides. They did aerobatics near Boulder and I watched them from my porch. The 450-HP R-985 Pratt & Whitneys they run sound impressive (read *loud*). I suspect the pizza team Stearmans are fully IFR-capable or they wouldn't be running them around the country eight months of the year like they do.

"They don't have naked women on their planes," Chuck said, and grinned. "Just a lot of little pizzas."

The vision of a squadron of pepperoni pizzas adorning the *Cannibal Queen*'s flanks made me shudder. "Some people got no class," I agreed.

So here I was marooned in Niagara Falls. I decided to do what any normal person would do in Niagara Falls—rent a car and go see the thing. So I told Chuck I desired wheels. The rental place at the airport was closed Sundays, but he called the Hertz man at home. One car had been returned that morning, so he said he would come out and rent it to me, which he did.

At the Hertz office in the terminal he glanced at my Colorado driver's license, then advised, "Try and avoid the traffic over the bridges to Canada in the evening. Half of Canada comes here to shop now that they jacked taxes over there again. And they'll all be going home on Sunday evening."

Of course I wanted to know why they shopped here instead of Canada. I was told that everything in Ontario costs two or three times as much as it does in the States. "It's taxes. They tax the hell out of everything over there to pay for socialism. I don't know where they think Canada's going, but it sure is a bonanza for our businesses. Even gas costs twice as much over there. Every other car in the filling stations here has a Canadian

161

tag on it. Canadians come in here all the time and rent cars to drive to the malls. That's why I'm out of cars, as usual.

"Had a schoolteacher in here yesterday that claimed he made sixty thousand dollars a year in Canada and can retire at fifty-five. That's what's wrong with that country. He was painting his house, he said, and house paint over there costs thirty-five dollars a gallon. Imagine that! So he earns his huge salary over there and buys his house paint over here. And they're buying houses here—a house here costs a third of what it does in Ontario."

He got me a discount on a hotel room downtown and warned me not to park my car on the Canadian side. "Lots over there charge you six bucks a pop. Walk across the bridge."

My hotel had a maple leaf flag flying out front and a big banner hanging in the lobby. "Welcome Canadians!" In my room was a give-away newspaper that told Canadians where to shop in Niagara Falls and Buffalo.

Americans know a good thing when they see it. They're cashing in.

When I was growing up in West Virginia everyone, and I mean *everyone*, honeymooned in Niagara Falls. I heard the hotels had whole floors full of bridal suites with mirrors on the ceilings. My hotel did not give me a bridal suite, probably because I was paying a discounted rate and had no nervous bride fidgeting beside me. There was no mirror on the ceiling, either.

The pay telephones and pop machines in the lobby had prominent signs posted about the evil things that would happen if you fed them Canadian coins, which jam them. Banks won't change these coins into American money, so they are essentially worthless unless you're planning a trip to Canada in the near future. Unwary American merchants end up with a till full. Some of these coins then get passed as change to unsophisticated rustics like me.

Standing on Goat Island and watching the cataract, I was seized by a powerful urge to throw coins in. This urge also struck many of my fellow observers of this natural wonder, especially boys under ten years. I thus got rid of the three Canadian coins I had pocketed during my travels—one quarter and two dimes. I suspect a good percentage of the Canadian mint's production goes into this river. Someday this riverbed will be a tin mine.

The observation platforms on Goat Island were like a sauna. The mist off the falls raised the humidity to 99.99 percent, which combined with the 85-to-90-degree July heat to make the sweat roll off everybody like they were fat ladies at a Labor Day picnic.

The Niagara Falls Chamber of Commerce should be justly proud of the public relations job it has done worldwide. From the look of the international crowd and the sounds of Spanish, Japanese, Swedish, German and Italian that I heard, this waterfall is on the itinerary of every foreigner alive who's planning a trip to the States.

On a sour note, part of the river below the falls is covered with foam caused by industrial chemicals and other pollutants in the water. Americans will be pleased to hear that the soapsuds are mostly on the Canadian side of the river. However, most of the stuff that made the suds came from cities and factories on the U.S. side of the Great Lakes.

Still, even with the suds, it's a heck of a waterfall. Best I've ever seen. This is the Grand Canyon of waterfalls, absolutely the biggest and most stunning, so standing here in the heat and humidity parboiling slowly, American hearts swell with pride. It's too darn bad we have to share this waterfall with the Canadians. If we could only get them to sell us a hundred-yard-wide strip of Ontario shoreline for a mile in each direction, it would be all ours.

The thing that impressed me most was not the falls, which are indeed impressive, but the wide river coming down the chutes toward the falls. In the chutes this stupendous quantity of water accelerates, losing elevation quickly, and becomes a raging torrent racing toward the brink where it will shoot into space and fall the 160-odd feet to the rocks below. This white-water fury seems to possess infinite energy. No wonder the name of the river—Niagara—has taken on this connotation in our language.

The waters of the four upper Great Lakes have been racing these rapids to leap the falls since the end of the last ice age. This is the power of the eternal. We humans are but small motes in nature's scheme.

*   *   *

Before I came to the Falls, while I was waiting for the Hertz man to arrive at the airport, Chuck and I visited. He told me about the last air show they had at Niagara Falls International, three years ago.

It seems the two solo Blue Angels were doing an opposing loop—that is, one came racing in from the east, one from the west, and after passing each other they pulled up in a loop to pass again on the top, then a third time on the bottom. This time, Chuck said, instead of passing on the top, the two planes collided. One pilot was killed on impact. The other pilot ejected and his plane crashed in a junkyard off the east end of the runway.

Niagara Falls hasn't had an airshow since, Chuck told me. The insurance companies want $3 million now to insure the airshow, so it's history.

That story got me thinking again about the only ex–Blue Angel I ever met in my nine years of active duty in naval aviation. I met him on my second combat cruise aboard USS *Enterprise*, the last cruise of the Vietnam War.

The ex-Angel was the executive officer of one of the two F-4 fighter squadrons we had aboard. He stood out like a sore thumb. He was the only flyer I ever met who spit-shined his flight boots—they looked like patent leather but it was Kiwi shoe polish. This guy sat down in his stateroom at night and layered the stuff on and polished and polished. Me? I never shined my boots, not once. I thought shoe polish might melt or burn, and anyway, I had better things to do, like read *Playboy* or play poker.

In those days the attack community to which I belonged feuded endlessly with the fighter guys, and vice versa, a rivalry assiduously cultivated over the years with mutual insults and one-upsmanship. The fighters in those days were F-4 Phantoms, which were designed as interceptors and were fuel thirsty. The Navy used them as fighters from necessity—it was the only fighter the Navy had except for the F-8 Crusader, which lacked the Phantom's sophisticated radar system. But since the North Vietnamese rarely sent a MiG aloft for the Phantoms to jump and shoot down, the fighter crowd insisted that their Phantoms be loaded with bombs so they could get into the war.

You must understand the irony here—for twenty years the

fighter jocks had talked about attack pukes dropping bombs because they didn't know any better, laughed about the air-to-mud guys, usually to their faces. Now they wanted six 500-pound bombs—all their plane would carry—and they wanted an A-6 tanker aloft to give them enough gas to get to the target and back. Six 500-pound bombs was a joke to the A-6 squadrons. Our airplane would carry up to twenty-eight 500-pounders, although twelve or eighteen was a more usual load. Yet we had to devote half our flight time and half our maintenance effort to keeping tankers aloft so the fighter guys could drop their pissy little bomb loads on Vietnam in addition to their aerial guard-duty chores. Now these prima donnas *wanted* to drop bombs, because otherwise, without MiGs to fight, they wouldn't get any Air Medals.

And they wanted medals. Whenever any reporter showed up aboard *Enterprise*, the fighter jocks would roll out the red carpet to ensure they got plenty of press. They wore little silk dickies all the time aboard ship, even when flying. The dickies were the last straw with us, flaming proof, if any more were needed, that our comrades in arms were totally devoid of couth and class.

So imagine our ex-Angel on the very last day of fighting before the armistice went into effect, decked out in his spit-shined boots and tastefully arranged yellow dickie. He mounted his trusty F-4 Phantom and blasted into the blue with his six little green bombs, hit the KA-6D tanker for gas and headed for the DMZ to give the gomers hell.

Meanwhile our skipper was leading a flight of four A-6s to the DMZ. He was given orbit instructions—which meant that he held his flight of four overhead while the ex-Angel and his wingman made their runs.

The ex-Angel told the Forward Air Controller, the FAC, that he could make *six* runs. That meant he would drop *one* lousy bomb per run. On the last day of the war. With the armistice signed, sealed, and delivered. If he had put one into General Giap's outhouse with Giap on the throne, it would have made no difference at all—the war was *over*. Well, you guessed it— the North Vietnamese got the lead just right on the fourth or fifth pass and shot our hero out of the sky.

The Radar Intercept Officer—the guy in back—never got out.

He was killed in the crash. The ex-Angel got on his survival radio and the FAC went in for a look. The bad guys blew the FAC out of the sky with a shoulder-launched heat-seeking missile, a Strella. He didn't get out of his plane.

The ex-Angel was never heard from again. Apparently the North Vietnamese weren't taking any prisoners that day. Maybe they had all the POWs they wanted. Maybe they were irritated about being bombed.

Our skipper called an all-officers meeting that night after the last plane landed. The war was over. The shooting had stopped. No peace treaty, just a ceasefire. Yet the skipper knew and we junior officers knew and the North Vietnamese knew that the United States wasn't going back to Vietnam unless the North Viets detonated a thermonuclear device on Los Angeles.

However, that wasn't what the AOM was about. Even though the war was over, the skipper wanted to tell us what he would do to anyone in *his* squadron who was damn fool enough to make multiple runs in a hot area. And he wanted to say what he thought about Lyndon Johnson and Robert McNamara and all that political crowd that had gotten so many good men killed for seven long years for no reason. And he wanted to tell us what he really thought about asshole fighter pilots. And asshole ex-Angels.

Then he stalked out and went to his stateroom, where he probably got stinking drunk. It was that kind of war.

That memory from the early months of 1973 came flooding back as I listened to Chuck tell about the Niagara Falls airshow crash three years ago. I'll bet after they landed, the four surviving Blue Angels taxied in and shut down in tight formation, put on their khaki fore-and-aft caps and marched away in a neat row, in step, the sun gleaming on their spit-shined boots. Being Blue Angels, that's what they should have done.

That's showmanship of course, the P. T. Barnum side of the job. The military is in love with that kind of showmanship, and occasionally it gets substituted for thinking. Too often.

Vietnam left me with a profound distrust of politicians, an antipathy bordering on contempt. As a writer I have to work to put it in my pocket and sit on it because the general public doesn't share it and wouldn't understand. For seventeen years newspaper and magazine journalists have liked to refer to the so-called theory that the U.S. military could have won in Vietnam if they had been given free rein by the politicians to win the war. I think Desert Storm showed what a professional, well-led modern armed force can do. The U.S. military could have crushed the North Vietnamese just as easily. But our politicians didn't want to "win," they didn't want to take the chance that Red China would be drawn into the war. Yet they were afraid to leave. So 58,000 Americans died and God only knows how many Vietnamese. For nothing.

I don't think about Vietnam very much anymore and I don't want to write about it again. *Flight of the Intruder* was my first and last Vietnam novel. Yet I *am* a Vietnam veteran. I know full well the scope of the tragedy that occurred when a generation of young men was betrayed by incompetent, foolish politicians interested only in self-aggrandizement and reelection. I know that war is not spit-shined boots or a geopolitical chess game or a football game with bodies.

I know what real war is.

But my antipathy for politicians has another side. My Vietnam experience turned my simple-minded acceptance of democracy into a deep-rooted faith. Vietnam proved that democracy works, slowly and inefficiently and inevitably—the rascals who got us into Vietnam were thrown out by the voters when they saw what a mess it was, and the replacement rascals were thrown out when the press showed the public the smoking gun.

Democracy is built on the simplest premise that has ever supported a political system, that a majority of the voters will be right more often than they are wrong. The inevitable errors will be corrected by the voters—when they perceive those errors. Democracy assumes that saints won't run for public office. The human condition being what it is, many of those that seek power successfully are charlatans, hypocrites, liars, thieves, and nincompoops, yet democracy provides a way to deprive these people of power when their excesses prove too much. The voters weigh the follies of fallible politicians against their contributions at every election.

Messy and inefficient as it is, the system works. Not very well and with agonizing slowness, but it does work.

* * *

Talking to a Flight Service Station briefer on Monday morning, I resist the urge to tear out my hair. Another front is moving across Michigan and Lake Erie on its way to western New York and Pennsylvania and eastern Ohio. But the scud might lift if I wait until early afternoon, when isolated thunderstorms will be doing their thing.

Out onto the parking mat to look at the sky. Maybe 1,500 scattered or broken, the dark gray scud whipping along at about twenty knots. I get back into Mr. Hertz's 1987 Corsica and drive to a McDonald's for a linger over coffee. Then slowly back to the airport to turn in the car and stroll across the parking lot to the FBO for a visit with Chuck. Finally I load my stuff into the plane and sit on one wheel contemplating the sky and the sad state of my tennis shoes. I pull the sectional from my hip pocket and study it one more time.

The matchbox where I keep my patience is empty at 10 minutes past 10 A.M. Aaagh! Ten minutes later the *Cannibal Queen* is airborne headed for the Falls. The powers that rule the skies have agreed that sightseeing aircraft will orbit the Falls clockwise at 2,500 feet, but I can get up only to 2,000 and still stay under this overcast. Fortunately the *Queen* is the only machine aloft over the Falls. In the cockpit I snap a few photos as a gap in the clouds admits a shaft of sunlight. The sunlight looks better to me than the Falls. I do love it so.

Leaving the circle over the Falls, the *Queen* takes me southward along the western shore of the Niagara River and along the western side of Grand Island. The buildings of downtown Buffalo slowly materialize out of the haze. At 2,000 feet I am just two hundred feet below the floor of the Greater Buffalo ARSA while my course takes me just offshore of the downtown and the empty docks and seemingly dead loading yards and factories adjoining them. To my right Lake Erie stretches westward until the gray water merges into the gray haze. As far as I can see the surface of the lake is empty—not a boat, not an ore freighter, not a wake of any kind. It's as if the city waits at the end of the lake for ships that don't come anymore.

I am about ten miles past Buffalo following the shoreline of the lake southwestward when the Lycoming stumbles. The adrenaline jolt is milder this time, but it still has a kick.

Yet *now* I know what causes the hiccups. I had just finished leaning the mixture knob another sixteenth of an inch thirty seconds before the hiccup occurred, so now I give back that sixteenth of an inch, then another because I don't like to do adrenaline on an hourly basis. I just leaned the air-gas mixture too much, that's all. Ha! And I was worried that something was wrong with that engine.

That engine is *forty-nine* years old! It didn't survive to this great age by indulging in mechanical shenanigans while airborne. Why, some ace without my vast aeronautical skill would have shattered that pretty engine against a granite cloud decades ago if it liked to stop running when provoked.

Cannibal Queen, you baby doll—we're on our *way!*

17

THE FLIGHT SERVICE BRIEFER I CALLED FROM THE ERIE, PENN-sylvania, FBO's office began like he was reading my obituary. "VFR flight southward is not recommended. The front is currently passing over Erie. Pittsburgh is predicting thunderstorms and severe rain showers."

"What does Pittsburgh have right now?"

"Forty-five hundred feet scattered, eighty-five hundred broken, ten miles."

"Youngstown?"

"Forty-five hundred scattered, eight thousand overcast, eight miles."

"And forecast?"

"Chance of thunderstorms with ceilings down to fifteen hundred overcast."

I gave him my politest thank-you and hung up the phone. I had just landed in the midst of this front passing over Erie, and it wasn't bad—a couple thousand feet scattered to broken, eight miles or so visibility, just about the conditions I have come to refer to as an Eastern Standard Day. Forty-five hundred scattered and ten miles visibility would be an improvement, about twice as good as the weather I had flying over Florida, the

Carolinas, and New England. Definitely flyable. Chance of thunderstorms. Talk about weaseling! Not one chance in ten, or one in two, or one in a hundred, but just a chance! Obviously one must just avoid the thunderstorms. When that looks like it's going to be impossible, land.

Listening to weather briefings, one must try to visualize the sky the patter of words is describing. This can be difficult if one pays more attention to the intonation of the briefer's voice than what is being said or fails to ask questions. You should turn in your pilot's license if you're willing to let the briefer make the decision on when to fly. On the other hand, you should also turn in your license if you don't carefully weigh his advice. The license is in your pocket, Jack!

Climbing out of Erie I pick up the interstate heading south for Pittsburgh, I-79. The sky is relatively clear and soon I am up at 3,500 feet to get my piece of that tailwind.

I cover the fifteen nautical miles between my first two checkpoints in nine and a half minutes. Holding the stick between my knees, I try my hand at higher mathematics. My calculations yield a ground speed of 95 knots. I am indicating my usual 84 at 2,000 RPM and 22 inches, which at this altitude and temperature would give me a true airspeed of about 90, so I'm getting a free ride of five knots. My next check, fourteen miles in eight minutes, gives me a computed ground speed of 105 knots. Better yet, if true. Call it an even 100 knots over the ground with a tailwind component of ten knots. I'll take that.

Tailwinds are like smiles from beautiful women—rare and to be cherished. Scientists say that headwinds and tailwinds average each other out over time, but any pilot will tell you he spends most of his flying hours subtracting winds from his ground speed, not adding them. It certainly seems so.

The sky darkens off to the west, over Youngstown, but I stay over the highway and pass safely without meeting rain. I seem to be racing southward over the scattered farms and towns of the rolling Pennsylvania countryside.

Approaching Pittsburgh I let the Queen down to 2,000 feet and stare southwestward for my first view of the Ohio River. I catch a glimpse, a place where a break in the overcast admits a beam of sunlight that reflects from the water. I turn in that direction. In seven or eight minutes I am westbound along the

171

river, then am turning to follow it southward around the Pitts-burgh TCA.

I had planned to land at Steubenville, Ohio, for fuel, but the field appears deserted from the air—only one airplane visible parked outside—and no one answers my calls on Unicom. If there is a fuel pump I can't see it. I turn southeast to return to the river while I consult the chart.

Wheeling has an airport, one with a control tower. And it isn't far from here. So I swoop into Wheeling for fuel. I am in luck. The building the FBO is housed in also contains a short-order lunch counter.

Airborne again, the route is southeastward away from the Ohio River over a landscape that offers few places to set down in an emergency. The roads meander along twisty, winding streams draining mostly wooded hills. Hills and streams and roads seem to wander crazily in a random pattern across this rugged terrain. Only villages and an occasional farm break the montage of green hillsides. Of necessity I fly a compass course.

Air mail pilots were among the first aviators to record their fear of flying over this terrain devoid of flat places to make emergency landings. These forested hills were not pretty sights to airmen nursing sick or dying engines. Emergency landings were common, everyday occurrences in the 1920s, before truly reliable aircraft engines came along.

I sight the smoke coming from the big power generation sta-tion at Mannington, West Virginia, and use that as a navigation waypoint. I pass it to the north and cross Fairmont. From there I follow the Tygart River southward.

Before long I am circling the Lambert Chapel church site and cemetery just north of Belington. The abandoned church has just been torn down—the shrinking congregation could no longer afford to pay a preacher. Circling, I stare down across the top of the lower left wing at the old cemetery and the empty spot where the church stood until last month.

My father's parents are buried there along with other Coontses back for four or five generations. Once this valley of the Tygart was the setting for hundreds of farms that supported large families, but no more. Now the farms that haven't gone back to trees provide only supplemental income for their own-ers, and not much of that.

When my father was a boy his parents sent him to this valley to stay with his grandparents for the summer and go with them to Lambert Chapel on Sunday mornings, just as they had done when they were children. Dad played with his many cousins and helped with chores and acquired a collection of wonderful memories.

The farmers were almost gone by the time I was old enough to hear Dad's stories. I knew only old men and women living on Social Security checks. And I went with my parents to their funerals in Lambert Chapel when they died, one by one. All that remains today to be seen from the *Cannibal Queen* are tombstones and naked dirt where the chapel stood.

Across Laurel Mountain is Elkins, with its airport built by the WPA in the late 1930s that still sells fuel. The town used to be serviced by feeders of major airlines; now only one commuter offers flights—two a day to Newark, New Jersey. I guess when you get to Newark the world awaits.

The town slides beneath the *Queen's* left wing as I make my approach.

My father's parents lived in Elkins while I was growing up. They didn't make their last journey to Lambert Chapel until 1981, when they died just nine days apart. When I was a teenager my grandmother worked in Phil's Restaurant in downtown Elkins as the evening cashier. I liked to drive to Elkins and visit with her at the restaurant on summer evenings. We would sit in one of the booths and have coffee, and every so often she would walk over to the register when people were leaving. It seemed as if she knew half the people in Elkins. "Hello, Mrs. Coonts," they would say, and she would give them a warm smile and thank them for coming to Phil's.

Sometimes I would drive over to their house and pick up Granddad and take him to *his* favorite restaurant, The Seneca Trail. He never ate at Phil's. Claimed Phil had a dirty kitchen and poisoned everybody, which infuriated Grandmother.

Oh, how pleasant it would be to take a taxi from the airport and find Phil's still in business and my grandmother Ruby perched on her stool behind the register, greeting all the regulars by name and giving directions to strangers. And to go to South Davis Avenue and find Granddad sitting in the glider on the front porch, wearing his hat, watching the world go by on a hazy summer afternoon.

I miss them both.

Twenty nautical miles west of Elkins lies Buckhannon, my favorite American small town. You guessed it, it's my hometown, the place where I grew up. My parents still live here, and this coming Saturday will celebrate their 50th wedding anniversary. Most of my parents' friends are still here and many merchants I remember from my youth. Even some of the youngsters I went to school with elected to stay. So I know people here and people know me.

The downtown has some vacant stores, but its decline is due more to the sad state of West Virginia's economy than mall blight, although that too has had an effect. The nearest mall is about twenty-five miles away in Clarksburg and nowadays people go there for serious shopping.

This year they're building a four-lane bypass on U.S. Route 33 that will take traffic blasting around the north end of Buckhannon at the national speed limit, 55 MPH, which that congressman from New Jersey foisted on an American public that had done him no evil. When I was a kid all that traffic went right down the two lanes of Main Street. Cars and coal trucks rumbled through bumper-to-bumper five days a week, and on Saturdays all the farmers in bib overalls came to town in pickup trucks.

The farmers liked to stand on the corner of Kanawha and Main in front of the G. C. Murphy Five-and-Dime trading watches and spitting tobacco juice on the curb. My mother was always appalled by men chewing tobacco, but I thought it would be a fine thing to be an accurate casual spitter and even tried chewing a few times, though I never told her that. I never could get the hang of spitting just so. My mouth watered too much.

Saturday mornings I liked to stand inside Murphy's Five-and-Dime and read comic books. Then in the afternoon my brother and I would go to a movie. There were three theaters to choose from back then—today they are all closed—and they all had matinees. Our choice of theaters was often dictated by the state of our finances. The Saturday matinee at the Kanawha

Theatre cost a quarter, at the West fifteen cents, and at the Opera House a whole dime. One year my dad did a bunch of work for Garland West, who owned the West Theatre, and didn't charge him anything, so from then on my brother and I got into the West absolutely *free*. That was a deal!

In the finest American tradition my mom routinely used the car to taxi us boys around town. I grew up thinking of Buckhannon as a big place. Today when I go back I am stunned when I see how small it really is. From my parents' house to the West Theatre in the heart of the business district is three-quarters of a mile, and the same from their house to the grade school and junior high I attended. If I cut across fields the distance to school is less than half a mile and can be walked at a comfortable pace in ten minutes.

After I graduated from law school in December 1979, at the age of thirty-three, I came back to Buckhannon to practice law in my father's firm. He had had a major stroke six months before and been forced to retire. My mother needed help taking care of him and the other lawyers in the firm wanted me. The fly in the wine was that my wife refused to leave Colorado. Her invalid mother was living with us in Colorado and the alternative to that arrangement was a nursing home. So trusting that it would all work out somehow, I came back to Buckhannon alone.

It didn't work out. After Nancy's mother passed away in the summer of 1980 she still refused to join me. Dad's health improved enough so that Mom could take care of him by herself. And I learned that you can't go back. You can't go back to your boyhood home after being away for fifteen years and expect to find it the comfortable, delightful place you remember. Buckhannon wasn't that for me in 1980 and '81. It was a small coal town in a depressed area, and the coal mines were shutting down, one by one.

One day I advised a divorce client wailing about her finances and job prospects to pack the kids in the car and get out of West Virginia. Desperate to be with my wife and children, that evening I decided to take my own advice. I eventually landed a job in Denver as an in-house attorney for an oil company. In July 1981 I truly left Buckhannon.

I go back occasionally to visit my parents. On these short

175

visits I can recapture the hometown that I remember. It is once again a delightful little town of 8,000 people, complete with an excellent private college, West Virginia Wesleyan, pretty homes on shady streets, and good people who can be good friends if you will only take the time to get to know them. I have. I still have friends in Buckhannon that I visit every time I am there.

I am thinking of them when the spire of Wesleyan's chapel appears in the haze. There's the courthouse! And the First Methodist Church and Frank Hartman's house next to it! And the college, and that tree on the corner of Camden and Meade that I passed out under the Saturday I got drunk for the first time. There's the house where my first girlfriend lived. . . . From a thousand feet you can see it all, so neat and appealing, people and cars coming and going, folks in their yards. . . .

I circle my parents' house, hoping Mom will hear the Queen and come out into the yard. Today the house is surrounded by big trees; when we moved in this was naked cow pasture on a hillside. I was eleven that summer. I helped plant all those trees.

The Queen floats round and round, the wings almost vertical, the engine noise surely audible to those below. From this height I can even see their barbecue grill. But no one appears in the yard.

I level the wings and head for the airport, a strip in a little valley a mile west of town. A hill guards the approach end of runway 26, so I cautiously S-turn around it to line the Queen up with the narrow ribbon of asphalt.

Another plane lands just ahead on me. This is unusual. Normally there are only three planes in the hangar north of the runway and I have rarely seen them fly. The FBO here went out of business fifteen years ago. His fuel pumps are rusting just as he left them.

I swing the Queen into the grass a little off the mat. The owner and pilot of the plane that landed before me walks over to inspect her. His name is Gary. He has never ridden in an open-cockpit plane. After a bit he asks, "What would it cost to get a ride?"

"Not a nickel. Would you like to go now?"

Yes. Now would be just perfect. I strap him into the front

cockpit and together we roar off over the town where I grew up.

Gary and his friend helped me push the *Queen* into the hangar. While I was installing the cockpit cover, the fuel sight-gauge began to leak. Again. Rotating it counterclockwise 90 degrees didn't help—the plastic or Plexiglas is not a screw-in affair—but the leak stopped when I twisted it back the other way a whole turn.

The next day Dusters & Sprayers Supply in Chickasha, Oklahoma, agreed to send a new sight-gauge in the overnight mail, the whole assembly. Armed with a five-gallon bucket and my meager collection of tools, I went back to the airport to change the *Queen's* oil. To my disgust I discovered that the weld that Siggy did on the cowl latch in Poughkeepsie had broken. At least the sight-gauge wasn't leaking just now.

With the help of Ernie Samples, who works for my folks, the cowling and left-side inspection panel came off the *Queen* as my father watched from his wheelchair in the shadow of a wing and a tractor cut hay on the adjacent hillside. Thinking about the busted cowl latch, I stared at the old oil running out of the sump drain. It looked as black and grungy as raw crude. I should have done this a week ago.

At the hardware store on Main Street the clerk waved away any payment for the four feet of wire he had just cut off a huge roll. "We sell it by the pound," he said with a smile.

I used the wire to safety-wire the cowl latch with the broken part. Sweating in the hazy sunshine and filthy with oil, I inspected the job carefully. I thought it looked pretty neat. The baling wire repair didn't seem to detract from the *Queen's* dignity in the slightest. Were the truth known, this was probably not the first time she had been so adorned.

After lunch, sitting alone in the grass by the wheel in the shade of the top wing, I smoked my pipe and waited for my afternoon joyriders. If I had lived during the Roaring Twenties I would have been a barnstormer, would have kept Jennys flying with baling wire and old shirts cut up for patches, would have sat contentedly in pastures all across America waiting for passengers who could afford five dollars for five minutes aloft in the summer blue. I might even have joined a gypsy airshow

177

and looped and twirled over county fairgrounds. Sure. But it wouldn't have been any better than this sunny afternoon sitting in the grass, the smoke from my pipe drifting upward past the *Cannibal Queen*'s yellow wings.

On Thursday the guys at KCI Aviation in Clarksburg drained the fuel from the *Cannibal Queen,* installed the new sight-gauge that came in the overnight mail from Chickasha, Oklahoma, then helped me refuel her.

She took 42.3 gallons, full to the brim. I think the only way anyone could get 46 gallons in that tank would be to lift the tail to the in-flight attitude, which would be impractical to do on a daily basis. With all the gasoline aboard, the new sight-gauge didn't leak a drop. The whole operation took less than an hour. Most of KCI's employees came over to watch and examine the Stearman.

The president of the company, Charles A. Koukoulis, led me to a corner of the hangar where his pride and joy was parked. She was a 1956 Cessna 172, the 488th off the production line in the first year of manufacture. With only 400 hours of time on her tach she still had the look and feel of a brand-new plane, resplendent with original as-new interior, upholstery, paint, instruments and avionics. Even the paint on the rudder pedals showed almost no wear. It was as if I'd been transported back to the year 1956 and a Cessna dealer was showing off the latest model, ready to carry me through the skies to every adventure I ever dreamed of.

That afternoon in Buckhannon I got back to the serious business of giving Stearman rides. The next day I gave three more, one to a real aviation enthusiast (read "nut") named Leon "Buck" Harpold, whom I had never met before today. He saw the airplane at the airport, asked around, then called and asked for a ride. I never say no unless the airplane's broken and I didn't this time. Buck owns six planes, one of them a pristine 1947 J-3 Cub.

I made the takeoff and let Buck fly us to Elkins for gas. I made that landing. Then I let him make the takeoff as I followed him through on the controls, fly back to Buckhannon and make the landing, again with me backing him up. I told him to use J-3 techniques and not to fight the controls if he felt me making an input. The only time I had to do that was on landing, when he needed just a little help.

Buck's prowess proved, to me at least, that the Stearman is very similar in handling characteristics to a J-3. I assured Buck he would have no trouble transitioning if he got a Stearman, as he swore he would.

The *Cannibal Queen* has that effect on people. Even people who detest small airplanes walk away wearing a wide smile. I described her to one rider as sort of a convertible with wings, and he agreed. There's really little thrill, not in the roller coaster or motorcycle sense. The Stearman is just pure *fun*. The strange sensation of the wind playing at you, the snoring of the engine, the feeling of freedom and also security as you take in those bright yellow, art-deco wings arranged around you as she banks and wheels at a stately pace and the earth slides slowly past—that first ride is a sensation to be savored and recalled. I tell riders to stick their arms out, to let the prop blast tear at their hands and clothes, to make them feel the power of the air that holds us aloft.

On Saturday before the big anniversary party that afternoon I gave seven rides. Sunday I pulled out all the stops. My brother, John, strapped the riders in and arranged goggles over their eyes, then I took them up for ten-minute excursions over town. After John and his family left to go back to Washington, Terry Reed took over as the official strapper. That afternoon I gave seventeen rides and made two trips to Clarksburg for gas.

When I started flying Sunday the winds were out of the north at about eight knots. It was hard to tell for sure because the metal hoop that holds the wind sock open was frozen—rusted—pointing toward the usual prevailing wind, northwest. But the tail of the sock was streaming and I could feel the wind as I worked to get the *Queen* onto that narrow east-west runway.

And I did work. On Thursday with my second rider a gust of wind had caught the plane as I was flaring and I made my second-worst Stearman landing ever, almost dragging the right wingtip before I saved it with right rudder and left aileron. The *Cannibal Queen* hadn't lost her taste for flesh.

Still, this Sunday afternoon in West Virginia I felt my confidence growing as I slipped off excess altitude and airspeed, eased her over the center of the narrow asphalt with a lowered

179

wing, then leveled her with rudder and aileron just as the left main touched.

When it was time for John and his family to leave for Washington, his wife, Nancy, came over to the plane to say goodbye as John strapped in his last passenger. She stood on tiptoe and kissed me. Now I have been kissed in the cockpit by both the Nancys in my life. Then they drove away waving.

For some reason the wind immediately died and the clouds dissipated. Kisses are powerful stuff, even kisses from sisters-in-law. Dead calm conditions under a sunny blue sky—oooh boy!

Back when I flew A-6s I had a trick of setting the power off the 180-degree position and not touching it again until the wheels kissed the asphalt. It took a sure eye to judge the height, distance and wind just right and a bit of skill to set the power just so. But I could really fly that plane.

Now, with no apparent wind, I gave it a try. About twelve inches of manifold pressure seemed right, and about a third of the time it worked out. My eye isn't good enough yet. I hope it comes. I do like that sense of satisfaction that I get when it works out just right and I think about it afterward.

If you try this, keep the airspeed needle exactly where it's supposed to be, and no slipping—that's cheating. Just set the power at the 180 and fly a constant angle-of-bank turn at your proper approach speed and reduce power to idle just as you flare. If you've judged everything perfectly the airplane will land exactly where you wanted it to when you eyed the landing area from the 180-degree position.

That night after the folks were in bed I took a walk. The streets were empty. The streetlights cast circles on the lawns and trees; the empty swings on the porches awaited the morrow. Even the dogs seemed to be asleep.

Tomorrow these sleeping people would swarm out of the well-kept little houses and charge off on the business of making a living. And tomorrow evening the swings would once again be busy, the lawnmowers buzzing, the neighbors talking back and forth. Tomorrow.

This visit to my hometown was a perfect one. My parents

spent two hours shaking hands and receiving friends and rela-
tives, some of whom I hadn't seen in over twenty years. Cousins with grown kids, aunts and uncles, longtime friends of my
parents, they all helped make this a delightful, memorable
occasion.

I doubt that I'll make it to a golden wedding anniversary. If
I get married sometime this next year, I'll have to live to the
age of ninety-five.

The way I feel tonight, I just might make it.

18

THE FIRST 60 OR SO MILES WEST OF THE TOWN OF PARKERSBURG on the Ohio River the country looks like a continuation of West Virginia with heavily wooded hills that run in random directions. Then 60 nautical miles west of the river the hills end abruptly. So do the trees. From this point westward as far as the eye can see in this haze every square yard of the land below is devoted to growing crops. Strangely, the land is not set off in the neat north-south, east-west sections of the Midwest and plains. Here the boundary fences seem to run northeast-southwest, northwest-southeast. Odd.

Today the *Cannibal Queen* carries me westward toward Colorado. There she will receive a careful look from Steve Hall, the royal mechanic, before she and I go on to the West Coast. That's the plan, anyway.

And today the sky is clear, the wind out of the southeast, a nice quartering tailwind. Visibility is about twenty miles and I am flying at 4,500 feet to enjoy it. I wish I knew what I did to deserve flying conditions like this so I could do it more often.

I am still glowing over the thirty-one rides I gave this past week in West Virginia. Cousins, friends, people I never saw before, I took everyone who wanted to go in the time I had available. Several of the strangers wanted to pay for their rides but I refused. The look of wonder on their faces when they got out of the plane and thanked me was payment enough.

Symbols of flight abound in contemporary society. They are everywhere, ubiquitous.

Yet humans used symbols of flight long before powered flight became a reality. Throughout history people dreamed of flight, drew pictures of it and speculated about it. They left us myths of Icarus and Daedalus, drawings by Da Vinci, paintings of the blessed ones—the angels—with wings upon their backs. The Greek gods flitted around Mount Olympus. Jesus ascended into heaven in a white cloud. Mohammed rode up mounted upon a white stallion. Notice where heaven always was—up. Up there where man could not go, up where only birds and gods, prophets and angels are allowed.

When I was a boy I had recurring dreams of flight in which I could raise myself off the ground and soar because I willed it. People whose only experience with aviation is riding in a window seat on an airliner tell me they have had similar dreams. I suspect many people have.

Flight has a subconscious, almost instinctive attraction for members of our species. To break the bonds of gravity that tie us to the earth and soar freely is an image that stirs us in unexpected, profound ways.

I have yet to carry a passenger in the *Cannibal Queen* who is unmoved by the experience. To see the ground dropping gently away as the yellow wings carry you sedately upward and the wind swirls against your face, to fly above the countryside at an altitude that allows everything below to be distinguished plainly, to see the clouds up close, to watch a hawk circling at your altitude, to truly *be* a part of the sky, and then to return to earth in a gentle, controlled glide—this experience moves even people who thought they would hate it. People with an active fear of heights enjoy this without a twinge. Nobody complains of feeling queasy.

The Stearman's wings allow one to feel contained and safe, yet the openness of the cockpit allows one to feel the sensations of flight in a unique way that appeals to that subconscious instinctive urge to fly that is fundamental in all of us.

I like to give people rides. It's a gift they'll carry with them all of their days.

*   *   *

Passing just south of Circleville, Ohio, I keep the *Queen*'s nose pointed straight west toward Washington Court House. When Dayton is visible off to my right the power comes back and the *Queen* drops into Dayton General, a general aviation airport in the southern suburb of Miamisburg. Airborne again, it's pretty much straight westward across Connersville, Indiana, over Rushville, Shelbyville, Franklin, and Martinsville to Terre Haute.

The southeasterly wind holds all the way across the intensively farmed state of Illinois as the sun marches westward and I fly over Mattoon, Assumption, Taylorville and Auburn to Jacksonville. This is Stearman country, where good airplanes dusted for the fathers and sprayed for the sons until even the most cunning mechanics had to admit that their working days were over.

At Jacksonville I get out and take a good stretch. I've been flying for six hours today, all in the bright sun, and I'm tired. To quit or go on?

Tomorrow will be a long day flying the Great Plains, especially if this tailwind doesn't last. Really, how much luck can one guy have? I resolve to fly another leg.

Just west of Jacksonville I see the village of New Salem depicted on the chart. I am already cruising at 4,500 feet, but I can't resist. New Salem is the village where Abraham Lincoln came when he was twenty-one, when he left his father's house. He clerked in a store in New Salem, studied surveying, did odd jobs, even got himself elected to the state legislature. I pull the power and head down. New Salem I have to see.

It is just a tiny village. From a thousand feet I estimate that New Salem contains no more than 150 people. The houses are not concentrated, but spread out, only three or four to a block. The streets run precisely true north-south, east-west. I wonder if Abe Lincoln helped survey the town. I can see one church and a cemetery. No obvious tourist attractions, yet from my experience with American entrepreneurs, I have no doubt that there's at least one log cabin Abe Lincoln museum.*

---

*Author's Note: Further research has revealed that the village of New Salem I flew over is not the one young Abe Lincoln lived in. His New Salem was about 25 miles northwest of Springfield, Illinois, and is now only a memory. There are a variety of Lincoln museums on the site, however.

I add power and climb westward for the Mississippi, which lies just a few miles ahead. Hmmm, Hannibal, Missouri, is dead ahead, Mark Twain's hometown. Should I stop?

Mark Twain grew up in the 1840s in Hannibal, I know, just west of New Salem where Lincoln was keeping a store. How many miles? I use my pen on the chart to estimate the distance. About 25 nautical miles. There's an odd fact—the young man destined to become America's greatest political leader and the savior of the republic tended store just a few miles from where the boy destined to become America's greatest writer was fishing in the great river and playing robbers with his chums.

The river doesn't look as if it drains half a continent, but it does. I cross above Hannibal at a thousand feet, craning my neck. Not too crowded.

The airport lies northwest of town. I had planned to fly on to Kirksville, Missouri, and spend the night. When I see the fuel pump at the Hannibal airport, I change my mind. After a squint at the wind sock I announce my intentions on Unicom and make an approach to runway 17. The crosswind is about 90 degrees, right out of the east at eight knots. All that practice yesterday in West Virginia pays off now: I settle the *Queen* onto the runway and taxi in feeling like Lindbergh after landing in Paris.

The man in his fifties who pumps the gas can't do enough for me. He calls the hotel, a Best Western known as the Clemens Hotel, and loans me his mechanic's van for the night. The key is in it. It has gone at least 130,000 miles and I can look through the rust holes in the floorboard at the ground, but it carries me off for town.

After dinner in the Mark Twain Family Restaurant and Dinette right across the street from the Clemens Hotel, I took a walk as the evening shadows deepened. I didn't have far to go. Right around the corner was the house where young Sam Clemens, the future Mark Twain, grew up. It's a museum now.

Running along the sidewalk downhill to the corner of Main Street is a white board fence, "the fence that Tom Sawyer's friends paid him to paint." Across the street is the building where Sam's father kept a law office. It's right beside the Becky

Thatcher House! Somehow fact and fiction are badly intertwined here.

Main Street parallels the river. Looking north, I could see a genuinely good, larger-than-life heroic bronze of two barefoot boys standing on a pedestal. Tom and Huck. After all, Mark Twain mythologized childhood.

But turning south, Main Street is lined with buildings from the 1830s and '40s. These buildings house shops selling souvenirs of Twaintown—please! I'm not making this up.

The brochure the hotel handed out stated that two and a half miles south is Tom Sawyer Cave, a must-see attraction. And across the river is Tom Sawyer Island, where Huck and Jim hid for a day or two before setting off down the river on a raft. It's obvious the National Park Service never laid eyes on this place.

If you don't know much about Mark Twain or the books he wrote, and I suspect most tourists don't, this interplay of fact and fantasy must be pretty confusing. I'll bet ten bucks of real money that the majority of tourists leave here thinking that Tom Sawyer really painted that fence, that Becky Thatcher lived right across the street, and that Twain just scribbled down all the things that went on in his hometown when he was a kid.

I wandered on, looking at the old buildings in the dusk. A block or two south on Main Street I turned east for the river. After crossing a double set of railroad tracks, I found myself on the edge of a boat basin. I wanted to get beside the water. I chose a path through a little park that led out onto the levee.

I estimated the river here is about three-quarters of a mile wide. Off to the south a replica paddle-wheel steamer moved slowly against the current. Off to the north, my left, a set of grain elevators block Twaintown from the river. Beyond that a highway bridge spans the Mississippi.

Two boys sat on the side of the levee fishing. "What're you fishing for?"

"Everything," the eldest replied, and turned to look at me. "We're using worms and corn."

Corn?

I examined their rigs when the youngest reeled in to check

186

his bait. He was using a weight and no bobber, so his bait, a worm, laid on the bottom.

I could see insects playing on the water's surface and every now and then a fish would jump and make an audible smack. The fish were going after the bugs. These boys should have been fishing with flies. As if I knew. Boys have been fishing along this bank every summer evening for over a hundred and fifty years.

These two weren't catching anything, but they were doing all right for themselves. "Ain't nothing else to do around here but fish," the eldest said.

He was leaning back against a rock with his feet braced and looked quite comfortable with his pole on his knees and his hands behind his head. Like me, he was watching the lights on the paddle-wheel excursion boat and monitoring its leisurely progress upstream against the current.

This, I decided, was the real Hannibal, the memory that stood out when Sam Clemens was my age and sat down to write of his boyhood. The huge river flowing lazily along in the twilight, the boys fishing on the bank and looking south toward the bend in the river, the boats going upriver and down, down to St. Louis, Memphis, Natchez, New Orleans. Those names must have resonated in the imagination of small-town boys growing up along this river who had never been anyplace much. This was what Sam Clemens remembered. This was the material he wrought into his finest masterpiece, *The Adventures of Huckleberry Finn*, my favorite American novel.

When he was grown Clemens went down the river. He became a steamboat pilot and worked at the trade until the Civil War and railroads ended that way of life. And young Abe Lincoln from New Salem, he went down the river. Abe and another farmer's son built a raft and floated a cargo of hogs all the way down the river to New Orleans, where he saw the slave markets and exotic women and tall ships. One wishes the thoughtful young man from the prairies, the rail-splitter who could read human hearts, had left us a journal, but he didn't.

To go down the river. That was the universal ambition that Huckleberry Finn fulfilled so magnificently.

If Sam Clemens were here tonight, he wouldn't be up on

Main Street looking into shop windows at Twaintown souvenirs—he'd be watching these boys fish and contemplating the river. Maybe he'd offer them some advice about bait. Young Sam Clemens caught a lot of fish out of this river.

I woke up at 3:30 in the morning at the Clemens Hotel and couldn't get back to sleep. After a half hour of tossing and turning, I got out of bed and performed my morning ablutions.

Out at the airport the *Cannibal Queen* sat waiting. I had filled the mechanic's van with gasoline and now I left it where I'd found it, the keys on the dash.

The sun is trying to come up in the east but is having its troubles shining through the low clouds that lie in that direction. Overhead the sky is clear. Another gorgeous day to fly.

At 6:30 in the morning I lift off into the still air. Climbing to the northwest for Kirksville, Missouri, the rising sun catches the yellow wings and makes them glow.

I waggle the rudder and watch how the shadow of the tail moves back and forth along the lower left wing. This amuses me and raises my spirits. Before long I am singing in the cockpit, roaring snatches of an old love song about "it's now or never, my love won't wait."

It's good to be flying, good to have such a beautiful country to fly over, good to be at peace with one's fellow man. It's good to be alive early on this summer morning.

Away from the river the northern Missouri countryside becomes a landscape of low wooded hills and irregular pastures. Little ribbons of asphalt wind their way along the ridges and valleys past widely separated farmhouses. Northwest of Kirksville, where I stopped for coffee and fuel, I fly under a layer of scattered clouds that diffuse the sunlight still coming in from a low angle. The land below takes on a bluish tinge in the shadows cast by the clouds.

I am still enjoying this southeast wind, now right on the Queen's tail, as we scoot up out of Missouri into Iowa, where I turn straight west.

Making my approach into Shenandoah, Iowa, at about 1,200 feet above the ground on a left base-leg I set the power at 12 inches and say a little prayer. Here goes nothing.

Down she glides at 80, looking very nice. Miracle of miracles, I have judged the wind right, about twelve knots out of the south.

With only a little fudging I make the landing area and retard the throttle as I pull her back into the flare.

At the pump a guy in bib overalls is waiting with the fuel nozzle in his hand as I shut down. The prop has barely stopped turning when he says without preliminaries, "It's gonna break your heart to hear this, but I bought three of these things one time for eight hundred dollars. That's eight hundred for the lot."

"After the war?"

"Yep. Government surplus."

I extract myself from the rear cockpit and step onto the back of the front seat. He passes up the hose. "Yep, we crashed one of them Stearmans and sprayed with the other two for years. Finally we retired one and used it for parts. Then we sold the last one. Wish we hadn't done that. Wish I had it now."

"Be worth a bit more than a third of eight hundred."

"Yep." He shakes his head regretfully.

Inside the new terminal-FBO building he tells me, "I'm an airport bum. Been retired for five years now and just hang out at the airport. Got a son spraying down in Oklahoma, flying one of them Pawnees. Now I think ag flying is the best flying there is. Ain't nothing else like it. Course it turns into work on a real hot day."

We talk about the weather. "Reason there's so much beans planted this year is that it was too wet for corn until about a month ago. Why, the end of May we was half flooded out here. So everybody put in beans."

Crossing the Missouri River just north of Nebraska City, it is obvious that the tailwind is now a crosswind, and substantial. The wind is right out of the south. I use a significant crab to hold myself on the section line road running west. But I am out from under the scattered cloud layer and am flying in clear skies. The Lincoln ATIS says the visibility is twenty miles. I believe it.

Syracuse, Palmyra, Crete, Friend, Exeter, Fairmont, Sutton, Harvard—the small towns and villages slowly pass beneath the *Cannibal Queen*. How did Harvard, Nebraska, get its name?

I get lunch at Hastings, Nebraska, and keep flying west, across Minden, Holdrege, Arapahoe, Cambridge. Scattered clouds reappear several thousand feet above me. Their shadows are moving briskly north right up the section lines. I am holding the Queen in a twenty-degree left crab and the turbulence is light to moderate. She bumps and grinds and rolls and flying becomes work.

David would not enjoy this. Most people wouldn't unless they were flying the plane.

McCook, Nebraska, has two paved runways that make a neat X, but the third one intrigues me. It is a short, 1,300-foot turf strip pointed 170 degrees. I ask the Unicom man if it's in good shape and he assures me it is.

A concrete taxiway crosses the approach end and I resolve to land just beyond it. The surface wind is out of the south at twelve knots gusting to twenty-two. The Queen gyrates down the final approach path. As I pull the power to idle and go into the flare—the worst possible moment, just as the Queen is the most vulnerable—a gust hits and she sinks abruptly. I add power. Not enough. Instead of landing in the grass beyond the concrete, the main mounts hit the lip. We bounce.

Dang nab it!

Taxiing back to the taxiway, I see that on landing I barely missed a blue taxiway light mounted on a rod eighteen inches high. What the heck—if this were easy, everybody would be doing it.

On the ground the heat is breathtaking. At least 95 degrees with that strong furnace wind. As soon as I am out of the seat I tie the controls in place with the seatbelt. I am inspecting the wheels and tires when the owner of the FBO comes trotting out to look the Queen over. "You were in St. Francis, weren't you?"

I admit it. I can see no damage at all to the tires or the wheels. Stearmans are tough. They wouldn't have lasted this long if they weren't.

"I had the white Stearman there," the owner tells me. He is a young man, in his midthirties I guess. "You been flying around ever since St. Francis?"

"Sure have. Been to Florida and New England. Doing a good bit of flying."

"Longest flight I made in mine was back from Illinois when I bought it. That wore me out."

"Little windy here today."

"Yep. Been like this for three days. Too windy for me and my Stearman."

I have no trouble getting off the grass strip, even in this heat. The tail comes up instantly in response to this wind and she's off after a modest run. Climbing out over the town of McCook I examine the engine instruments. Oil temperature is 160 degrees and cylinder head temp is 200 degrees Fahrenheit. You couldn't even boil water on those heads.

One of the primary reasons this round Lycoming engine is still running like new forty-nine years after manufacture is that it runs so cool. It has no turbocharger and the compression ratio is only six to one. That's the prescription if you want an engine to last—get a big one and go easy on it.

The route now is west up the Republican River, past Swanson Reservoir and the towns of Stratton, Benkelman and Haigler. The river valley is farmed but to the north and south the plains are used for grazing and occasional winter wheat. The colors are changing again. The green of the watered east has given way to yellows, ochres and browns under a brilliant sun in a cloudless sky. The visibility has also improved.

And I'm climbing. The elevation of the airport at Wray, Colorado, is 3,662 feet, so I let the thermals lift the Queen higher and higher. After twenty minutes of this I am at 8,500 feet. Now the winds have shifted and I'm no longer crabbing to follow the two-lane asphalt below. It seems the wind is out of the east, right on my tail.

I'm back at this altitude for the first time since I left Colorado and I notice the difference in the Queen's performance. Full throttle yields just 22 inches of manifold pressure. I let her cruise at 20 inches, which gives me 95 MPH indicated. And I have a substantial amount of right rudder constantly applied to keep the ball centered. At the low altitudes of the east the Queen is so well rigged you can fly her with your feet flat on the floor and the ball will stay centered. At this altitude you need right rudder. This is the origin of the term, "Stearman leg."

Rudder trim would be nice, I tell myself, then grin at my

impertinence. And Raquel Welch needs a few little improvements. Yeah.

The Queen is pointed true west, right down a section line. I casually scan the wet compass. The reading, 270 degrees, finally sinks in. Something's wrong here. I crane my neck and examine the compass in the front cockpit. It reads 260 degrees. I examine the chart. Yes, just as I thought, the magnetic variation hereabouts is eleven degrees east—call it ten degrees since even Lindbergh couldn't see one degree on these old army compasses. So 260 is the proper reading, and the rear compass is ten degrees in error. How long has it been that way? Is this why I got in trouble flying a compass course southwest from Cooperstown, New York? Perhaps. I should have noticed this problem weeks ago. Ah me . . .

I am anxious to get home. Past Yuma, past Akron at 4,694 feet MSL, then out over the high, empty plains toward the Rockies, which are still hidden in the haze. I scan the blue horizon repeatedly looking for mountains. After five weeks away I want to see them again.

At last, a half hour later, there they are, all purple-blue and indistinct with dark anvil clouds crowning their peaks. Summer in the Rockies. Approaching Longmont I pick out Pike's Peak, 90 nautical miles away to the south. Visibility is down today, only 90 miles in haze.

A storm is just north of Boulder. I descend toward the base of it and enter its shadow. The air is so clear that it seems I can reach out and touch the houses and trees on the land below. The eastern United States has crystal-clear air like this only in the winter after a cold front has moved through.

The wind over Longmont is out of the east, but at the Boulder Airport in close to the foothills it's out of the northwest. And strong, maybe twelve to fifteen knots. Field elevation here is 5,300 feet and pattern altitude is 6,100. I swing into a right downwind for runway 26.

"Welcome back, *Cannibal Queen*," someone says on the Unicom.

On final I decide to land on the grass glider strip parallel to the paved runway. A little right wing down, power off, a waggle of the rudder and I'm home.

Eight-point-four hours of flying today. Even this fool is tired.

Colorado makes the 30th state I've visited since the 8th of June. Only eighteen more to go. But they're big ones, not those little eastern-U.S. postage-stamp states.

The guys working in the hangar turn to watch as the *Cannibal Queen* taxis up. Steve Hall comes walking out.

When the prop stops, I pull off the headset and call, "Bet you thought you'd never see this ol' gal in one piece again."

He throws back his head and laughs.

19

WHATEVER HAPPENED TO THE LONG-HAIRED SANDAL-WEARING anti-everything hippies of the '60s and '70s? Remember them? They renounced materialism, Republicans, corporations and soap, and dedicated their lives to cheap drugs and free love. Their fate is one of the minor mysteries of our time. You've probably puzzled about it.

They moved to Boulder, Colorado, the little city where I live.

An endangered species in most parts of America, they are quite common in Boulder and seem to thrive here. Balding, graying, with varicose veins bulging above their Birkenstocks, they can be seen on street corners and in restaurants and espresso coffee shops all over town. They also like to hang out on the Pearl Street pedestrian mall, which is perhaps the best place for tourists to observe these creatures in a natural habitat.

Not everyone in Boulder is an aging hippie, of course. Humans could not survive here if that were true. But the hippies with their drug-fried synapses and political lobotomies give the town a distinctive tone that we locals have a phrase to describe. When you see something really screwy or kinky, you nod knowingly and say how "very Boulder" that is. Try it the next time you visit the People's Republic of Boulder. You'll impress the natives.

The Boulderist thing in Boulder is probably the Naropa Institute, "a private, non-sectarian, upper division college of the arts and humanities . . . founded in 1974 by Tibetan meditation master and scholar, Vidyadhara the Venerable Chögyam Trungpa, Rinpoche. It is the only North American college whose educational philosophy is rooted in the Buddhist contemplative tradition." This quote is from the Naropa Institute course catalog.

For years the institute's most famous faculty member was Allen Ginsberg, the gay antiwar guru poet. He achieved fame not because of his poetry, which not one person in ten thousand ever read, but because when his turn came to speak at an antiwar rally at the 1968 Democratic Convention in Chicago, he took the microphone and said, "Oooommmm," and kept saying it for seven straight hours, pausing only to inhale.

Ginsberg the Profound "co-founded" something called "The Jack Kerouac School of Disembodied Poetics" at Naropa way back in the dark ages of 1974. He still teaches there summers. Perhaps we should be thankful he didn't give us the Ginsberg Institute of Public Speaking. Oooommmm.

For $7,500 a year you can enroll in the Naropa Institute and take courses like "Discovering Your Personal Clown," taught by David Godsey and one Janet McAlpin, whom the catalog advertises as "an enthusiastic wiggler." Or Joanne Kyger's course on "Beats and Other Rebel Angels."

If you are ready for a graduate-level challenge, try "Ethnopoetics," where students scribble "brief scholarly papers" and work on "poetic projects founded on the bedrock of the archaic art." Think I'm lying? Send for the course catalog and see for yourself. But even if you enroll here and get so educated you need a custom-made hat, don't expect a degree. They don't give degrees or do commencements.

Yet you don't have to enroll in college to participate in the Boulder experience. There's all kinds of weird stuff going on all the time. Some of it costs a lot less than $7,500. This past May they only wanted $65 from everyone who wanted to hear Betty Dodson, an "expert on women's sexuality." You know she's an expert—she came from out of town and talked for five straight hours on one subject. The flier announcing this event said:

> For the past 17 years she has taught thousands of women how to increase erotic pleasures. In this presentation, Betty will discuss a variety of rituals that enhance sexual self-knowledge. This presentation is for all women who are committed to their sexual growth. From those wanting techniques to achieve their first orgasm to those wanting to enhance their present experience of sexual pleasure.

If you missed this presentation Ms. Dodson will probably be back next year, although that's a hell of a long time to wait for an orgasm if you need one now. (I haven't mentioned this before, but I too am something of an expert on women's sexuality, and if . . . But no! I probably shouldn't use this forum to advertise. Still, I wish I had a list of the names and telephone numbers of the women who attended Ms. Dodson's presento.)

While you're suffering you might take in the Biokinesiology Institute's "Holistic Health, Nutrition, and Biokinesiology Intensive" the first week of August. The institute says, "Biokinesiology is a highly sensitive system of muscle testing, used to test and balance the organs of the physical body, determine and correct allergies, discover the emotional causes of physical illness, and determine individualized nutritional needs."

God knows my organs are out of balance, but I'm going to be flying during this intensive. I'll try to hold on until next year. Yet if I weren't having orgasms I'd probably forget the flying. First things first.

When they're not going to intensives of one sort or another, the natives of Boulder do political things. The more unpopular the cause, the more they like it. These people worshiped Daniel Ortega, the self-anointed Sandinista saint of Nicaragua, sent him money and invitations and speechified endlessly about his virtues; then the jerk had the audacity to let himself be voted out of office in a free election. That was a somber, black day in this little city where the plains meet the mountains. They haven't yet forgiven him. Mention Ortega at a party and conversation stops dead.

Every left-wing cause I've ever heard of has a fund-raising

political action group here in Boulder. On any given night there is a rally about something you would be outraged about if you had only given it a thought. The poor devil I pity is the congressman who has to read and answer mail from this crowd.

But the right-wingers have found Boulder too. *Soldier of Fortune* magazine has its editorial offices here. Trees die so that you can read articles on obscure wars in Africa, how to survive in guerrilla-infested jungles, cooking for the combat gourmet, reviews of nifty new weapons, and so on. If you've missed this slick monthly in your dentist's waiting room you might ask him to subscribe.

After you've had your orgasm, gotten all your organs in holistic balance and are politically correct, if you still need to clean out the pipes Boulder has just the thing. This is world headquarters for Adrenaline Adventures, a collection of seriously disturbed wackos who will introduce you to the joys of bungee jumping, "the ultimate test of the human mind vs. a universally held fear of heights. The freefall sensation followed by the first gravity-defying recoil to the point of total weightlessness produces an adrenaline rush that will have you wired for days."

The lunatics of Adrenaline Adventures claim they have jumped from over twenty-five bridges across America, including a 590-foot leap from the 650-foot-high Rio Grande Bridge near Taos, New Mexico.

For neophytes, an Adrenaline Adventures jump of 110 feet with an 84-foot recoil will set you back only $89 plus tax, but be advised, "Advance reservations and payment required." You'd think they'd wait for their money until afterward, when you might be so adrenaline-drenched you'd throw in a tip, but no.

The 110-foot drop comes with a money-back guarantee. I'm not sure about the recoil. Better ask before you leap if recoil is important to you.

In the midst of all this craziness are 20,000-plus basically normal college students who call the University of Colorado home. They enjoy football, sweaty sex, skiing at nearby resorts and traditional college activities like beer busts, co-ed dorms, and frat parties that keep the brothers in more-or-less permanent hot water with the powers that be. They try to sandwich in a little studying. It's a good school. I even have a law degree from the place.

One of the things I like best about Boulder is the way the free spirits here use language. Use of adjectives like "intensive" as a noun is one delightful example, but that is only the beginning. Tell me, if you can, the meaning of some of these typical Boulder expressions:

"Disembodied poetics"? I'd like to hear Jack Kerouac's definition. Oh, now I get it! This is poetry that Jack whispers into your ear from wherever it is he is. Maybe.

"Biokinesiology"? According to my dictionary kinesiology is the study of the principles of mechanics and *anatomy* in relation to *human* movement, so what does the bio add?

Astrologers here like to say things like "raise the spiritual vibration." Do you have a clue?

"Holotropic Breathwork"? That's the title of a seminar offered here this summer. The ad says that individual sessions and psychotherapy are also available. If you paid real money to attend this seminar you probably need psychotherapy.

"Deep Ecology"? I like this phrase and plan to use it as often as possible even though I have no idea what it means.

Here is an announcement from the July-August 1991 issue of *Nexus*, a free newspaper distributed hereabouts. Savor the words, even if you don't understand them:

Dr. Farida Sharan, Naturopath, Master Herbalist, Iridologist, Founder of the School of Natural Medicine in England and America, international educator, author . . . is opening a holistic practice in Boulder.

Preventive health education * body/mind/spirit karmic iris print readings * eliminative activation * harmonize your interior ecology * strengthen your weaknesses, make the most of your strengths * relieve stress. Learn to nourish the adrenals & the nervous system * gain higher levels of health, energy and well-being * fertility counseling * herbs, naturopathy, nutrition * bodywork support * purification, regeneration, transformation programs * wellness retreats.

One of those karmic iris print readings would be a great gift. And you probably have a loved one whose interior ecology needs harmonizing. Eliminative activation? Use Ex-Lax for that.

Always on the lookout for a new way to make a buck, I have

designed and patented a board game called How Boulder Can
You Get?™ This is a parlor game for groups tired of wife swap-
ping. Each person in turn draws a card and reads a Boulder
phrase, such as "etheric founts." The first person who provides
the correct definition of the word or phrase rolls a die and
advances his piece upon the board, which is a map of Boulder.
The players race their pieces through the downtown, past the
Boulderado Hotel and along the Pearl Street Mall to City Hall.
The first person to City Hall becomes mayor of Boulder.

Etheric founts? Those are the portals of energy through which
your soul-body aura emanates. Or is that the chakras? My research staff's report is unclear. Whatever.

Boulder isn't for everyone although I call it home. It's flaky,
weird, skewed slightly off-center and a lot of the women don't
shave their legs. After they read this the Boulderites may ride
me out on a rail. I'll have to chance it.

For my forty-fifth birthday David and I went to see Arnold
Schwarzenegger in *Terminator II*. Naturally David and the girls
saw it when it first came out, and Nancy couldn't have been
dragged there by wild horses, but David had this itch to see it
again. From hints he's been dropping, I think he's joined the
Arnold Schwarzenegger fan club. He sent away for some
"literature."

If you haven't seen it, you should treat yourself to *Terminator
II*. Your adrenals will need nourishment after you see this flick.
But first see *Terminator I*.

Whenever I hear someone sniff about the low quality of Hollywood movies these days, I just shake my head. Hollywood is
still making great entertainment, just as they had been doing
for seventy years. *Terminator*, *Predator*, the Indiana Jones movies and a dozen other recent movies I could name are entertainment in its purest form, worth every cent of the six bucks they
charge you to get inside and the $1.50 they clip you for a little
box of Milk Duds. I never liked Milk Duds that well anyhow.

Movies are the second-best entertainment bargain in town.
The best, of course, is books. Six bucks will still buy you ten
or twelve hours of entertainment, depending on how fast you
read, at any bookstore, convenience store, grocery store or

newsstand. As an intellectual and an expert on women's sexuality, I assure you this is true.

The night after my birthday Nancy and the kids treated me to a Chinese dinner at the Double Happy Restaurant. Somehow I bit into a red-hot pepper and whew! Two glasses of water later I was still burning.

Steve Hall and his assistants gave the *Cannibal Queen* a good lookover and fixed a few problems. They had a machine shop make a new cowl latch from billet aluminum. They changed the engine oil, lubed everything, found that the ring that the cowling attaches to was broken and fixed it. The most serious problem they discovered was a broken primer line to the top cylinder. Every time I primed the engine I was squirting fuel through this broken line onto the exhaust system. But I didn't have an engine fire and it's fixed now.

They tell me the *Queen*'s ready to fly. I am too. I've polished my journal while they worked on the *Queen,* washed my underwear and replenished my wallet.

I've sat on my deck and stared at the blue mountains to the west. The last four days storms have come down off those mountains every afternoon. I've also done some squinting at some charts.

Flying the American West in an 84-knot biplane will be a bit different than aviating back east. The deserts are hot and vast, the mountains huge, the canyons straight up and down, the storms more severe, the distances from anywhere to anyplace a whole lot longer. By God, this is a *big* country! I love it as I do no other place on earth.

I'm ready. Come with me, won't you? Together we'll see it from the *Cannibal Queen.*

PART TWO

Thou liftest me up to the wind;
thou causest me to ride upon it . . .
                                                Job 30:22

20

My departure for Whidbey Island in Washington State was planned for Tuesday, July 23. It didn't happen that way. Which didn't surprise me much.

Summers on the Front Range of the Colorado Rockies define the season for everyone else. The days are cloudless with low humidity and not much wind, and about every other afternoon a thunderstorm will be born over the Rockies and come drifting eastward as it grows. It usually passes over Boulder and Denver without doing much of anything and continues eastward to grow to maturity in the thermals over the high plains.

We had four days of that, then on Monday, July 22, the wind shifted and blew from the northeast. This condition is known as an upslope. Warm, moist air circulating around a low over Kansas and Nebraska rose as it crossed the high plains and became saturated, then turned to rain and mist and cloud when it hit the steep slopes of the Rockies. This weather pattern is common on the Front Range in the spring and late autumn, when it often brings blizzards; it's rare as hen's teeth in summer.

The upslope brought rain early Monday afternoon, a gentle soaker. The temperature dropped twenty degrees. A drizzle developed. Unheard of this time of year!

Monday night the rain was still falling. Tuesday morning at 5 A.M. as I packed my bags, it was still coming down. Out on my deck I surveyed the sky in the moments before a gray dawn and contemplated my luck. Whatever I mumbled out there didn't set well with the weather angel. Back inside I turned on my laptop computer to update my journal only to find the computer was as dead as Julius Caesar. It refused to boot.

Last week in West Virginia, on the morning I left, the computer fell out of the back of Mom and Dad's Jeep as they were driving to the airport. Apparently I hadn't closed the rear door properly. The impact of a fall from a moving vehicle onto a concrete street broke the screen. In Colorado my computer doctor, a wizard named Fred Kleinberg, replaced the screen and ran the computer through its diagnostics program, then gave it a clean bill of health.

But it apparently expired last night while I was sleeping! Imagine the scene—there I was at 6 A.M., the world's most patient man, drizzle falling from endless low clouds on the morning I was to fly, staring at a dead computer and listening to Fred's wife's cheerful voice on her answering machine. No fools they, the Kleinbergs rig up their answering machine when they go to bed so that they won't be disturbed by the Steve Coontses of the world, people who are constitutionally incapable of waiting until normal business hours to inflict their woes upon others.

Fred arrived at 8:30. He would have to ship my laptop away for repairs, so I borrowed my daughter Rachael's.

The computer crisis resolved, I went to the airport and hung out.

I called the folks at Flight Service every few hours. They weren't hopeful. This upslope was going to be around awhile. By noon the rain stopped but the visibility improved only a little and the clouds were as low as ever. That night the rain began again.

Wednesday was more of the same. At 10 A.M. I called a taxi and started out the door with my bags, only to pause in the driveway and grope wildly for the ignition key to the *Cannibal Queen*. A mad search ensued. It was lost. Luckily the guys at the hangar had another, but dang nab it!

I crawled into the taxi with Rachael's computer and my soft

bag filled with underwear. At the airport John Weisbart and I went to breakfast while the *Cannibal Queen* got a wash from the Hotsy machine and rain continued to mist down.

The weather problem was only here on the Front Range, the briefer told me yet again. Cheyenne, Wyoming, was 2,500 broken, 10 miles visibility; Billings, Montana, was clear and 50. Yet the Rockies and the Snowy Range west of Cheyenne were obscured by clouds. If I could just get east to the interstate and fly north to Cheyenne, I could continue north until the mountains peter out, then turn west. I could fly around the northern end of this entire weather system.

As the guys were wiping the *Queen* down the misty rain ceased, so we broke out the touch-up paint and John polished the prop and hub. These are a neat bunch of guys, sensing my frustration and helping me carry it by fussing over the plane with me.

By noon I guessed the visibility was four or five miles and the clouds looked to be a thousand feet up, so I loaded the plane and shook hands all around.

"Don't fly into any granite clouds," John says.

The big Lycoming catches immediately. Even the oil cloud from the exhaust stack is modest and ladylike.

On the roll the tail takes at least fifteen seconds to come off the ground. At 5,300 feet above sea level the engine only has 23 inches of manifold pressure to use, so the takeoff run is leisurely and the breaking of contact with the ground a graceful good-bye caress.

The *Queen* rises slowly into the gray sky, climbing at about 300 feet a minute at her best climb speed, 70 MPH indicated. At this altitude everything happens slowly, sedately, as befits the dignity of a lady of forty-nine years. And this regal lady has dignity, even if she is a cannibal and wears only a smile.

I have no trouble flying under the overcast. As I fly northward the weather immediately improves. Cheyenne is 3,000 scattered, at least a dozen miles visibility, with a broken layer well above. As I fly through the airport traffic area the man in the tower is telling someone that the field will close in twenty minutes for an airshow. Frontier Days in Cheyenne, Wyoming— ten wonderful July days of rodeo and airshows and horses and cowgirls, an annual celebration of summer called "The Daddy of 'Em All."

I can see the crowd on the ramp and several dozen different types of military planes, all Air Force and National Guard by the look of them. The Navy rarely sends planes to these things, and those they do send are forbidden to fly—the only Navy airplanes that can fly at civilian airshows are the Blue Angels. I think the admirals are missing the best chance they'll ever get to sell naval aviation to the American public. The Air Force types figured this out long ago.

North of Cheyenne the clouds break up enough so that splotches of sunlight reach the prairie. To the west the hazy mountains still wreathed in clouds appear blue and mysterious. In contrast the prairie below is a wonderland of greens and browns as the sunlight and shadow play upon it in a surreal way. All this and a modest tailwind too!

My spirits soar even higher than the Queen as my frustrations are swept from me by the swirling cockpit breeze.

There are scattered showers around Casper but I skillfully avoid them and drop in for gas. As I fly northward again the rolling prairie appears empty. Only the four-lane highway below me snaking northward breaks the grassy perfection. I look carefully and see occasional ranch complexes; still, this is the emptiest land I've flown over yet.

To my left the Bighorn Mountains crowned in clouds rise boldly from the empty prairie. They too are blue, vague, with their summits cloaked in storms. Somewhere over there is Hole-in-the-Wall, where Butch Cassidy and the Sundance Kid hid from the law and outraged neighbors between robberies.

Armed robbery in this lonesome land couldn't have been an easy life, not when you consider all the riding those guys had to do. They must have ridden for days, weeks, to get someplace where they could steal money, then ridden for days, weeks, to get back to Hole-in-the-Wall, where there was nothing to spend the money on. Still, maybe they got to town more often than their honest neighbors, who probably could afford to make the trip only once a year. If that.

I fly over Buffalo, Wyoming, a town that Butch and Sundance must have thought was the Big Apple, and continue following the interstate, now I-90. Soon Sheridan appears on the horizon. The visibility is at least 20 miles now. I land for another load of gas.

On the ramp sits a 1937 Fairchild monoplane, a cabin machine with four seats. Mounted on the nose is the original engine, a 1937 Wright that the proud owner tells me develops 440 horsepower. I stand back for a good look. The wings are unlike anything I've ever seen: they jut straight out from the fuselage for about four feet on each side, then sweep back at about a thirty-degree angle. The effect is striking. The plane looks like it's doing a thousand knots sitting on the ground.

"Fairchild only made seventeen of these," the owner tells me, "and there are only two left." He looks at her, measuring her with his eye, wondering why fortune favored him so. I too have moments like that.

The owner and his friend are on their way to Oshkosh, Wisconsin, for the world's biggest airshow, the annual EAA fly-in. I tell them I'm going the other way, west, for an airshow at the Whidbey Island Naval Air Station. The commanding officer of the base invited me to bring the *Queen*, and the family wants to fly up commercial to wallow in nostalgia with me over the weekend, so that's my destination. I'll visit Oshkosh later in the summer after the crowds are gone.

The creeks flowing down the east side of the Bighorns made the valley that Sheridan sits in. Flying north I follow the highway and the meandering river, the Little Bighorn, down the valley full of cultivated fields. To the east the grassy plains stretch away until they merge with the sky. To the west the sea of grass runs to the mountains, which are petering out.

After I pass Lodge Grass, Montana, I begin to look off the right side for my first glimpse of the Custer battlefield. Finally I spot it on a grass-covered bluff above the valley. An asphalt road leads up from the highway to a cemetery with all the gravestones arranged with military precision. It looks odd in this ocean of rolling, grass-covered plains, somehow jarring.

On the crest of a higher knoll is the monument to George Armstrong Custer. The road leading to it is lined with cars and campers. I guess it's on the itinerary of many Americans for after retirement, when they buy the camper and set forth for a life on the open road with occasional postcards to the kids. I always wondered what the attraction of that way of life was—now I know. While the lawnmowers and weed whackers rust they are staring at the monument to Custer and 263 troopers of the 7th Cavalry who died with him when they ran into several thousand angry Indian warriors in 1876.

History is a little hazy about the actual chain of events here: the Indians say Custer attacked an encampment of 10,000 Indians and the warriors counterattacked—Custer admirers say the colonel's command was ambushed. Everyone agrees on the result. The soldiers were annihilated.

Americans have always had a soft spot in their hearts for spectacular losers, and Custer certainly qualified. If he actually led 263 troopers in a cavalry charge against an encampment of 10,000 armed, belligerent Indians, he was also the stupidest soldier who ever graduated from West Point.

There's a big flap brewing in these parts over the name of this national monument. Indians point out that this is the only battlefield in the country named after the loser. What if Gettysburg were called Lee Battlefield? As you might suspect, this issue is about more than road signs. The Indians feel that the name of the monument is symbolic of America's approach to their problems.

I think they have a point. Under the rules whereby most American battles were named, this Sioux-cavalry engagement should be known as the Battle of the Little Bighorn, and the battlefield should be known as the Little Bighorn Battlefield, the river being the prominent geographical feature hereabouts.* After all, the 264 soldiers and the approximately 2,000 Indian warriors who fought here were all Americans, all fighting for what they believed to be right. We should honor them all, not just Ol' Yellowhair, who might have lived to die of natural causes if he had had a little more sense.

If we're going to name this battlefield after one of the generals, we should call it Sitting Bull Battlefield. I've seen the chief's photo taken after he was reduced to a bit part in Buffalo Bill's Wild West Show. He looked like the kind of guy you'd

---

*Editor's note. A few days after these words were written, the National Park Service announced its intention to change the name of this national monument to the Little Bighorn Battlefield.

like to get to know, a no-nonsense practical fellow who would make a good friend and a bad enemy. I've often wondered what he really thought of Buffalo Bill Cody, who was stamped from the same mold they used for P. T. Barnum. Perhaps it's better for Cody and Custer that Sitting Bull died before New York publishers started paying generals millions for their memoirs.

Ten miles north of the battlefield the road curves west, toward Billings, Montana. I follow the highway and the railroad.

It's past 6:30 P.M. and the sun is dropping toward the western horizon. Flying directly toward it, the sun illuminates the entire lower wing of the Queen. The brilliant yellow wing against the greens and yellows and browns of the earth must be seen to be believed—a play of color and form that would inspire a masterpiece if I were capable of painting one. That is not my talent. I fly on, enjoying this rare sight.

A young woman answers my call to Billings Approach Control. Traffic is light. She cheerfully grants me permission to fly through the ARSA. On the western side of town I ask if she has a readout of my ground speed. "You've been making one hundred ten since I acquired you."

One hundred ten knots! I'm living at the foot of the cross.

Forty-five minutes later I am abeam the Yellowstone massif, which lies to the south, my left. Towering dark-blue and purple thunderstorms crown the hulking mass of mountains. Yet the sunlight is still playing on my little plane and the green and brown fields beneath me. In my years of flying I have never seen a more spectacular sight, never felt so much a part of the land and the sky.

There is a shower in Bozeman Pass when I fly through. I don't get very wet and I am through in less than a minute. Once through and into the sunshine beyond, I glance back.

Behind me is a circular rainbow with every color of the spectrum clearly delineated. The rainbow forms a perfect circle, right, left, over and under the plane. It appears that the Queen has just flown through it. Never before in my life have I seen a rainbow below me.

At Bozeman the FBO is a man named Arlin Wass. He looks to be in his late sixties. Mr. Wass asks if I'm going to Oshkosh.

"Nope. Headed the other way."

"Fellow in here this morning on his way to Oshkosh was flying an old Fairchild, the first I ever saw. Watching that thing take off was a treat."

I tell him about seeing the Fairchild in Sheridan as we gas the plane and watch a BT-13, a Vultee "Vibrator," taxi out with a load of joyriders.

"That fellow flying the Vibrator spent two years restoring it," Mr. Wass said. "Told me on the First of July he was going to fly her on the Third, and somehow we got it done. Weighed her and everything. He's done a hell of a job on that plane."

Buried in one corner of his hangar is a Stearman that has been in restoration for fourteen years.

"Fourteen years?"

"Yep. I told them they're going to die before they get it done."

The Stearman is almost ready for the wings to be attached. Sitting on the nose in the place of honor is a baby Lycoming, looking better than brand-new. Mr. Wass tells me that it's 225 horsepower.

In his office I admire the photos of old airplanes mounted on the wall and we talk. On his desk is a cylinder of an OX-5 engine, the 90-HP engine that powered the Curtiss Jenny. "Got the crankcase and crank and everything except the cylinders for that engine. Someone stored it disassembled and some mice nested in the cylinders. The acid in their feces corroded the cylinders."

I tell him about Cole Palen at the Old Rhinebeck Aerodrome. Maybe he and Palen can strike a deal. Somewhere in Palen's treasure houses in a dusty old box he probably has a set of cylinders for an OX-5 engine that he bought at an estate auction. Or maybe he'll want the engine to keep the Jenny flying.

On the way back to my plane, Mr. Wass asks where I'm going to spend the night. "Thought I'd try to get to Missoula, but it's getting dark."

"Just fly 290 degrees until you hit the highway north of Deer Lodge, then follow the canyon. Take you right into Missoula. You won't have any trouble."

He seems so confident I decide to give it a try. It's 8:30 P.M. and the sun won't set for forty-five minutes or so. Why not? Well, because I don't have a landing light, so I'll have to use the runway lights to flare and keep her drifting gently downward until the wheels touch. And I'll have to use the runway lights to ensure the nose doesn't swing.

Standing beside the plane, I think about how it will be and about the day not yet over. I'm tired, but it's been such a perfect day of flying, I'm reluctant to end it.

So I strap in and wish Mr. Wass good-bye. As I start the Queen the BT-13 taxis in to pick up another load of joyriders.

I climb to 10,500 feet in the twilight to ensure I'll not hit a granite cloud, and flip on the Queen's exterior lights and the two little red lights that shine on the cockpit instruments. Steve Hall installed the instrument lights. Their glow is comforting. The route is as ridiculously easy as Mr. Wass suggested. Even with the sun gone I have no trouble. What more could a fellow wish for?

As the sun fades behind a layer of clouds on the western horizon and the great valleys below me turn gloomy and dark, I wish for a landing light.

Boy, Coonts, talk about a dumb stunt! You dingdong! You could crack up this forty-nine-year-old masterpiece that Skid Henley spent thirteen months rebuilding and you sweated blood to pay for. Bozo! Idiot!

Yeah, but Skid built this thing to fly. He wouldn't hesitate to fly it over this terrain as night comes on.

True, but he's got 15,000 hours in Stearmans—you got what, a few more than a couple hundred? Don't make me giggle. I can't fly and giggle too.

But when I was in the Navy I made at least a thousand night landings without a landing light. Navy pilots don't use landing lights—they're for civilians and Air Force pilots. We only used landing lights when arriving at Air Force bases because the guys in the tower got nervous.

Yeah, and you didn't flare those Navy jets—you just drove them into the runway at 600-feet-a-minute rate of sink. You do that to this Stearman and that's the last landing she'll ever make.

Oh, shut up! I can hack it. Just watch me.

I am flying under a high thin stratus layer and now the moon is visible through it. And I can now see the flame that comes

211

out the exhaust stack. It's a yellowish blue, about six inches or so long, and in the growing darkness it is quite plain. It even casts a small amount of bluish light on the left wing root area. Neat!

I watch the flame, fascinated. And I would never have seen this if I hadn't flown the Queen at night!

I am wearing two sweatshirts and a leather flight jacket, but still I am chilly. And hungry. My 10 A.M. breakfast with John was a long time ago.

An hour passes and I'm still flying northwest down the valley toward Missoula. I have quit looking for landmarks: there is nothing to be seen below but the outline of the valley and the headlights on the highway.

Then I pick up the Missoula ATIS. Wind out of the east at ten, still a tailwind. Am I the luckiest man alive?

Finally I round a bend in the valley and catch sight of the lights of Missoula dead ahead. I spot the airport beacon on the first glance.

Tower tells me to make a right base entry for runway 9. Okay. Power to twelve inches, prop to full increase, down we come over the ridge east of town and across the lights of the city, the yellow-blue flame still quite prominent from the exhaust stack.

I must judge this just so. No religious experiences, no driving her into the ground, no wing dips, just a perfect landing. Please! You'll never forgive yourself if you hamburger this one, Steve.

The crosswind is about twenty degrees from the right. I tweak in a little rudder and hold her level with aileron. There is just a trace of light, just enough. Stick gently back now, an ounce more rudder ... let the mains touch first ... gently now ... there! The mains kiss and I pull the tail down with the stick. She settles in like she had Skid Henley at the controls.

I shut her down at the FBO and have to pry myself from the cockpit. I am exhausted. It's almost 10 P.M. and my stomach is so empty it aches. Yet I am the most contented man alive. To have such a day to fly ...

The next morning the sun is out. The man driving the motel's van just nods when I comment on how beautiful the morning is. With my stuff on the backseat I sit beside him. He is in his late fifties and pleasantly plump. He merely nods at all my comments.

Halfway to the airport, in response to some remark or other, he says, "No speak English."

I eye him. Speaking slowly and distinctly, and with added volume, I ask, "Where you from?"

"Russia."

"How long you been here?"

He takes a while to process it. "One year," he says at last.

I am itching to ask more, but refrain. Everyone can't understand English, even if you shout it. I've tried it often enough to know.

Maybe he's a Soviet Jew. Maybe he's a KGB colonel who defected, telling our guys a million secrets, everything from the serial numbers of the Soviet missile subs to the layout of the bathrooms in Gorbachev's dacha. Maybe he's a spy who came in from the cold. Maybe . . .

When he drops me in front of the FBO I stop speculating and tell him, "Thanks a lot."

He just nods his closely cropped head, then drives away, back toward the Econo-Lodge of Missoula, Montana. To leave home, friends, perhaps children and grandchildren, forever, and to come to live out the remainder of your life in this little city nestled in the Rocky Mountains where you don't speak a word of the language, that takes a form of courage I don't have. Few people would do it unless they had something really nasty that they wanted to leave behind. I don't have that either.

This morning navigation is a piece of cake—I'll simply follow the interstate highway northwest down the Clark's Fork of the Columbia river to St. Regis, where the river S-turns north. I'll stick with the highway after St. Regis, cross the spine of the Bitterroot Mountains at Mullan Pass and zip down the valley into Coeur d'Alene, Idaho. Or I could stay with the river after St. Regis and follow it all the way to Lake Pend Oreille, then fly westward above the lake to Coeur d'Alene.

Mountains on both sides of the Clark's Fork valley reach to six or seven thousand feet. I fly several thousand feet above the valley floor looking at the green mountains and the sky. The blue over Missoula quickly gives way to clouds with bases at about the height of the tallest peak. At first the clouds are scattered, then broken, then solid. And they are coming down. Now the clouds obscure the peaks.

Uneasy, I scan my chart. About a half hour west of Missoula near the village of Superior is a small airport. On a whim I pull the power and study the wind sock, then swing into a downwind leg for the western runway.

Taxiing in I see that there is a fuel pump. It is locked and there is no FBO. No phone. A few airplanes, but no place to call Flight Service to have my nervousness assuaged. I back taxi and take off heading west.

In another quarter of an hour I am over St. Regis, where the river turns north, then back east for ten miles or so before it loops around to the northwest for the straight shot to Lake Pend Oreille. The valley northward looks clear, the mountains to the northwest still free of clouds. That's my bolthole if Mullan Pass is socked in.

So I'll try Mullan Pass. It was supposed to be open this morning. Coeur d'Alene is supposed to be pretty good—why am I so goosey?

On the way to Mullan Pass I pass a high-wing aircraft flying the other way, east. Did he fly east through the pass from Coeur d'Alene, or did he try to go westward and find the weather too bad?

The clouds are coming down. There is a saddle through the mountains leading northward to an airport at Thompson Falls on the river, and it's still open. Another bolthole. But is there gas at Thompson Falls? I don't need gas, but in these mountains and clouds, the more the better.

The pass is listed at 4,738 feet above sea level. I am flying at 5,500. But the clouds continue to come down. Soon I am down to 5,000 feet and the clouds are just above me, seemingly close enough to reach up and touch. The way ahead into the narrowing, rising valley doesn't look good.

I resolve to give the pass a peek. One peek and an instant decision.

Why am I so nervous? Because I had better do my turning around while I have the room. But there is room—the *Cannibal Queen* will spin on a dime. So stomach, calm thyself.

I get my peek. Through the pass I see only gray, and on the

ground coming up the western slope of the pass, tendrils of ground fog. That is the face of death.

Prop full forward, mixture up, throttle to the stop and left wing down smartly, 80 degrees angle-of-bank and pull hard to whip her around. Wings level and eastbound with heart pounding, I reset the engine controls for cruise.

You wanted a peek, Coonts, and by God you got it.

The saddle leading north across the ridges to Thompson Falls is still open, so I turn the *Queen* north.

Over Thompson Falls Airport, a single 4,000-foot-long strip of asphalt, I look down the Clark's Fork valley at a white haze. Time to find a phone, even if I have to walk to town.

No answer on Unicom, but the wind sock tells me the wind is out of the west, as I suspected it would be. All these clouds are coming from that direction.

Taxiing in I see a fuel truck and a man and two children standing beside it in front of a hangar several hundred feet east of the parking mat. As I kill the engine I look at my watch. It's 10:30 A.M. and I have been flying for 1.4 hours.

The man from the hangar comes walking over trailed by the children. His name is Jim Carstens. He's in his sixties, wearing bib overalls and a small blue cap with a tiny bill, the kind that heavy equipment mechanics wear to keep grease out of their hair. The children are his grandchildren, visiting from Washington state for a few weeks.

He compliments me on the condition of the plane, then adds, "Boy, we sure are getting some old ones this summer. Couple days ago two guys in an old Fairchild stopped here on their way to Oshkosh."

"A 1937 Fairchild?"

"Think so. Wearing a Wright engine."

"Saw them at Sheridan, Wyoming, yesterday and heard about them in Bozeman. Small world."

After we fueled the plane and added a couple quarts of oil, I called Flight Service. "I don't have a current observation for Sand Point, and no forecast. Coeur d'Alene is fifteen hundred overcast, rain showers about. No forecast for them either. You know, the weather wasn't supposed to get this bad."

I knew. "Call you back in an hour or so. Maybe you'll have a forecast then."

215

"Maybe."

I hung up the phone on the workbench of Carstens' hangar and walked outside for a look. The wall of white was still there. Mr. Carstens offered to loan me his Jeep to go to town for lunch, and I accepted.

As I parked in front of Granny's Restaurant the rain began. And I had left the cockpit cover off the Queen.

For some reason I developed a headache.

After a hamburger I filled the Jeep with gas as the rain continued to fall, then drove the three miles back to the airport to get the cockpit cover installed. I finished that chore thirty seconds before the rain stopped. Thirty minutes later another shower came though, obscuring the valley to the west.

Mr. Carstens, the kids, and I were having a pleasant visit outside when we heard an airplane. Automatically the chins rose and four pairs of eyes scanned the cloudy sky.

There! A high-wing tail-dragger. It passed over Thompson Falls and continued westward down the valley into the opaque rain squall. It disappeared into the rain as Mr. Carstens shook his head and I made a flip comment about people without good sense, one I instantly regretted. Who just flew into Mullan Pass for a peek?

The words were no more than out of my mouth when the plane popped back out of the rain. It passed overhead and set up for a left downwind approach. When it landed Mr. Carstens and the children walked over to greet the pilot and his passenger, a woman. As the little party came back to the hangar, another rain squall arrived.

This couple were from a city in coastal Washington and were returning from the annual Cessna 180 fly-in this past weekend at Cody, Wyoming. Over 150 of these airplanes were there and many people camped out under their plane, they informed us, as they did.

They were nice people and Mr. Carstens loaned them his Jeep for the jaunt to town for lunch.

As the afternoon progressed and two more showers came and went, Mr. Carstens and I talked about flying. He learned to fly in 1958, he said, but soon dropped it when money got tight.

"I tried farming and didn't make it, tried trucking and didn't

216

make it, so I told my wife that if we weren't going to make it, we might as well do something fun. So I bought this hangar and got a lease from the county and got into the FBO business. There never has been an FBO here, so I figured to give it a try. We aren't in the books yet and most people are surprised when they find gas here, but the word will get around and things will pick up."

It's painful to hear such optimism. You hope it's true, you suspect it isn't. If it were that easy someone would have tried to float an FBO here years ago.

Carstens has plans—he was building a picnic table to put out front as I watched; he's going to build a little office building beside the hangar. Then he wants to put up four tee-hangars that people have told him they would rent.

He went back to work on the picnic table and I got out of his way. I examined every airplane on the line—all five—and watched the clouds roll in from the west.

The children visited with me in turn. The girl likes to ride in her granddad's Cessna 172, and she and her brother were going to visit for three weeks unless her grandmother tired of them sooner and sent them home. The boy's favorite radio station in Washington was KORD, which plays all of his favorite songs, including his very favorite "All My Ex's Live in Texas." His granddad learned welding the hard way.

"Which way is that?"

"I don't know. But I heard him tell someone yesterday that he learned it the hard way."

I was on the phone to Flight Service when the Cessna 180 couple returned from town. I shared what I had learned from the briefer with them—Sand Point weather was unknown, but Coeur d'Alene was 2,500 scattered. They decided to give it a try. I was dubious. All I could see down the valley to the northwest was clouds. I decided to wait awhile after they left and then go myself if they didn't come back.

This free ride on the courage of others may sound sneaky smart, but it has a rather large flaw. If the weather is so atrocious the recce pilot kills himself, the folks waiting to see if he made it will erroneously assume he did. Yet the Cessna pilot looked intelligent enough, reasonably sober, and he had made it here from Cody, Wyoming, without altering the appearance

217

of his airplane. I thought he might have sense enough to turn around if he ran into an opaque wall of rain.

I watched him go as I took the cockpit cover off the *Queen* and got her ready. The speck that was the Cessna moved over to the west wall of the valley and disappeared behind the cloud at a very low angle.

Aha! Now I see. There is a little hill between me and that cloud and it really doesn't reach the ground.

I strapped in and cranked the Lycoming. In minutes I was airborne and could see that my revelation had been correct. But I was thankful the Cessna pilot had dropped into Thompson Falls. Having that other airplane on the ground made my waiting easier.

An hour and ten minutes later I landed uneventfully in Coeur d'Alene.

As I cross the great basin of western Washington the wind begins to blow from the northwest. At first the only indications are the dust plumes from the tractors plowing the wheat fields, then the noticeable crab, and at last the realization that my progress across the ground has become glacial. I have gained an hour by crossing into the Pacific Time Zone, so it is still only a few minutes before 6 P.M. when I cross over Moses Lake.

The weather here in the basin is clear and the mountains to the west plainly visible. Also plainly visible are the tops of the clouds pushed up behind the mountains by the westerly wind and trickling through the passes.

The Flight Service briefer I called from Coeur d'Alene said everything west of the Cascades was overcast and would stay that way for the next two days, so I am going to land in Ellensburg and call again. If the cloud deck is solid tomorrow, I'll leave the plane, rent a car and meet Nancy and the kids at Whidbey tomorrow night. They're returning to Whidbey Island for the first time in fifteen years. Spending the weekend with them seems more important than getting the *Queen* to the airshow.

Over Moses Lake I decide to land at Wenatchee instead of Ellensburg. If there are any cloud breaks over Puget Sound, I can hop the mountains from Wenatchee.

The last ten miles of the flight take ten minutes as I descend into the teeth of a terrific headwind. I fly directly northwest up the Columbia River gorge with the runway at Wenatchee in plain sight dead ahead. But I can't get there. This is life in painfully slow motion. Remember those dreams you had as a kid when you were racing for your life from some slobbering monster but you couldn't run?

The wind is at least twenty to twenty-five knots straight down the runway—the *Cannibal Queen* stops like they have glue on the asphalt. She touches down and is instantly taxiing. I have to add power to keep her rolling.

"I'm flying a Stearman," I told the briefer, "strictly VFR. I'm in Wenatchee and want to get to Whidbey Island. I can't sneak through a pass and down a valley because the clouds are too bad. So I need to fly over the overcast and find a hole. I need a hole."

"I understand," he said crisply. "I've been briefing this area for a lot of years and I know exactly what you're up against. Let's see. . . ." He played with his computer a bit, then said, "The San Juans have scattered clouds, clear above. Bellingham is broken and so is Navy Whidbey. Solid over Seattle."

So the clouds feathered out over Puget Sound. Hmmm. Could I count on this? "What's the forecast?"

"Going to stay scattered in the islands until dark. Supposed to be a low solid overcast west of the mountains tomorrow and Saturday, clearing Sunday. There's a trough to the northwest driving this stuff down on us."

"And the winds at nine thousand feet?"

"Northwest at twelve to fifteen."

After I thanked him I sat staring at the chart. I have fuel for two and a half hours of flying. I'll be bucking a hell of a wind to get high enough to get over the Cascades and the clouds, yet if what the briefer said is accurate, the winds probably drop off once I get west of the divide. But what if I get over the sound and there is no hole?

Well, unless I have the gas to go with the wind back to Wenatchee, my goose is well and truly fried. So say I fly northwest for an hour and a half, and if I don't actually see indications that there is a hole over the sound, I turn around? An hour's flying with this wind right on my tail should put me back in Wenatchee. What's wrong with that plan?

Well, the wind could die, then you would need an hour and a half to get back to Wenatchee. That's three hours aloft, my slow child, and you'll be burning fumes. Twelve gallons an hour times three is 36 gallons, plus the extra fuel burned in the taxi and climbout. Your plane holds 42. Maybe three gallons or so left after three hours of flying. If the wind dies completely, which is not very likely.

I play with it and use my pencil on the chart to measure distances. I'll give it a try.

It's 6:45 P.M. when I start the engine. At 8:15 I must fish or cut bait. If I keep going, the hole had better be there or I'll be in big big trouble.

Aided by this brisk warm wind the *Cannibal Queen* leaps off the runway. She climbs willingly enough above the city of Wenatchee. I level at 10,500 feet and check her progress over the ground by watching the topography slide under the leading edge of the left wing. Slow.

And already I am cold. Not chilly—truly cold. I'm wearing an undershirt, a long-sleeved cotton shirt, two sweatshirts and a leather jacket, but I forgot to put on gloves. My hands are cold and the cold seeps around the collar of the jacket and my legs and feet chill. It couldn't be more than forty degrees up here and the humidity gives the air a bite.

I fly 290 degrees toward my first and last navigation checkpoint, Lake Wenatchee. I can see it dead ahead when I swing the nose a little left or right. Beyond the lake are the mountains and the cloud deck. I can see more than a hundred miles from this altitude. West beyond the crest of the divide is an unbroken deck of clouds with the sun shining on fairly level tops. Way, way off to the northwest is a higher, darker cloud wall, but that looks to be over Vancouver Island in British Columbia, or even beyond. The angle is too low to tell.

Thirty minutes into the flight I am staring at the fuel sight-gauge. I'm not even across the crest yet and it seems that I've used a lot of fuel. Well, an 8,000-foot climb costs gasoline. Still, the little float bobber looks to be about where it usually rides after an hour's flying.

Oh, you're just nervous. Lean the engine until she stumbles

and forget the fuel gauge. Try to stay warm. Hold your heading. Look for holes. Damnation, boy, this is supposed to be *fun!*

Thirty-four minutes after takeoff, at 7:19 P.M., I am abeam Lake Wenatchee. Just ahead are the mountains and the clouds. If the engine stops over the mountains the problem will not be saving this forty-nine-year-old antique airplane—it'll be saving my forty-five-year-old neck. Jimmy Hanks and George Dustin, you knew it might come to this.

Oh well. The bets are down and the wheel is turning.

What's out there? What can I see? The sun is low and diffused, but I'm still looking in the sun's direction and the glare makes me squint. What I can see is clouds.

Cold. I'm sitting hunched up to stay as much out of the wind as possible, so now my back is hurting. There's a muscle above my left shoulder blade that likes to act up when I'm tired or have been sitting too long, and I certainly qualify on both counts today.

I'm staring at several rocky crags, peaks, sticking up just above the clouds, and wondering which ones they are when I realize that I can see Mount Baker ahead and slightly to my right. Baker is an old friend from my A-6 days, a 10,800-foot snowcapped volcano that dominates the northern Cascades. I study the chart. My heading is too northerly. If Baker is there, I need maybe 270 degrees.

I make the change and study the white mountain. She's a great lady, a smaller version of Mount Rainier, which is visible behind my left wing. Rainier never captivated me like Baker did, and I have no idea why.

After an hour's flying the cloud tops are descending. I'm across the crest. But are there holes over Puget Sound, over the San Juans? There's an upper layer out there, and lots of clouds over Vancouver Island that the sun is sinking behind. But yes, I think that the clouds descend and get choppy.

I let the *Queen* descend into warmer air, down to 8,500 feet. I would like to go lower but dare not until I am sure of the holes. I check my watch again. Fifteen minutes, then I must make the decision to go back or go on.

I remember another time years ago when I crossed the Cascades above an overcast. I was flying an A-6 then and the sun had been down for several hours. There was a slice of moon

221

that night, just enough to let us plainly see the top of the overcast at ten or eleven thousand feet and entice us down to fly just above it. A cloud layer at night looks like a swell-filled gray sea, but the swells are frozen and you speed just above it on magic wings, as if you were living a dream.

That night years ago we saw the glow of Seattle making the clouds incandescent, so we steered for it. As fate would have it there was a hole over Seattle and we could stare straight down to the twinkling lights of the great city. And we were young, my bombardier and I, so I rolled the Intruder on her side and we spiraled down into the hole until we were only a thousand feet or so above the housetops and streets and boulevards.

Back then they didn't have TCAs, ARSAs, or similar positive control nonsense. As long as we stayed out of airport traffic areas and stayed VFR, we were legal. We hoped. Of course, even if this wasn't legal, the chances of our getting caught were very small.

There was no way out of the hole except the way we had come in. So throttles forward, stick back, and we spiraled back up and out while the thunder of our engines shook every window in northern Seattle, even windows belonging to selfrighteous hippies dedicated to saving the world. Especially their windows.

Occasionally a night sky or an undercast makes me remember that evening, and the memory is always sweet.

Ah, shake it off. That was long ago, when you were very young.

Where might I be this evening over the earth? Judging from the position of Baker, I suspect I'm over the upper reaches of the Skagit River. With all the clouds it's impossible to be sure.

I look down, studying the clouds. Through occasional breaks in the gray I can see sheer cliffs of darker gray granite, with foggy air underneath the cloud deck. The fact that there are breaks is a good sign, but I am not tempted to descend into one of them. It's plain there is no open space to fly in underneath— the clouds go down to the ground.

Ahead, is that a gap over the sound? Isn't that water I see? Well, it looks like water. It might be sky reflecting off fog. Looks like water though.

And now it's 8:15. Time to decide.

Well, it looks like water way out there in that gap, and the cloud deck is much lower, and there are breaks in the clouds around the peaks and ridges below me, so yes. On we go.

Now I let the *Queen* drift down another 2,000 feet. Mount Baker is off my right wing, so I must be paralleling the Skagit River, just south of it. That must be the Skagit Valley visible through the cloud gaps with fog rising up the ridges.

I dial in Whidbey Approach on the radio, 120.7. My fingers are so numb with cold that I have difficulty with the knobs. The female controller is talking to some guy in a Cessna flying at 1,700 feet through the San Juans. He must be VFR.

Islands! I see islands ahead! The San Juan Islands. The *Queen's* nose is down and we are clipping along at 115 MPH indicated. I scrutinize the chart, study the islands I can see, then look again at the chart. But I can't recognize anything.

Isn't that the cove on Orcas Island? Well, it could be, except for the fact it seems to be attached to the mainland. But where is a cove like that on the chart?

Exasperated, I abandon the features I can't identify and try to find one I can. Fixating on a feature that stymies you is one of the common errors of pilotage. I am searching for something familiar.

A town! Now that has to be Bellingham. Only town it could be there on the coast with the water to the west like that. So if that's Bellingham, then Anacortes is under this cloud on my left.

Okay.

Flying at 4,500 feet, I give Whidbey Approach a call. The young woman assigns me a discrete squawk and I manage to get it into the IFF by using first one hand, then the other. My fingers are like sausages tonight.

"Stearman 58700, I have you seven miles east of Orcas Island. Say your destination."

"Oak Harbor Airpark."

"Roger." I assume that's a clearance into the Whidbey ARSA.

I pass the western edge of the cloud under me and am out over the water. Swooping down with the power on, letting the *Queen* accelerate, I descend past the lip of the cloud and spot Anacortes underneath. I level at 1,800 feet and fly south along the west coast of Fidalgo Island with the lights of the Naval Air Station on Whidbey plainly visible ahead.

The controller wants me to climb back to 2,000 to cross through the Whidbey airport traffic area, so I do. That altitude puts me right at the base of a cloud. When the cloud starts to come down on me I have the airpark in sight and the controller releases me to the Unicom frequency.

The wind is from the west, so I swing out over Penn Cove on the downwind and line up on the narrow ribbon of asphalt they so blithely call a runway. When I first transitioned from jets to light civilian airplanes at the Naval Air Station's Flying Club, my instructor liked to bring me here to practice landings on the theory that if I didn't crash here, I never would.

I land downhill on a strip so narrow I can't see if I'm lined up on it. When I flare the nose completely blocks my forward vision. After three or four panicky swerves, the *Queen* is safely slowed to taxi speed.

I put her in a tiedown spot in the grass and pull the mixture knob to cutoff. It's 8:45 P.M. It's taken two hours to get here from Wenatchee.

But I'm back on Whidbey Island, where I really learned to fly and got married and became a father and spent the better part of six years, the parts when I wasn't at sea. Not exactly years of bliss, but damned good ones.

Tonight I pry myself out of the cockpit and go inside the little Harbor Airlines commuter terminal for a cup of coffee. It's been a long day and I'm tired.

21

FRIDAY MORNING I WENT OVER TO THE AIRPARK AND FUELED THE plane. She took 28.3 gallons. Normally she drinks eleven or twelve an hour, so that 8,000-foot climb out of Wenatchee cost me four or five gallons.

This morning the air was clear and the overcast very high, so high that I could see the peaks of the Cascades to the east. This weather was much better than forecast. I would have had no difficulty getting across the mountains from Wenatchee this morning.

Weather forecasting is not science, not art—it's guesswork. There are too many variables for it to be anything else.

I flew the Queen to the Naval Air Station and parked her right in front of base operations. A half dozen junior officers in khaki shorts and blue pullover shirts with the words "Whidbey Sea and Sky Fest 1991" on their left breast were greeting air-show arrivals and handing out cans of beer and pop. They were also handing out rental car and BOQ room keys. I assured them I was taken care of and hitched a ride back to the airpark to pick up my rental car.

That evening I met Nancy and the kids at the airpark when they arrived on the 7:10 P.M. commuter from Sea-Tac airport.

After dinner we drove around the island a little, while Nancy marveled.

I was serving a tour aboard USS *Nimitz* out of Norfolk, Virginia, when Nancy loaded the girls in the car in September 1976 and set off for Boulder. She was pregnant with David, who was born in Colorado. This was the first visit to Whidbey for Nancy and the girls since that day fifteen years ago.

Whidbey has changed a lot in the last twenty years. The town and the Navy base have doubled in size, and tourism has become a large chunk of the economy. What once was a sleepy little community of 2,500 to 3,000 people nestled in the heart of one of America's most scenic regions has grown into a bustling little city filled with motels and fast-food emporiums. McDonald's has come, as have Burger King, Taco Bell, Taco Time, Arby's, Best Western, etc. Sears even has a mortgage company here. Everywhere you look are new commercial buildings, new condos, new subdivisions.

Saturday morning we visited each of the four houses we had lived in during our Whidbey years. We even called on the next-door neighbors at the last house we lived in, on 900 Avenue East. Bob and Denise Nelson remembered the girls as tots. The girls remembered the Nelsons too, and the little park right beside the Nelsons' house with its slide and merry-go-round.

I used to let them go down the slide by themselves and catch them at the bottom. Kids in diapers slide slow on those things. Still, they wanted me there. "Catch me, Daddy," they used to shout. "Catch me!"

They remembered my carving their initials in the park logs that they walked on with me holding their hands, but the logs are gone. I took photos of these two college-age young women posed at the top of the slide. They were laughing.

Saturday evening was airshow time. My little yellow biplane looked odd surrounded by an F-111, an A-6E, and a B-1 bomber. Rather an eclectic mix.

The Canadian Snowbirds were there and the U.S. Air Force had sent F-16 and F-15 demo pilots who, as usual, put on a great show. But then the clouds dissipated, almost at a fingersnap, and we were treated to the most spectacular flying exhibition I have ever witnessed. A gentleman named Manfred Radius was towed over the field in his sailplane and released at 5,000 feet. He had a smoke canister on each wingtip. As the evening sun reflected off the sailplane and the smoke trails, Radius did aerobatics against the blue sky. He spun, he looped, he did vertical 8s, he did every aerobatic maneuver I know about as the loudspeaker system played classical music. No engine noise, just classical music and the sailplane soaring against the blue vault of heaven.

The silent crowd watched, mesmerized.

Lower and lower the sailplane came, then Radius flipped it inverted and dove at a ribbon stretched across the runway between two poles. He was too high by about a yard.

He rolled the sailplane upright, did a couple more whifferdills, then a 180-degree turn to a perfect landing. His mastery of his craft was total, his exhibition a tour de force.

The next day, Sunday, he successfully cut the ribbon.

Sunday we loafed through the streets of downtown Oak Harbor, now all spiffed up for tourists, then drove to Anacortes and caught the ferry for Friday Harbor on San Juan Island.

Nancy and the kids thought we were just going for a ferry ride, but I had a secret motive. Friday Harbor is the home of Ernest K. Gann, who is merely the greatest flying writer who ever lived. *Fate Is the Hunter, The High and the Mighty, Island in the Sky, Blaze of Noon*—the list is a lot longer and mighty impressive. I hear Ernie Gann is now devoting his time to oil painting. Not much of a chance, of course, but Friday Harbor isn't a big place, so maybe, just maybe, I'll see him strolling along the street and lean out the window and say, Thanks for changing my life with your books, Mr. Gann, and for making it richer.

But on the ferry I saw a poster that convinced me we had made a major mistake. Friday Harbor had hosted a Dixieland jazz festival all weekend, and that crowd would be trying to board the ferry that evening for the trip back. So we just drove around San Juan Island for forty-five minutes, then joined the traffic trying to get on the ferry. A wasted afternoon. If I had caught a glimpse of Mr. Gann amid that mob, I wouldn't have had the heart to shout a greeting.

Monday morning I drove Nancy and the kids to Seattle to catch an airplane since we had been unable to get them seats on the commuter airline. When I got back from Seattle I went over to the base to get the *Cannibal Queen*.

Navy and Air Force crews were preflighting their craft and filing flight plans. On the observation platform of base ops a female aviator in a flight suit watched me preflight the *Queen* and man up. Actually she spent most of her time watching a ground crew ready a B-52 for flight and glanced at me occasionally to see if I'd fallen off the wing or tripped over a pad eye.

Her Whidbey years are still going on. Like me, she will probably realize their meaning only in retrospect. But maybe she's wiser than I was.

After I tied the *Queen* down at the airpark, I returned to the Captain Whidbey Inn depressed. As usual when I am in that condition, I took a nap.

Whidbey was an important time in my life. On this island I learned that dreams don't always come true, that I would get out of life only what I put into it, that happiness is a state of mind, not a condition to be achieved or a commodity that can be bought and sold. I grew up here.

Seeing it again is bittersweet—I don't know anyone here anymore and I am only an invited guest at the Naval Air Station. The young pilots and bombardiers treat me as an outsider, which I am. I am no longer a part of naval aviation.

But Whidbey occupies a special place in my heart. It is important to Nancy too. I got an inkling how she feels when we were driving around San Juan Island Sunday afternoon. To my eye the vegetation, topography and modest, weather-beaten homes were indistinguishable from those on Whidbey, but Nancy announced, "Whidbey is prettier." I didn't argue.

Tuesday morning arrives foggy. I play with the journal on Rachael's computer and drink too much coffee and brush my teeth three times. By 9 A.M. the fog is thinning, so I check out of the Captain Whidbey Inn and drive to the airpark.

By ten I have the *Queen* preflighted, untied and loaded, and the sun is shining down from a blue sky. She rises off the narrow runway like a kite in a strong breeze.

From a thousand feet I can see the fog that still remains over the eastern waters of the sound. South of Whidbey Puget Sound is clear, not a cloud in the sky. Blue sky, blue water, green land, mountains to the east and west, a modest quartering tail-wind, what more could anyone ask of life?

I stop at Olympia for gas since I didn't refuel after my hops to and from the base. The FBO loans me a car for the drive to a McDonald's in town for lunch.

South of Olympia I turn the plane southeast for the 8,300-foot cone of Mt. St. Helens, the volcano that blew her top in 1980. I have flown over this mountain several times since then, but it has always been obscured by clouds. It's clear today so I'm going to see it.

With the prop full forward and the throttle to the stop, the *Queen* climbs slowly into the cold, moist upper air as I survey the hills and low mountains that rise gradually toward the grand climax, the giant shattered mountain that dominates the area.

One of the misconceptions popular among people who don't fly light airplanes is that the coastal mountains of Washington and Oregon are forests, full of wild animals and scenic vistas. There is some of that, it's true, but most of the mountains comprise one gigantic tree farm. Here trees are grown as crops and harvested periodically in clear cuts, vast areas where every tree is taken down and hauled away to be turned into plywood and two-by-fours. A lot of the scenic vistas are of naked mountainsides infected with tree-stumps and logging roads.

The timber industry has argued for many years that clear cuts are the most economical way to harvest the trees, and they are probably correct. But everything else in the clear-cut package is not so good. To get the trees off the mountains and down to the mills the timber companies bulldoze roads. The dozer operators go at it with a will. From the air you can see that every ridge, every knoll, every hillside has had dirt roads gouged into it. The roads cover the terrain like veins and capillaries. No valley, cove or glen is spared.

Denuding steep terrain and cutting roads ensures that the natural erosion process will be speeded up, so centuries' worth of erosion can occur in the decade or two it takes for the area to reseed itself. Rivers and lakes silt up and the numbers of salmon and other fish decrease drastically.

Wildlife also has a hard time making it in these tree plantations with their huge tracts of trees all the same age. The plight

229

of several endangered species may eventually force the timber companies to change the way they do business, which will have a catastrophic effect on many families and whole towns. Between sixty and eighty thousand jobs will be lost in the Pacific Northwest in the next few years if clear-cutting is drastically curtailed to protect the spotted owl and other endangered species. That's a lot of families.

There would be a lot less hue and cry over the timber companies' harvesting practices if they were clear-cutting private property, but they are not. Most of these mountains are public lands, owned by all the citizens of the United States. We citizens seem to want the mountains and rivers protected, wildlife given a chance to thrive, cheap lumber for homes, and jobs for everyone. The American way is for industry, government and the environmental groups to fight it out in the courts and legislatures. They will. I suspect the timber industry will be forced to cut only selected mature trees in the most unobtrusive way possible. It's that or no cutting at all, an option that only the most zealous eco-crackpots advocate.

Looking down at the leaf-vein roads and the naked hillsides, I have this gut feeling that we haven't been good stewards of the land.

Rising above the Pacific Northwest tree farm is Mt. St. Helens, tangible proof that God hasn't finished with creation. I remember the pictures—everyone does—of the inconceivable, a cubic mile or two of solid rock turned instantly to dust and blown into the atmosphere by the incomprehensible forces at work inside the earth. It seems only yesterday that the mountain exploded, yet it happened in 1980.

Eleven years later—an eyeblink in real time, cosmic time— the volcano is still gray and bald. The trees are gone, the creeks are still choked with dust and debris, stark testaments to the power of nature. But life has a foothold. From 8,500 feet I can see a greenish tinge to the gray slopes below the peak.

The peak itself resembles color photos of the moon. It's just a bald, pockmarked gray rock cone with the northern face missing. Inside this gash is the caldera, and in the middle of the caldera is a mound from which steam wisps skyward in three or four places. The mountain is still alive.

The contrast between the way nature and man work is vivid

here. Nature made an instant change in just one place, a catastrophe, yet man works like a zillion deranged ants to change the whole ecosystem, a fatal disaster. Most species can survive nature's whims. They succumb under man's ministrations. Our planet is a tiny lifeboat adrift in the infinity of hostile space, yet we persist in chopping holes in the bottom.

I feel extraordinarily small against this volcano, a tiny blob of protoplasm adrift on the wind above something so massive and powerful that my mind cannot comprehend it. A rising column of air forced aloft by the peak reinforces my mood by making the Queen quiver and dance. I wrestle the stick and let the rising air lift her higher.

Then the peak is behind and I am heading southward toward Portland. After a while I look behind, past the tail at the receding mountain.

Mountains are so big and I am so small—God must be like that. Mountains remind me of Him.

South of Portland is the Willamette River Valley, a wide fertile valley with apparently every square foot under intense cultivation. To the east and west rise tree-farm mountains.

I fly south up the valley under a clear sky, helped along by a wind from the northwest, a quartering tailwind.

I once knew a man who lived in the Willamette Valley. He had a farm here. I got to know him because he also had an airplane, a Grumman Hellcat. I met him at the Canadian National Airshow in Abbotsford, British Columbia, in 1974. I let him sit in the cockpit of the A-6 Intruder I had flown to the show and he let me sit in the cockpit of his Hellcat. Of course I was intensely curious about how he came to own and fly one of the premier naval fighters of World War II. So he told me the story.

It seems the president of Alaska Airlines got into trouble with his board of directors and was shown the door. The board decided to immediately rid itself of one of the president's more flashy toys, the Hellcat, which was sitting at Boeing Field in Seattle. The farmer read about the airline's desire to sell this plane in the newspaper one morning at breakfast. He invested in a long-distance telephone call and was told the price was $25,000 and the plane had to be off Boeing Field by five o'clock.

Like any true airplane enthusiast, our hero was a man who

could make up his mind in a hurry. He stopped by the bank on the way to the airport and cleaned out his savings account. In Seattle he paid cash for the plane and presumably they gave him a ride to the hangar.

Although our hero had never flown a plane more powerful than a Cessna 172, he strapped himself into the captain's seat of the Hellcat, successfully started the engine and aviated the fighter into the sky. He flew it home filled with emotions that can only be imagined.

Gasoline was expensive, he told me, and the Hellcat had a powerful thirst for it, so he logged his hours flying to and from airshows. When he arrived they filled the tanks for free. He flew it in flight demonstrations all weekend; then they filled up his tanks gratis when he left for home.

He never used the supercharger on that double-row radial engine, which made his flight demonstrations look a little anemic. He didn't want to risk blowing one of those thirty-year-old jugs, he told me, because the cost of overhauling that engine would be more money than he had in the plane. He couldn't afford it.

And he had a lot of jugs at risk. The Hellcat used an engine with two rows of nine cylinders each, a total of eighteen. That's thirty-six spark plugs, eighteen intake valves, eighteen exhaust valves. Mechanics qualified and willing to work on these engines are an endangered species. Spare parts? Better have your own machine shop.

I always wondered whatever became of the Willamette farmer and his Hellcat, and a year or so ago I found a book that listed the owners and location of every flying warbird in the world. His name was in it. According to the book he was killed in 1977 when the Hellcat was totally destroyed in a crash.

I have no idea why he crashed and I'm not about to look up his widow to ask. I don't know if the weather got him or that old engine failed at the wrong time. I don't know if he properly maintained the engine and airframe. I don't know anything and I probably never will.

Still, flying over this valley I can see his smiling face and that beautiful airplane, and I envy him the joy it gave him. Every person should have a passion like that once in his life.

*   *   *

The valley narrows the farther south one goes. Past Eugene the farms peter out and the valley winds through mountains. The character of the vegetation is changing. The southern slopes of the hills and mountains have huge meadows that appear golden in the midday sun. The amount of rain carried in from the sea is apparently not enough to sustain forests on the southern-facing slopes. So the residents raise cattle.

The valley rises steeply south of Medford. Just short of the pass is the small city of Ashland, Oregon. I drop in for fuel. Inside the FBO office building I call an artist I know, Bill Phillips, to see if he would like a Stearman ride. I get his answering machine and leave a message.

The FBO building is crammed with aviation memorabilia and out-of-print books about flying. I take my time and peruse everything. Photos of Amelia Earhart, Charles Lindbergh, other famous aviators and planes, old goggles, model planes, posters—the place is a small aviation museum, a shrine to flight.

The collection belongs to the owner of the FBO, Jerry Scott, whom I meet later that evening when Bill and his wife, Cynthia, pick me up at the motel and we come back to the airport to fly. Jerry wears a blue flight suit and has white hair. Aviation never lost its magic for him. And he's the kind of guy that you would like to get to know.

Successful fixed base operators, I have noticed, all have this trait. To succeed at a fixed base operation you must have repeat customers, the same people over and over. People who own or fly airplanes are like everyone else—they return to do business with people they like who like them. In this book I have followed the practice of not saying anything if I couldn't say something nice, which is not to say that I have included every good person I met, because I haven't. But I have purposely omitted references to those FBOs that operate like they were running a convenience store–gas station on a freeway exit.

Those FBOs are often owned by investors who are in business for the money, so they hire the cheapest desk help they can find, usually a young person, usually a female, who knows absolutely nothing about aviation and has no desire to learn. The office person can be pried away from her paperback novel or telephone conversation with her boyfriend only long enough to process your credit card invoice. She doesn't care where you flew in from or where you're going. She has no idea if the weather is good or bad to the east or west. She doesn't know one plane from another and so would have no comment if you arrived in *The Spirit of St. Louis* which you had just stolen from the Smithsonian Air and Space Museum. She would merely punch up your credit card invoice and go back to the romance novel. And the owner wonders why his business gets worse with each passing month.

It's not that I am the world's most gregarious guy, but after a couple hours of flying by myself I appreciate a friendly face and smile. Most people do. Which is why FBOs like Jerry Scott make decent livings in out-of-the-way airports like Ashland, Oregon, only a few minutes' flying time south of the big airport at Medford. His ramp is full. His line boy is busy most of the time. And his aviation collection isn't dusty.

The next time you see him, tell him I said Hi.

Bill Phillips goes flying with me first. I circle to climb out of the valley into the clear evening sky. The air is smooth. The sun low on the western horizon illuminates the *Queen* like a giant spotlight. She flies against a green and yellow landscape with Mt. McLoughlin on the eastern horizon and Mt. Shasta to the south. Both these old volcanos seem close enough to touch in this clear air.

I take Bill to the pass and circle Pilot Rock, the core of an ancient volcano, then pull the power and let the *Queen* descend back into the valley for a landing. Cynthia is my next passenger. She sticks her hands up, then puts her elbows on the rail.

The delight on my passengers' faces gives me great pleasure.

Wednesday morning the cloud deck that the low-pressure trough off the Washington coast was supposed to push inland doesn't arrive. Which is great for me.

I top the pass that leads down into California and head straight as a bullet for Mt. Shasta, a truly impressive mountain. Unlike Rainier, which is about the same height, 14,400 feet above sea level, Shasta rises from a river basin that is only several thousand feet in elevation. So Shasta is a genuinely large mountain to delight people who like genuinely large mountains, which I do.

Another old volcano, Shasta's giant cone has a lesser cone of ash and soft stuff sticking up from the west side. I approach the monster from 11,000 feet with my camera out. The wind here is out of the south, very light, but it is breeding a cloud on the peak that streams off northward. When I get around to the south side of the mountain the updraft lifts the *Queen* another 500 feet.

I wheel and turn next to the mountain, making sure I don't get too close. Prudence and experience dictate that one not rely on Mother Nature and luck to keep light aircraft out of severe up- or downdrafts. A strong gust of wind from the wrong direction when you are in close to a colossal rock like this could ruin your whole day.

The Redding-Benson airport has a deli on the second-floor above the FBO office, and I sit on the deck there drinking coffee and looking northward at Shasta. The wind here is out of the south at about fifteen knots, which means every mile of my progress south will be earned.

An hour down the valley of the Sacramento River, I decide to stop for fuel and to take off the leather jacket, which is too much in the warm air at 3,500 feet. It's over 90 degrees on the ground.

The airport I land at has no FBO office, merely a trailer for the guy who pumps the gas. There is a fuel pump, a pay phone against a hangar wall, a little restroom building beside the mat, and near the fuel man's trailer, a fountain shaded by four trees. Flat plowed fields stretch away in every direction. To the west one can clearly see the coastal range.

The FBO man comes out of his trailer as I taxi up. He is portly, in his fifties, and wears bib overalls. I'm going to get a pair of those. They make a definite statement.

As he tots up the charge for gas and oil using the top of the pump as a desk, I pronounce the name of the airport.

"A good place to be from," he grunts. "I been here thirty years too long. Married one of the local broads"—he jabs his thumb at the trailer—"and she won't leave her mama."

With the paperwork done, he announces, "Well, I gotta go inside and get fatter," and nods his good-bye.

It is lunchtime, I notice with surprise. I get a drink from the fountain and stand in the shade smoking my pipe.

Well, everyone has his problems. I've had places I wanted

to leave too. When I finish my pipe I leave this one without ceremony.

An hour later I landed in Petaluma and called my sister-in-law's brother, Jack Williams, at the administration office at Point Reyes National Seashore. He is the head engineer there. With the *Cannibal Queen* tied down, I am soon on my way to Point Reyes Station in a rental car.

I confess, California has always charmed me. There is nothing attractive about the sprawl of Los Angeles, but that is the only boil on this fair state. The countryside between Petaluma and Point Reyes is rural California at its best. Straw-yellow hills accented by groves of green trees are occupied by dairy farms and beef ranches and little else. No shacks with collections of junk cars, no abandoned refrigerators, just straw-yellow hills under a brilliant blue sky and cattle lolling in the shade of the trees.

The road winds and traffic is light.

I could live in a place like this.

That evening Jack and I drove out to the seashore to meet my nephew Jack when he got off work. He won a lottery and qualified for a summer's employment with the Youth Conservation Corps at Point Reyes National Seashore. It worked out well—he is spending the summer with his aunt and uncle and their two young daughters and having a great time on his first summer away from home at the ripe old age of sixteen.

The park lies on the west side of the San Andreas Fault and will become one of the Aleutian Islands in ten years or so. In the interim the northern half of the 94,000-acre park is a grassland on which hundred-year-old ranches still raise cattle for milk and meat. The southern half of the point is wooded.

After recovering from the surprise of finding ranches on property administered by the National Park Service, I was enchanted by the pastoral beauty of the place. Surrounded on three sides by water, the point is often covered by fog and low clouds in summer. This afternoon the clouds whipped in off the ocean and the air smelled of the sea.

The next morning after the two Jacks had gone to work and Dino and the girls had departed for errands, I drove back to the national seashore. The low clouds were solid, the wind at least twenty knots. After passing through Point Reyes Station and the village of Inverness, the road followed the western shore of Tomales Bay for another few miles, then cut up onto the point.

In the gloom and wind the seashore was a lonely place. Empty roads, cattle cropping grass in the pastures, every now and then a ranch complex. And I had it all to myself.

Out on the point near the lighthouse the fog blew up the ridge from the sea. Here and there I got glimpses of the surf smashing on the beach below.

This wild, lonely place seemed to me very British, like a moor from a Thomas Hardy novel. Or perhaps Scotland. All I have seen of Britain is London, but I suspect one could drop a Scotsman onto Point Reyes and he would think it was home until he met his first Texan driving an RV.

But no RVs this morning. I drove slowly out of the park on Sir Francis Drake Drive—he was supposed to have landed on South Beach while on vacation from sacking Spanish galleons in the tropics. If it was a day like today he must have felt right at home. Then I stopped in the village of Inverness for coffee.

Inverness looks like a lot of other villages near major tourist attractions, picturesque bric-a-brac on the buildings and cutesy little signs on boutique shops, but its real claim to fame is that it is or once was home to one John Francis, a serious eccentric.

The local paper, the Point Reyes *Light*, ran an article about him and I had to admit, jaded as I am, that Francis is something out of the ordinary. This is a man that the locals justly point to with pride.

In fact, he is so kooky I would have gone to look him up, except that he isn't there anymore. In 1983 he set off on an eighteen-year trek around the world by foot, bicycle, and sailboat.

That isn't why he rates as one of the world's premier eccentrics. Oh no. Guys that set off to hike around the world are a dime a dozen in California. Every day in this state women tell divorce judges, "He walked to the corner convenience store for a pack of cigarettes and decided to keep going, all the way around the world, and here is the postcard he sent to let me know." They then display a card postmarked San Francisco or Vegas or Gloversville, New York, occasionally one from Europe.

What makes Francis special is that in 1973 he took a vow of

silence and didn't speak again for seventeen years, until 1990. According to the paper, he communicated during this period by "pantomime, giggling, and grunting."

Imagine how your life would change if you tried this. Say you go to work tomorrow and don't speak. Not a word to anyone. Just giggling and grunting. Your boss finally comes in and says the secretaries are upset, so what's your problem?

You write a little note: "I have taken a vow of silence."

At 10 A.M. on a weekday you go home to give your wife the news that you have joined the ranks of the unemployed. You write her a note: "I've been fired." She shrieks, she demands an explanation.

You do another little note: "I have taken a vow of silence."

She is stunned. "What will my friends think?" she wails. "What will I tell them?"

Finally the truth will dawn on her—that all this is your fault—and she will crown you with an ashtray, then grab the checkbook and keys to the car as she announces in a quivering voice, "I'm getting a divorce."

Sitting there amid the shattered ruins of your life, crying, giggling and grunting, it will come to you as it did to John Francis, you need to take an eighteen-year trek around the world. Since you have no car, of necessity the journey will be by foot, bicycle, and sailboat. You write notes to all your friends who will understand—both of them—and tuck your toothbrush into your shirt pocket, then lock the front door behind you on your way out. After all, you don't want to be burgled while you're away.

As you walk along the highway on your way out of town, a police car pulls up and the officer gets out. Remembering your vow of silence, you say nothing, merely giggle and grunt. He runs you in.

At the police station you keep your vow. Not a word passes your lips. They examine your wallet and call your wife. She tells them she never heard of you.

In jail you refuse to speak to the turnkey and other inhabitants. You refuse to talk to the psychologist when he makes his weekly visit. Before you know it, you are in front of a judge for a competency hearing. You write His Honor a note: "I have taken a vow of silence." He sends you to a padded room at the funny farm.

How John Francis avoided this fate I have no idea. Since he's talking again after seventeen years, maybe he would share his experiences. If he were still living in Inverness, I would have looked him up and gotten that explanation. But Francis has gone on to a new career out there in the real world.

With a resumé like that, what on earth could this man do to earn a living? I'm glad you asked that question. I wondered too.

Well, John Francis, world-class eccentric, is now an envoy for the United Nations.

Honestly!

According to the Point Reyes *Light,* a newspaper that once won a Pulitzer Prize, John Francis has been appointed Goodwill Ambassador to the World's Grassroots Communities by the United Nations Environmental Programme (I know it's spelled funny, but that's what it is). After seventeen years of silence this guy came out waving a diplomatic passport!

As I drove out of Inverness and tried to keep from spilling my coffee in my lap, my hat was off to these proud people who helped mold the character of this extraordinary man.

That afternoon the fog cleared and I gave rides in the *Cannibal Queen.* First to risk life and limb with me was my nephew, Jack Coonts. Earlier that afternoon he had looked sun-bronzed and handsome as hell when he introduced me to his girlfriend, a cute blonde who also worked on the summer crew. His cousins, ages four and six, caught the two of them kissing one evening a few weeks ago and promptly reported them to the authorities, their parents. Jack just shrugged it off.

The marine layer of cool air seemed to top out about 2,000 feet, so I cruised from Petaluma to Point Reyes and back at 2,500, where the air was at least fifteen degrees warmer and smooth as silk. The sea looked like it was covered with frosted glass as the sun got lower and lower.

Next to go was Dino with six-year-old Carolyn on her lap. I forgot to give them cotton balls for their ears so Dino rode the whole way with her fingers jammed in hers. She said she enjoyed it though.

Jack Williams and four-year-old Ashley were the final passengers. I took them past the village of Point Reyes out over the national seashore almost to the lighthouse. The wings of the *Cannibal Queen* passed over South Beach outward-bound. We were on our way to Hawaii but I decided we couldn't make it before dark, so I turned around.

The sun set just as I landed for the third time. My passengers stood on the ramp in the twilight comparing notes. If only all my days could end like this.

22

PETE BAUR WAS AN F-14 PILOT FOR UNCLE SUGAR'S NAVY UNTIL last month. In September he'll become a cattle-car pilot for Delta Airlines. Right now he's hanging out at the Petaluma Airport.

When I arrived two days ago he watched me tie down the Queen and carry my stuff through the gate to the porch of the FBO building. I didn't know him then, of course.

As I fished in my pockets for coins for the pay phone, Pete said. "You're Steve Coonts, aren't you?"

I never know quite what to say when accosted in this manner. Do I owe this guy money? Did I make a pass at his wife? Hell, I don't even know any women in California!

Since I was about his height and outweighed him by thirty pounds, I cautiously admitted that he was correct.

"I love your books."

I exhaled. When you puff up your chest they think you're bigger. "Terrific. Keep reading them." Actually I want people to keep buying them—I didn't pay for the Queen with lottery winnings.

We shot the breeze a while that Wednesday afternoon, and he was here on the porch when I arrived on Friday morning.

We leaned on the rail and waited for the overcast layer to burn off while talking about the Navy and getting out and what kind of airplane a fellow should buy when he gets a few bucks ahead.

The scud did burn off, suddenly, as if a curtain went up. In minutes the sky was blue and empty.

Pete helped me untie the Queen and push her to the fuel pump. When she was gassed and oiled, I asked him if he wanted to go for a ride. This was a mere formality. No guy who wore Navy wings would turn down a ride in a plane like this unless he were terminally ill and due to expire this afternoon.

When we were level and headed south for the Golden Gate, I turned the stick and rudder over to Pete. He made gentle turns and climbs to get the feel of her. The ball stayed centered. His experience in light planes was immediately evident. Here was a jet pilot that knew what a rudder was for!

Over Hamilton, the closed Army field, we could see the fog layer above the entrance to the bay. I took the controls and trimmed the Queen nose down. We went under the goo at a thousand feet at the water's edge and had to keep descending to about six hundred. We flew by the Golden Gate and turned eastward to fly between Alcatraz and the promontory of the north shore. The buildings of downtown San Francisco, the Embarcadero, Fisherman's Wharf, all of the great city lay on our right glowing in the diffused sunlight under the cloud.

With sailboats and powerboats and ships plowing the water of the bay under us, we flew northeast across the San Rafael Bridge, where we came out from under the cloud. I climbed back to altitude and turned the Queen over to Pete. In the mirror I could see his wide grin.

To write about flying is not easy. To write about it well is extremely difficult. I don't know that I do it well, but that is my goal.

Jaded airline passengers who don't fly themselves usually look skeptical when one tries to explain that flying is more than stick, rudder and airspeed control. It is more than manifold pressure and engine RPM. To catch the emotion of it, the feel, the wonder, on paper is the challenge.

Those who don't fly can easily envision the thrill associated with flying hot jets, the tactical military machines. They suspect those birds are the unholy offspring of a roller coaster and a Grand Prix race car and can easily believe that being at the controls is a gas, which it is.

What they find more difficult to understand is that flying anything is fun, challenging, rewarding. Any airplane. Any machine that will leave the ground. The fun factor cannot be measured by reference to the airspeed indicator or the amount of money the aircraft would bring if sold.

But flying is more than thrills, more than fun. Intertwined with all the tasks and sensations of aviation are some deep emotions that have stirred pilots since the Wright brothers. If those two ever felt any of it they didn't try to let us know. Yet many of those who followed the Wrights into the sky have tried to tell us in words the essence of what they felt when aloft.

Lindbergh and his wife were both excellent writers and gave us flying as exploration of the world and the human spirit. Saint-Exupéry gave us the experience as poetry, Ernest Gann found both challenge and peace aloft, Richard Bach tried to show us the beauty. Alas, my writing is less focused. Flying gives me all of these emotions and a host of others that will probably take a lifetime of sorting and cataloging to get right.

And language seems so pale when compared to the richness of the aviation experience. What words can I use to tell you how I felt when the Sierra Nevadas lay before me and I coaxed my little plane higher and higher into the clean moist sky?

This cunning contraption of welded steel tubing, wood and fabric rose readily, willingly, until the upper tree line of those ragged summits was even with her, then below. Slowly, aided by five or six knots of quartering tailwind, she carried me toward the peaks. As my heart thudded out some of the allotted moments of my life and the pistons spun the crankshaft, she carried me across the reddish crests toward the sunlight and shadow playing on the emerald blue lake of Tahoe.

Shivering in the cockpit I watched the panorama change and thought how life resembles flight. We grow, mature, age slowly, imperceptibly, while the landscape of our lives changes at a steady, merciless pace. One day we realize we have traveled far on a journey that cannot be repeated or retraced. We turn and look back and find the perspective much different than it was coming through facing forward. Yet the past recedes at the inexorable pace necessary to sustain our forward progress. At some point the past is no longer visible—it is hidden by the crests we have crossed, and the haze. Then we have only our memory of it as we fly on toward an unknown destination.

How does one capture all that on paper? How to say it so the reader will comprehend, feel, the essence?

To write well of flying is not easy.

An electronic billboard beside the taxiway at the Lake Tahoe airport gives me the current density altitude. Today it reads 7,400 feet. Actual field elevation above sea level is 6,264.

The higher one goes, the thinner the air gets, until at some point way up there for every airplane the molecules are so far apart that an absolute ceiling is reached. The machine can go no higher without additional speed, which the engine cannot give. This altitude is different for every machine. The service ceiling is that altitude at which the aircraft can climb at only 200 feet per minute. The absolute ceiling is, of course, higher.

And as air gets warmer, it gets thinner. Density altitude is a term that describes the density of the air that your craft must fly in by comparing it to a so-called "standard day"—29.92 inches of mercury and 59 degrees Fahrenheit. Today the air here at 6,264 feet is equivalent to 7,400 on a standard day.

Density altitude is not an esoteric gee-whiz number. Like indicated airspeed—which is a mechanical measurement of the actual molecules available to fly in—density altitude is a computation of the actual molecules available to provide lift. Both numbers are equally important. Lift is what flight is all about. Without lift we are firmly grounded.

At this density altitude at Lake Tahoe the *Cannibal Queen* takes her own sweet time about accelerating, rolling for a significant time before the tail lightens, then rises slowly to the flight altitude. The airspeed indicator needle has also got a case of the slows. The engine is sucking in this warm, thin air and so produces less power. How much less is recorded on the manifold pressure gauge, which reads a mere 22 inches. The propeller thrashes the thin air and gets less bite. And the wings must be going faster—a higher true airspeed—to get sufficient molecules passing under them to provide the lift necessary to raise our weight from the ground. The amount of lift necessary to support the plane never changes.

When the Queen finally achieves an indicated 65 MPH I tweak the nose up and she reluctantly leaves the ground. I say reluctantly because the rate of climb is quite modest.

I cross over the airport boundary and climb straight ahead. I am a thousand feet above the ground when I cross the shoreline of the lake. Still climbing I continue northerly along the west shore.

When I finally reach 8,500 feet on the altimeter, only 2,300 feet above the lake, I level off and reduce power. Soon the Queen settles at an indicated airspeed of 95 MPH. Our true airspeed is much higher, but that doesn't matter. What matters are the 95 MPH-worth of molecules passing around the wings.

Halfway up the lake U.S. Route 50 cuts east through a pass in the mountains and drops down to Carson City on the high desert below. I angle for the pass.

East of the mountains lies the central basin of the western United States at about 4,000 feet above sea level. The Sierras are a wall running north and south, the result, I suspect, of an uplift along an ancient fault line, much like the eastern slope of the Rockies in Colorado.

Over the brown desert the air is turbulent, roiled by thermals, and the Queen bounces along. I fight the stick and try to maintain altitude as I fly northeast for Fallon, Nevada. My efforts yield mixed results. I manage to hold altitude plus or minus 200 feet, yet the airspeed varies between 80 MPH in downdrafts and 125 in updrafts. And we are rocking and rolling.

I call Fallon Approach to see if Restricted Area 4803 is hot, and while we are trying to establish who I am and what I'm flying, an F/A-18 Hornet goes squirting across the desert down in the weeds. He's subsonic but moving right along.

Naval Air Station Fallon, Nevada, has no fleet squadrons that call it home, but every air wing in the Navy spends at least two to four weeks here before every cruise. Flight crews need to learn to drop real bombs in a safe, controlled practice area before they are called upon to do it in combat. Fallon is where they do that. A civilian pilot literally takes his life in his hands if he enters without permission one of the restricted areas that ring the base. Yet amazingly, every so often a Cessna or Piper putts across a target that a half-dozen Hornets or Intruders are in the process of pulverizing.

R-4803 is cold just now, so Approach gives me permission to cross it. As I do I look for the run-in line to the target. There! I used to go roaring up that line at 500 knots while the bombardier worked the system.

Fallon Municipal lies to the north of the Naval Air Station. Fallon Muni now has about 5,000 feet of asphalt, the air base 14,000 feet. You wonder how any fool could mistake one for the other. Especially at night when the runway lights are illuminated.

The thermals and a crosswind make my approach to the municipal airstrip tricky. But I have her nailed until five feet above the runway, when I hit a wind shear. The bottom drops out. I add power but not enough—another crummy landing.

The air on the desert floor is furnace hot. Over 90 degrees. In my sweatshirt and leather jacket I am sweltering. I kill the engine by the fuel pump, stand up in the cockpit and start stripping off clothes.

Two women come out to greet me—one is a lady who works here to get flying money and the other is the mother of the owner of the FBO. They help me gas the *Queen;* then I ask, "Any jets from the base ever landed here by accident?"

They laugh. "No, never."

Well, I did it twenty years ago this summer, so the proper answer is, Not lately. Navy pilots now are probably smarter than they used to be. I did it one night while giving the squadron flight surgeon a ride. And I wasn't the first one. A year or two before my misadventure an F-8 Crusader landed here instead of at the base and went off the end of the runway trying to get stopped. The fighter flipped over in the dirt and the pilot was killed.

How could such a thing happen? Easy, if you are complacent, not devoting all your attention to the task of flying. Then visual cues arrive and register, but your brain refuses to process them. You expect only routine and subconsciously reject anything that doesn't fit the expected. Complacency, or mental unpreparedness, probably causes more accidents in and out of aviation than all other causes combined.

I remember my skipper telling the commander of the air wing

that a lesser pilot than Coonts would have killed himself land-ing an A-6 at night at Fallon Muni, which only had 4,200 feet of asphalt then. The air wing commander agreed, but tartly observed that a better pilot wouldn't have landed there at all.

As they say, there are two kinds of pilots—them that has and them that will. My fear is that I will do it a second time. In a plane like the *Cannibal Queen* that lacks any electronic naviga-tion aids, this mistake is ridiculously easy to make. I identify a town based on prominent landmarks, and the airport by its position in relation to the town and the direction of its run-ways. I've never seen a lot of these towns and fields before, so it would be easy as pie to think little strip B is really A and plant it, only to find that Oops! Dang, did it again!

I suspect more than a few pilots have made this mistake and never told a soul.

The *Cannibal Queen* rises off the runway at Fallon like a fly leaving molasses. The density altitude must be over 8,000 feet. Safely airborne, I call Approach and make sure R-4803 is still cold, then head northwest to join I-80 for the trip west across the pass to Reno.

More turbulence. This is the worst bouncing I have yet en-dured in this airplane. It's lucky David is not with me—he would not enjoy this ride.

Coming into Reno, Approach tells me the wind is out of the west at twelve knots, then assigns me runway 16 Left. I think about it for half a minute, then ask if I could use runway 25 instead. This request is granted.

My landing here is better than the one at Fallon. I am ex-pecting a wind shear near the desert floor so am not surprised when it comes.

At 7 P.M. I tie down the *Queen* at the Reno Jet Center amid the hot twins and corporate jets and stroll across the ramp pretending I am somebody. Now for the bright lights and big city.

My hotel had a variety of fliers displayed on the registration desk advertising marriage chapels. This is a cottage industry that thrives in Reno and Vegas. Several of the big casinos even have a chapel in the basement. As the desk lady examined my credit card I helped myself to the chapel brochures.

"Are you getting married?" she asked.

"Not today," I told her. "I've taken the cure. But if I catch another bad case of romance I want to be prepared."

Two of these matrimonial emporiums are visible from my ninth-floor balcony. I stand there watching the evening deepen and enjoying the cooling breezes and inspect the brochures.

"Do The Deed Before They Change Their Minds" is the credo of one establishment. They accept five kinds of credit cards and offer "simple fast service." There is courtesy transportation for all clients, a florist and wedding boutique on the premises, professional-quality color photography, and they video-record all weddings "for your review." With the video out there it will be difficult to later claim that you were drunk. Apparently you have to pay extra for all these extras, but if you present the brochure you get a $10 discount on your wedding.

The best deal is probably the other one, which advertises "free witness, free audio cassette, free marriage scroll, candle-light and organ music, and flowers, pictures and video available." Each of these bullets is preceded by a little heart, which is a nice touch, I think.

This establishment gives a ten percent discount if you present the brochure, but only "one discount per wedding." This proviso is obviously designed to prevent you from saving the discounts and demanding that your eleventh wedding be a freebie.

If The Donald gets in a marrying mood while he's in town partying with Marla or Carla, I'll bet he'd go to this second chapel. A free witness is nothing to sneeze at. Can you envision The Donald out on the sidewalk offering five bucks to a wino to come inside and watch him commit holy matrimony?

Three things make Nevada special—desert, prostitution, and gambling. Most of the state is desert so hot and arid it takes a thousand acres to keep a steer alive. If the miserable critter can find water. The state has no law criminalizing the oldest profession, so each county gets to say yea or nay. The only legal whorehouses in America are here.

Last year the Internal Revenue Service acquired title to one after the owner forgot to send in a check, so for a while there Uncle Sam had some practicing prostitutes on the federal payroll. Everyone snickered about it, but it was no big deal, really. We've had congressmen for over 200 years.

I considered bidding on the whorehouse but finally decided against it. I'd never get any writing done. Besides, I probably couldn't have afforded it. Still, if I had Clancy's money I might have sent in a bid just to see.

Gambling is the industry that pays the electric bills. Every wide spot in the road has a casino and almost every shack has a few slot machines. The airport terminals are full of them. The sound of Nevada is the clunk of levers being pulled and the whirring of spinning wheels. This clunk, whir, click, click, click is accented at random intervals by the clinking of coins falling into metal trays. Ever wonder why they don't make those trays out of plastic? Because they want everyone to hear those coins spitting out. There's another lucky winner!

It's hard to believe, but tens of thousands of people come from all over the United States by car, train, bus and airplane to feed quarters into the slots. Hordes of women with rolls of quarters in empty margarine containers work those arms day and night. Clunk, whir, click, click, click.

Only in Nevada can you put up a billboard that says "Hot Slots" and attract thousands of women. In New York City that sign would only get you a few curious teenagers and dirty old men.

The only cities of any size in Nevada are Las Vegas and Reno, and they have different cultures. Vegas is polyester pants and bouffant hairdos while Reno is more blue-collar. More blue-collar? Yeah, jeans and message T-shirts and lots of tattoos.

I wandered around several Reno casinos reading T-shirts and inspecting tattoos. This evening was the first of a three-day extravaganza they call Hot August Nights, which will bring 20,000 polished old cars to town and all the people that polish them. These tattooed people must be polishers. I haven't seen this many tattoos since the time my ship left Hong Kong after a ten-day visit.

Reno is soaked with atmosphere tonight and I'm collecting drippings. After all, I'm a working writer. Maybe I'm all wet, but the mood I sense in these get-rich-quick glitz joints is quiet desperation. It's the undercurrent that's always there, the background against which the drinking, the gambling, the nervous laughter occurs.

249

Money comes hard for 99% of the human race. The one percent for whom this isn't true aren't sitting in Reno at the blackjack tables or leaning over a crap table with a fistful of five-dollar chips watching dice roll around. The people here earned their money by working for it. Now it bleeds away as they assure themselves their luck will turn. They stand with a week's wages in their hand and watch someone much like themselves win fifty or a hundred on the roll of the dice. If only it would happen to me!

I parted with a fifty-dollar bill and got ten of those five-dollar chips. They're plastic, colorful, somehow without the emotional attachment that I have for five-dollar bills that I earned. This is funny money, Monopoly stuff, easy to wager, easy to lose. That's the theory anyway.

I selected a blackjack table without any other players. The dealer was a Korean lady, Mrs. Lee. With the skill acquired by thousands of hours of practice she flipped the cards across the green velvet. After I lost the first three hands I begin winning some. More people came to the table. The guy beside me won three in a row, then muttered something about how much he's lost already. He's one of the desperate ones.

I quit after sucking down two free drinks, while I was still $65 ahead. I was a hundred ahead at one point but I lost some of it. So I quit. Sure as God made man willing to take a chance, I would have lost the $65 and the $50 I started with if I had stayed at that table another twenty minutes.

The next morning I came down to the lobby of my hotel at 6 A.M. As in most Reno hotels, you must exit to the street through a bar filled with slot machines. A man and a woman unwilling to give up the night were still nursing beer and cigarettes. They were the only patrons. The windowless dark room smelled stuffy, stale.

"I'm thirty-three and I've never been married," the man said.

"I'm thirty-three and I've been married twice," she told him, and laughed nervously.

I walked on through the door into the new day.

23

At 11,500 feet over the Sierra Nevadas, the world looks mighty good. The thin patchy cirrus layer never seems to get between me and the sun. The wind is out of the west-northwest, just a tad behind the right wing. And the *Cannibal Queen* is purring along with Nevada dropping out of sight behind and Southern California over the horizon ahead. Today I will try for Chino, California, one of the eastern suburbs of Los Angeles. Chino airport is home to the Planes of Fame Museum, which people tell me is not to be missed if you like World War II warbirds. Me, I like everything that flies.

Today is Wednesday, August 7. I haven't been at the controls since Friday when I landed in Reno. Saturday morning I took an airliner from the Reno terminal and flew off to spend a few days with the family on their summer vacation. Tuesday I arrived back in Reno. This morning I finally got the *Queen* back into the sky.

First she needed an oil change. Len and Dave at the Reno Jet Center helped me with that.

Dave and I chatted while we worked on the plane. His hobby is designing airplanes and engines. He told me he has drawings of a turbine engine that he thinks would be better than anything in existence. His dream is to build the aircraft design he likes best—a steel-frame plane 16 feet long with P-51 performance—and market the plans as a kit once he has ironed out the bugs.

Watching Dave pour oil into the *Queen* and listening to him tell me about his plane, I reminded myself that Wilbur and Orville Wright had a dream once. So did Glenn Curtiss, Lloyd Stearman and Kelly Johnson. Perhaps Dave will one day make his dream come true.

Flying south from Reno at 7,500 feet I realized I was underdressed for the temperatures over the Sierras. I landed at Douglas County Airport south of Carson City to fix that. While I was there I topped off the *Queen* again.

Now over the Sierras I am still cold. Not freezing, but shivering cold. I lower the seat and hunker in the cockpit. I sit on my right hand awhile to warm it, then fly with it while I sit on my left.

Still, the Sierras are gorgeous this morning. I can't think of anywhere else I would rather be.

Safely past the crest, I drop a thousand feet to find slightly warmer air. Soon Yosemite National Park appears before me and I break out the camera. I click photos of the world's most beautiful valley and bemoan the sun's position. These would be world-class shots if the sun were setting and throwing the valley in direct, low-angle sunlight and intense shadow. Still I'll take these. Maybe one will turn out pretty well.

I keep letting down as the terrain allows. Soon the mountains give way to foothills, then the foothills give way to perfectly square and rectangular fields of growing crops. This is the San Joaquin Valley, the highly productive, irrigated market basket of California. A layer of haze in the valley limits visibility to about 20 miles. It is very noticeable after the 50 miles plus of the mountaintops.

I stop in Visalia for fuel, then follow the highway south to Bakersfield, where I turn east for Tehachapi Pass. South of the pass is the coastal range; north of it are the Sierras.

A few hours of flying has brought me to a different world. Here the mountains rise from essentially barren, low-elevation desert. Vegetation increases on the mountain slopes in a direct relationship with elevation—the summits of the mountains actually support pine forests.

Tehachapi Pass is a natural wind funnel. Man has tried to profit from that happy fact. At first I can't make out what they are, then I realize I am looking at windmills, hundreds of them, all turning in unison. There are easily a thousand of these big, three-bladed windmills, perhaps twice that many. I amuse myself by counting blades and decide they turn at about 50 RPM.

The Mohave Desert lies on the eastern side of Tehachapi Pass. The desert is yellowish-brown and looks barren from 7,500 feet. It stretches away pool-table flat until it disappears into the haze. Approaching Palmdale I can easily distinguish Edwards Air Force Base and the runway where the space shuttle lands. Beyond the base is Rogers Lake, a vast salt flat. To the south are the San Gabriel Mountains.

Looking at Edwards and the Mohave, I immediately think of Chuck Yeager, the first man to break the "sound barrier." Such is the power of a great writer. *The Right Stuff* by Tom Wolfe made Yeager a larger-than-life figure. Before Wolfe, Yeager was a retired Air Force brigadier general who had once enjoyed a sliver of public notice. After Wolfe, Chuck Yeager was the ultimate American hero, the determined, straight-arrow man of humble origin with no education who transformed himself into the world's greatest pilot by strength of will and sterling character. Wolfe ran wild with the hero dust, and such was the magnitude of his talent, he mythologized Yeager.

That base over there by the salt flat is where the great Odysseus Yeager, a kingly man beloved of the gods, strapped a bullet-shaped rocket-plane to his ass one day in 1947 and fulfilled his destiny.

Just flying in the same valley where the man-god did it gives me goose bumps.

I am enviously meditating on Tom Wolfe's talent when the bottom drops out. The *Queen* drops sharply enough that my derriere parts company with the rear seat for a heartbeat, just long enough for the adrenal glands to squirt a quart of the go-juice into my system. I get a firm grip with my left hand on a steel fuselage member. It's silly, I know, but it makes me feel better when the next jolt comes half a minute later.

These turbulence speedbumps that leave you weightless for an instant—they make me wish the *Queen* had a canopy. That feeling that you and the plane are parting company has a visceral impact on me, made all the worse by my experience in Australia in a Tiger Moth on my very first open-cockpit airplane ride. We weren't wearing parachutes. Without warning my pilot in the rear seat, a New Zealander, rolled the airplane upside down and put negative G on, which predictably catapulted me toward mother earth. Of course my progress downward was arrested by my shoulder harness and lap belt.

Still, I almost wet my pants. I jammed my knees sideways and grabbed. There I was, 2,000 feet over Australia with nothing between me and my creator but a harness with one buckle that I hadn't preflighted.

When my benefactor rolled the plane upright, I found that the throttle quadrant had a screw sticking out of it about half an inch. I noticed it because the screw was buried in the side of my left knee. I still have the scar.

Forty miles southeast of Palmdale is El Cajon Pass, the entrance to the Los Angeles basin. The pass is low, about 4,200 feet, so the Queen sails through at 7,500 with only a few wicked bounces. A thicker smog layer coats the L.A. basin. It looks like smoke and the upper limit has a definite edge. Visibility in the thick stuff is about six miles.

Approach calls traffic right, left, above, below, but I spot only one other plane, an airliner. Welcome to the big city, you bumpkin.

Ontario Approach vectors me right across their field at 3,500 feet. Just when I wonder if they've moved Chino Airport, I see it.

As I taxi in, a P-51 Mustang dressed for a Saturday night date taxis by on the way to the runway. A better-than-new B-24 is surrounded by a retinue on the ramp; an A-1 awaiting restoration sits rotting behind a hangar.

This is the place!

The Exxon dealer is a guy named Dave Lewis, who let me tie the Queen beside his building and borrow his Toyota pickup. The next morning I strolled along the parking mat taking photos.

Chino is warbird heaven. Here former military fighters, bombers and trainers are expertly and lovingly restored, painted, polished and flown. Small hangars belonging to outfits like Aero Traders and the Military Aircraft Restoration Company are chock full of these machines—they even stick out the open doors because there's no room for them inside.

Swarms of airframe and engine experts bustle about doing mechanical things, peering here, prodding there, talking to each other in the lingo of the aeronautically initiated. I won't reproduce any of it here because you wouldn't understand a word. I didn't.

Peering into the gloom of the hangars from the bright sunlight of the ramp, one sees all manner of gleaming, shining masterpieces: a MiG-19 under restoration, a T-28 dolled out with a Navy gray and off-white paint scheme, several P-51s, Corsairs, Hellcats, T-6s, a T-2 Buckeye, you name it.

On the ramp beside a pristine B-24 complete with fake guns is a C-1 Trader wearing the colors and markings of USS *Lexington.* This may be *Lexington*'s former carrier on-board delivery (COD) plane, but it never looked this good while flying for Uncle Sugar.

In silent awe I walked down the ramp to the Planes of Fame Museum, there to be overwhelmed. On the grass outside is a B-17 Flying Fortress, *Piccadilly Lilly,* and the fuselage of the first aircraft to fly nonstop around the world, a B-50.

They want $7.95 to let you inside the museum hangars. Pay it. It's worth every cent.

Hangar #1 houses the heavy iron, a couple of P-51 Mustangs, single examples of an F6F Hellcat, P-47 Thunderbolt, TBM-3 Avenger, P-40 Warhawk, SBD-5 Dauntless, and F8F Bearcat, among others. These are big airplanes. The Thunderbolt was called "the Jug" by its pilots, and looking at it one can see why. Did you know the Hellcat had fabric-covered elevators, rudder and ailerons?

Among the planes that caught my fancy in Hangar #2 was a Japanese A6M5 Zero, the only Zero in the world still flying with the original engine and prop. After capture in Saipan in 1944, it was brought back to the U.S. and wrung out by test pilots, among them Charles Lindbergh. Restored in 1978, it toured Japan, the only Zero to fly in Japanese airspace since World War II.

Here also you will find not one but two Messerschmitt BF

109s, both originals. One is a Spanish-built version with a Rolls-Royce Merlin upright V-12 engine, but the other is the real McCoy, with an inverted V-12, 1,475-HP Daimler-Benz. According to the museum catalog there are only four of these German-built 109s in the United States.

I grew up reading tales of these fighters, and here are two of them! Yet they're so small! The Germans wanted fighters with maneuverability optimized, yet the American fighters of that era had to fly tremendous distances, which meant large quantities of fuel, so they were of necessity much larger aircraft. The Americans were also fond of heavy armament, so the requirement to house six or eight 50-caliber machine guns and their ammo was also a major factor in the design process.

Hangar #2 houses two great American fighters from the '30s, a Boeing F4B-3 biplane and a P-26 Peashooter. This is the only Peashooter I have ever laid eyes on. Also here is a Bristol fighter from World War I, generally acknowledged as the best fighter of that war. But the *pièce de résistance* is the personal fighter of Charles Nungesser, a Hanriot HD-1 scout wearing its original 130-HP Clerget rotary engine. Nungesser shot down 45 German airplanes and survived World War I only to be killed with Raymond Coli in 1927 when the two of them tried to fly the Atlantic from east to west to win the Orteg Prize.

The Hanriot is unrestored and hangs from a dimly lit ceiling. Here is a plane that needs plenty of floorspace, a spotlight or two, and a tastefully arranged velvet rope to restrain the overly enthusiastic. She also needs new fabric. There are a thousand uses for duct tape, but patching holes in the fabric of priceless airplanes should not be one of them.

The jet hangar is a block down the street. A nice collection of Air Force hot stuff is parked outside. Inside you will find a MiG-15 and MiG-17, an F-11 Tiger that once flew with the Blue Angels, an F-104 Starfighter, a couple of F-86 Sabres, and the one that I would steal if I had keys to the place, an F-8 Crusader. She carried four 20-mm cannon and was known as "the last of the gunfighters." Crusader pilots were also partial to bumper stickers that proudly proclaimed, "When you're out of F-8s, you're out of fighters."

No interceptor, the supersonic F-8 was designed before air-to-air missiles became reliably operational. It was a dogfighter all the way. A Crusader pilot had to outmaneuver and outfly his opponent until he closed to gun range, which, as any real fighter pilot will tell you, is as close as humanly possible.

How close is humanly possible? "I opened fire only when the whole windshield was black with the enemy," said the Luftwaffe's Erich Hartman, the most successful fighter pilot who ever lived.

By the mid-sixties F-8s were also armed with heat-seeking Sidewinder missiles, but there were no hundred-mile missile shots for those guys.

Air-to-air combat as a joust of aerial knights reached its zenith with F-8s, the last U.S. Navy fighter without a computer or sophisticated radar. One man strapped himself into the airplane, took the catapult shot, and went to find the enemy with his eyes. When he found him, he attacked. A gun battle followed, one that Manfred von Richthofen, Charles Nungesser and the other aces of old would have understood. You didn't "shoot down" your enemy or launch a million-dollar missile that would do the dirty deed for you—you outflew him and closed to hammer him with your guns. You *killed* him. Then you flew home to live with it.

To win one of these highly personal aerial duels to the death required a warrior's heart. You could be the world's greatest pilot and that wouldn't be enough. Somewhere in your psyche there had to be the willingness, the desire, to get in close and kill. Nintendo didn't invent this—you had to have this streak of the savage or you were the hunted, not the hunter.

F-8 pilots were the keepers of the holy flame during the early dark years of the Vietnam War when they alone enjoyed a very favorable kill ratio against MiGs. The founding fathers of the Navy's Top Gun School were all F-8 pilots.

This blood lust is still essential for a fighter pilot, even if he or she is flying one of today's push-button missile-launching platforms. Does this apple-cheeked high-tech computer whiz have enough savage left when the veneers of civilization are ripped away and he is naked in the sky in a kill-or-be-killed situation? If he doesn't kill quickly enough and well, he will be killed. It's that simple.

257

*   *   *

After snarfing a gut-bomb at Flo's Airport Cafe, I wandered back to the FBO to say good-bye to Dave Lewis. As I walked toward the building a Navy-blue F4U gull-wing Corsair taxied in. The throaty rumble of that 2,100-HP radial engine touched something inside me that no torch singer ever reached.

"There's always something new and different happening here," Lewis told me. "History taxis by my window every day. And you never know what will go by next.

"The restorers are the key to Chino. Guys like Bruce Goessling, who went to Red China and thirty-nine days later came back with a batch of MiG-15s that still had the machine guns installed. And David Tallichet, who reportedly owns over three hundred airplanes. He's almost finished with a magnificent restoration of a B-26 that crashed in Alaska on a ferry flight. Guys like Charles Nichols, who cornered the world market on N3N wings when he drove by a salvage yard one day and saw them stacked up. He walked in and bought them all. Just couldn't bear the thought of those wings going in the smelter."

I asked him if these people ever sell their treasures.

Lewis laughed. "Goessling sold the MiGs. But most of them never sell anything. Oh, they'll trade you if you have something they want, but they don't sell airplanes."

We talked about the Planes of Fame Museum. "It's a flying museum. They fly about everything except the Hanriot. Steve Hinton flew their A-1 Skyraider when Paramount filmed your book, *Flight of the Intruder.* The museum used to give an airshow every year here at Chino, got all those planes out and flew them. That stopped about three years ago. The TCAs and ARSAs are growing like weeds in the L.A. basin. It's getting harder and harder to fly here.

"But we have a new airport manager, a retired Marine, and he knows a thing or two about airshows. He's working on one for next year, getting people to help. It's going to be a great one. I think Hartley Folstad is going to do his Stearman show."

Lewis rooted through the pile on his desk for a moment and found a brochure. A 25,000-hour former Navy pilot who now flies for United, Hartley Folstad has formed a company known as the Stearman Flight Center with headquarters at Chino. The company has five Stearmans, three with Pratt & Whitney 450s and two with Continental 220s. The company is in the airshow business, putting on aerial acts with the big-engined Stearmans and giving rides with the others. Folstad has personally restored seven Stearmans. I gotta meet this guy!

I thanked Dave Lewis for his hospitality and preflighted the *Cannibal Queen.*

Are warbirds the ultimate upscale status toy? Certainly. They're like beautiful women—if you have to ask what one costs, you can't afford it. But for your edification I will tell you that you could own a couple of Lamborghini Diablos and a Ferrari for the price of one good P-51. And the Mustang will cost you a fortune in maintenance and operating costs—plan on hiring a couple of full-time mechanics and buying gasoline by the truckload. You'd also better be a pretty good pilot or you and your toy will end up in the same smoking hole.

But Chino is more than a toy shop for the filthy rich. Here the heavy iron is restored and maintained by experts and continues to fly. Here and at airshows across the country people like you and me can thrill to the roar of big piston engines and watch with awe as Mustangs and Corsairs and Hellcats take off with 52 inches of manifold pressure and point their long, gleaming snouts skyward. There is more to aviation than airliners and Cessnas. Thank heavens!

Some warbirds obviously should be preserved in museums for future generations. Yet when an airplane is permanently moved inside and polished so slick a fly groundloops trying to land, somehow we are all a little poorer. Some of these machines should be flying, should be out there in their natural habitat, the great open spaces of the sky.

I think a warbird is the perfect way for a person with more money than he can count to lighten the load. On airframe restoration experts. On machine shops. On engine experts. On custom paint specialists. On experienced flight instructors. Liz Taylor's emeralds never gave me an ounce of satisfaction.

24

THE VISIBILITY IS ONLY THREE MILES WITH THE SKY PARTIALLY OBSCURED by haze. There's too much moisture in the air—humidity is about 35%. And the smog thickens the mix.

I study the sectional yet again and carefully note the ARSA approach frequencies. Chino is under the ARSA centered around Ontario Airport, eight miles north. East of Ontario is the Norton Air Force Base ARSA. West of Ontario is Pomona, with an airport traffic area that reaches up to 3,000 feet. Ten miles east of Chino is Riverside Airport, which also has an airport traffic area. March Air Force Base is southeast of Riverside. Eight miles south of Chino are hills, one with a peak of 3,085 feet. South of that row of hills are Marine Corps Air Station El Toro and John Wayne–Orange County Airport. To the west of Chino lies the great malignant mushroom of the Los Angeles TCA and all the airports in its shadow—LAX, Los Alamitos, Long Beach, Burbank, El Monte, Torrance and so on.

This basin is no place for a fellow without navigation aids to wander around semi-lost. You'll get a flight violation quicker than an IRS agent can clean out your wallet. Full of misgivings, I strap on the *Queen* and light off the Lycoming.

After an intersection takeoff the *Queen* climbs quickly to

1,500 feet. A left turn clears the traffic pattern; then I ask Tower if I can switch to Ontario Approach. They grant permission.

I want desperately to avoid getting lost in this soup in the two or ten minutes it will take for Approach to pick me up and grant me permission to enter the ARSA. I make a left turn and place Chino Airport on my left wing as I make my call. Straight east five or six miles is a four-lane highway running north and south. If I hold over that highway I should be clear of both the Chino and Riverside airport traffic areas and under the Ontario ARSA.

Approach answers immediately and assigns me a discrete squawk. I dial it in and look again for Chino Airport. Still visible. I am debating whether to make a tight 180 to keep it in sight or fly east to the highway when Approach announces radar contact and grants me permission to head north through the ARSA.

Well, that was easy. Today. They're obviously not very busy. A fellow wouldn't want to try this without nav aids on a soupy day with a flock of migratory airliners coming and going. Then Approach will just tell you to stay clear, if they condescend to talk to you at all.

Climbing through 3,000 feet I top the hazy marine layer and visibility instantly improves to maybe 15 miles. El Cajon Pass is ten degrees right. Beyond it is the Mohave.

I go through at 5,500 feet and follow the interstate toward Barstow. The air above the dirty, yellow-brown land is hot. Wispy high clouds merely diffuse the sunlight without weakening it. In minutes I am sweating in the cockpit under my leather jacket.

At Barstow the winds are supposedly calm. That is what the FBO man tells me on the radio. But on final approach I find they are shifting around all over the compass at four or five knots. The landing is a typical desert arrival—I'm proud that I didn't scrape a wingtip.

I shut down by the fuel pump and stow the jacket in the baggage bin. The temperature here is in the high nineties. Baking in the sun are rows of Army olive-drab helicopters in front of three long, white clapboard hangars. I've never seen anything quite like these hundred-yard-long sheds. They look like they might have once held a hundred cavalry horses each.

The FBO man asks where I'm bound and I tell him up toward Vegas. "Good luck at the tables," he says.

"Won't be doing any of that," I assure him. "I'm going on up toward Zion and Bryce Canyon."

Northeast of Barstow the desert seems lifeless from three thousand feet above it. The peaks are black rock. Alluvial skirts of sand and gravel fan out below them and peter out on the harsh brown flats. The watercourses are quite plain, but there is no water. Not a drop. All this erosion resulted from occasional showers and thunderstorms, only a few inches of water a year total. So the stark, eroded landscape is a profound monument to the immensity of time.

In this bleak wilderness of sand and stone there are few good places for an emergency landing. Inevitably any spot you choose will have a boulder or a gulley in the wrong place that will wipe off the landing gear or flip the plane onto its nose or back. A forced landing—that is one where the engine is still running and you can fly around down low for awhile to find a likely spot—has a better chance. If you can, find a road.

Passing Baker I look left, off to the northwest, at Death Valley. The heat shimmering off the desert up that way vaporizes my vague desire to land at Furnace Creek in the heart of Death Valley. At 211 feet below sea level, the airport there is the lowest in the United States. I've landed at Furnace Creek before in other airplanes in the winter or fall. In early August the heat will be truly awesome. I like the Lycoming engine on the *Cannibal Queen* too much to subject it to that kind of abuse.

That thought automatically brings my eyes to the engine gauges. Cylinder head temp is 220 degrees, the hottest I've ever seen it. Oil temp is 165 and pressure is steady at 50, the minimum safe pressure.

I'm bouncing again in desert thermals so I let the updrafts carry the *Queen* higher. The air will be cooler the higher I get and I have a 4,630-foot-high pass ahead, just south of Clark Mountain in the Tonopah Range. The turbulence in that pass may be fierce today, so I hit it high, at 7,500 feet, and cross with no problem.

Out here in the desert the visibility is excellent, easily a hundred miles, so Las Vegas is visible quite a distance away. I leave the interstate and head east across the McCullough Range. The highest peak here is under me at 7,026 feet, but the winds forced upward by the mountains slam the Queen around.

On the eastern side of the McCulloughs is a salt flat, then a gentle incline up to Boulder City overlooking Hoover Dam and Lake Mead. The airport is a new one on the southwest side of the city, on the slope below the town. It's 2,200 feet above the ocean.

The Unicom guy says the wind is out of the north and suggests runway 33. I make a left base entry and am soon floating down final, floating so much that I know the wind is behind me. Toying with the idea of going around, I keep descending.

There's a wind sock at the approach end and it verifies the wind is out of the south, behind me, at seven or eight knots. At least it's not a crosswind. I'll give it a try.

With the power at idle I begin my flare. A wind sock at midfield catches my eye—wind out of the west at seven or eight.

I fly through the shift just before the wheels touch. Left wing down, right rudder, stick slamming around to hold her, then she's on. As I roll out I see a third wind sock at the upwind end of this runway: this one indicates the wind is out of the north! At seven or eight knots.

The line boys who help me fuel the Queen are Indians. "How hot is it?" I ask.

"Last I looked, a hundred and four."

Well, Coonts, you wanted desert. By gum, boy, you got it!

Lake Mead is emerald green from 2,500 feet above it. The sand-colored rock ridges are visible after they enter the green water: they seem to descend into infinite green depths as shadows until finally the yellowish color is completely merged with the green of the water. Speedboats pulling water skiers plow the surface.

North of Lake Mead I pick up the interstate just east of the Mormon Mesa VOR. The white cone of the radio nav aid is quite prominent amid the rock and dirt of this hot, empty land. And Lordy, it is hot!

I take a squint at the engine instruments and my heart sinks. The oil temperature is up to 175 degrees and the pressure is down to 45, 5 PSI below the green. As oil gets hotter it gets thinner. Is it lubricating the engine properly? Cylinder head temp is only 190, so maybe.

How the heck would I know?

Now I fret. My eyes keep coming back to the oil temp and pressure gauges. If I try to climb to cooler air the climb will really cook the oil. I reduce power an inch. Maybe that will help. Since nothing is free, the immediate result is the loss of five miles per hour in airspeed. That means less air is going through the cooling fins of the cylinders.

Have I developed an oil leak? I use my hand to wipe the sides of the Queen. Dry as usual. No oil film on the forward windshield.

The air's just too darned hot. That's what it is.

St. George, Utah, is just ahead through the pass. I decide to land and sit for a couple hours until the air cools a little. That oil pressure needle below the green arc is impossible to disregard.

My call on Unicom is answered promptly. The wind is 240 at 12. Recommend runway 16. Okay.

My first look at the field makes my stomach churn. The single asphalt runway sits on top of a ridge that drops steeply away on all sides, especially the approach end. And the approach end of runway 16 is guarded by a huge hill to the west. The wind is coming around the south end of that prodigious hill and roaring up that steep slope to the runway. Hill? Big as it is, it's a mountain to this West Virginia boy.

I keep the right wing down as I flare and let the right wheel make first contact. I can feel the wind shift toward the right. She bounces. Stick back and right and lots of left rudder, and still I swerve alarmingly before I save it.

Disgust washes over me. Damn this desert flying! Another religious experience. Before this trip is over I'm going to be qualified to live in a monastery.

It's 102 degrees at the St. George airport, which is 2,938 feet above sea level. The wind is 12 knots gusting to 21. The line boy tells me about the wind. "Always comes humping from the west in the afternoon. You gotta get here before noon if you want to avoid it."

*   *   *

At 6 P.M. I'm rolling down the runway feeding in right stick and left rudder to keep the Queen straight as the strong right crosswind makes the plane goosey. Now I lift the left wheel, then the right. Airborne, crabbing, but she's climbing!

The wind squirts the Queen eastward across the town of St. George when I turn in that direction. Away from the ridge upon which the airport sits the air is calmer and the plane climbs smoothly but slowly. The shadows are lengthening in the little city below and streaming eastward off the mesas that stand to the north and south.

The two hours on the ground allowed the oil to cool. It stabilizes at 160 degrees and 60 PSI. Now if it will just stay there!

Heat and wind are part and parcel of the desert's stark beauty, which you either love or hate. There can be no in-between. The land is too primal for subtle emotions. And too big. Only mortal man is small here.

I steer the *Cannibal Queen* northward across Hurricane Mesa toward the great red cliffs of Zion, then turn and fly southeast with the cliffs off my left wing.

A gnat flying by the face of God, that is what I am. The size of the jagged red cliffs overwhelms me. The inanimate, basic power of stone that has resisted wind and water through the eons fills me with awe. Life is uncertain, life is short, life is filled with pain and joy, yet these great red cliffs endure the ages, only occasionally yielding a grain of sand.

All my ambitions, all my dreams, all my hopes, they are as a gust of evening wind against the grandeur of the red cliffs.

And what am I? The God who raised the stone from the place where it was made into this position and rejoices at its constancy, what does He expect of me? What could I possibly achieve to be worthy of His notice in my short span upon the earth?

Man is a foolish little creature, worried about transitory things. We are all, each of us, saturated with that egocentric silliness that causes some of the women in Boulder to fret about the intensity of their orgasms. Do you really think the Creator of billions of galaxies, each containing billions of stars, has time for silly, tiny man?

The gods of old were all little gods. Science has ripped away the veil of time and distance and shrunk us to our proper place

265

in the great scheme of things, yet we still cling to our ancient, little gods like a drowning man clings to a board.

Little people in little rooms in little places purport to tell us the eternal truths. People that don't understand the most basic laws of physics tell us with straight faces that they have mastered the incomprehensible. How could they know?

The airport at Bryce Canyon, Utah, has the only log hangar I've ever seen. Built in the 1930s by the WPA, the big hangar is visible for many miles if you have a good angle on the sun.

I like this airport and the location, 7,500 feet above sea level on a great mesa. The east side of the mesa is composed of soft pink stone that forms the spectacular cliffs of Bryce Canyon National Park. The south end of the mesa, which is in the park, is a high pine forest. Yet the gentle swale north of the park where the airport is located is treeless. A couple miles farther north the land rises and is covered with trees again.

Elevation is the key to life in this rugged country. The tree line is a contour line—only a few feet in elevation means the difference between enough water to sustain trees year after year and mere prairie grass. Lower still is the desert.

I cross above the national park shivering at 11,500, still flying in a short-sleeve shirt after my day in the desert, and slip the *Cannibal Queen* onto Bryce's 7,000-foot strip of asphalt. After taxiing forever I arrive at the little mat in front of the log hangar and maneuver the *Queen* into a tiedown spot for the night. The air temperature here is a mere 75 degrees.

Two men are sitting on a log bench in front of the hangar. One is elderly, the other I soon learn is the FBO man. I am barely out of the cockpit when they wander over to inspect the *Queen*. I have a reservation tonight at Ruby's Inn, the biggest of the three motels hereabouts, and they advertise they will send a car over to pick up folks at the airport. I call them from the phone inside and they say they'll be over in a bit.

So I sit on the log bench and talk to the old man. From Florida, he is living in an RV parked beside the hangar, has been here since July 7 and is going to stay until the desert down below cools off. Then he'll probably go down to Bullhead City, Arizona, on the Colorado River. Laughlin, Nevada, is right across the river. Every evening boats ferry people across the river to the gambling joints. But it's hotter than holy hell down in Bullhead right now, so the old man is whiling away the summer at the airport in Bryce.

"I'm an airport bum," he tells me. "Been one since 1946. Like to hang out at the airport and watch the planes come and go."

The daughter of the FBO man sits with us and plays with her cat. She talks to it and won't let it escape. Finally it jumps down and runs for the trailer behind the hangar where the family lives, the girl running after it.

The old man and I talk about airports and planes and Bryce Canyon. A half hour passes, then forty-five minutes, and I'm still waiting. Ruby's van is taking its time. But the company is pleasant, the sun is low on the horizon and, all in all, it's been another great day of flying, a fine day to be alive.

"They'll want five bucks now for the ride to Ruby's," the old man informs me. "When they get around to showing up."

"They never used to charge."

"They quit giving free rides from the airport the first of the year. Now they want five bucks a head and two dollars more if you have luggage."

"It's only a couple miles over there."

"I know. Ain't right. Some of the people arriving here have been arguing with them about it."

I can understand that. *Flight Guide* says Ruby's offers free airport pickup.

The van shows up an hour after I called. The sun is just setting. As we drive away I look over my shoulder at the lonesome log hangar and the *Cannibal Queen* sitting in front. The old man is still sitting on the bench.

The young woman driving apologizes for the delay and tells me cheerfully that she won't charge me tonight for the ride since she was so late.

Five dollars! The whole subject irritates me. Welcome back to earth!

Friday morning when I arrived at the airport a man and woman were preflighting an American Eagle biplane parked beside the Stearman. I visited a moment with the old man, who was back on the bench, then packed the *Queen* and taxied her to the fuel pump. The Eagle pilot and I started engines at about the same time and were soon ready to taxi. I got on the radio.

"Eagle, this is the Stearman. If you want to taxi down the runway behind me, you can swing around and take off first."

They took me up on it. When the smaller plane was safely airborne, I rolled the Stearman.

The *Cannibal Queen* climbs into the thin morning air at a pace suitable for a dowager. The Eagle slashes in and settles on my right wing as I swing the *Queen* southeast across the cliffs, then turn south.

Now the Eagle crosses under and surfaces on the left side. I snap a few with the camera. After a minute or two the pilot goes back to the right side. He's three or four wingspans away at all times, which I appreciate. I have no idea how good a formation pilot he is and I don't want him in tight trying to show me.

The Eagle is a snappy, fully aerobatic biplane much smaller than a Stearman. The two people sitting in tandem are covered by a bubble canopy. With a conventional, horizontally opposed flat engine, she has good performance and excellent economy. The paint job on this one is uninspired, but you can't hold that against the plane.

Finally the Eagle crosses under to my left wing, then turns away to the east as the pilot says good-bye on the radio. Soon she is tail on to me. In moments she disappears into the bright blue eastern sky and the *Cannibal Queen* is once again alone.

The Grand Canyon, which is Spanish for "big ditch," is a stupendous jagged tear in the earth's crust that mere words cannot describe. It must be seen and felt to be believed.

Of course nature displays her finest masterpiece to best advantage. Oriented east and west to catch the morning and evening sun, the canyon must be approached from north or south by man the insect. On the ground this journey is a gradual climb through pine forests as the land swells gently upward toward the rim. Then, like a curtain being raised, there it is!

Even jaded teenagers who have been everywhere and seen everything are stunned into silence by their first look. At the rim overlooks people point and whisper.

This morning as I fly south toward the north rim the rising terrain also obscures my vision. Under me is the pine forest and the twisting, winding road that leads up to the lodge and the overlooks.

I have the chart spread on my left knee and am watching it carefully. The National Park Service has been busy here. In the last eighteen months the Park Service, an outfit that really knows and cares about airplanes and the problems of the people who fly them, has managed to create a mandatory overflight system of such Byzantine complexity that even Odysseus Yeager couldn't figure it out. Which is what they intended. If you can't positively identify the turnpoints on the VFR tour routes or the boundaries of the segments with their varying altitude restrictions, you'd best avoid the place and leave canyon flying to commercial tour operators hauling planeloads of Japanese and Germans. If you want to keep your pilot's license, that is.

To avoid the hassles you need to fly over the Grand Canyon at an altitude above 14,499 feet above sea level. Better make it a good bit more than one foot higher because the thermals and downdrafts over this colossal ditch can be vicious.

The *Cannibal Queen* might stagger up to 15,000, but I'm not going to try it today. I'm at 10,500 feet coming up over the forest toward the north rim.

I can see little arms of the great canyon off to my right and left, but the main gorge is ahead and obscured by the rising terrain. I look longingly to my right at a finger of rim that I can see coming up from the south. There is a VFR corridor there that can be traversed above 10,000 feet, but only if you can hit the narrow north-rim entrance right on the money, and to do that you would need to acquire the FAA's new special chart that includes photographs of the waypoints. Then you should take a few flights with an experienced canyon pilot to ensure you know what you're looking at when you're looking at it. Today I decide to play it safe and forget the whole thing.

I turn eastward. I will fly around the eastern end of the canyon and then along the southern rim to Grand Canyon Airport. I dial in the radio frequency required for flight in the adjacent section of the canyon and listen to the tour pilots report their position and altitude.

"Over the dragon at ninety-five."

The dragon? Why not points A, B and so forth, points labeled as such on the charts?

I'll be honest—I resent the government's insistence that I avoid overflight of national landmarks so that environmental activists won't have their "wilderness experience" disrupted by aircraft noise. You and I carefully give national parks two thousand feet of clearance when overflying while the commercial tour operators are right down in the weeds with the paying customers. This system has been carried to the point of absurdity at the Grand Canyon as a direct result of political pressure by environmental activists on Congress, which decided to let the National Park Service make the rules. The fact that general aviation is getting a raw deal delights the "environmentalists," some of whom want jets rerouted so that *they* won't have to look at contrails.

There are a lot of people in this country who would like to see every private aircraft recycled into beer cans. The restrictions are only going to get worse unless the people who own and fly noncommercial aircraft fight back. According to the Aircraft Owners and Pilots Association, some state officials want *state parks* protected from overflights.

Are you listening out there? Do you care? Or are you going to wait until general aviation is stone cold dead, then tut-tut about the swine politicians and wax nostalgic?

This morning I do the only thing I can. I turn the damned radio off and sit looking at the view with just the engine for company.

The view is something to look at. Reds, yellows, grays, all shades of pink highlighted by the morning sun and contrasted by stark shadows. If God ever takes a vacation, I'll bet He comes here.

Visibility today is good, about 60 miles. I can see Navajo Mountain 60 miles away to the northeast across the Painted Desert.

It isn't always this good. There are days now that the smog from Los Angeles and the emissions from the Navajo Power Plant near Page, Arizona, combine to reduce visibility to the point that you can't see from one rim of the canyon to the other. That distance is about 12 nautical miles, call it 14 civilian miles.

In the humid east 12 miles visibility is terrific; out here in the great west that's the equivalent of a London fog. Things are bigger out here and the air is dry.

Yesterday an agreement was reached to clean up the emissions from the coal-fired Navajo Plant, a process that will take twenty years and cost $2 *billion*. But don't expect to see any improvement in the air until the next century. If the cleanup happens at all. And all that money will do nothing about those 14 million people in the L.A. basin.

Once again I get the feeling that I am seeing something that my grandchildren may not be able to see. If people keep moving to California the magnificent vistas of the west may become hidden in smog. What the Grand Canyon will look like then is something to contemplate the next time you are drunk. At least there won't be any airplane noise.

People say that birds don't do aerobatics. You've always heard that, I suspect. I have been told that by flight and aerodynamics instructors since I started in this game. And they're wrong. Someone in the FAA forgot to give the birds a copy of the rules.

A couple years ago I was standing on the south rim staring at the canyon and thinking big thoughts when I noticed some kind of swallow come shooting out over the canyon into the rising air. He rolled neatly upside down and did a one-G pull for a few seconds, then rolled upright. I saw another bird do it while I was getting the camera ready. Then I sat for an hour with the camera in hand, waiting, but the show was over.

An attraction on the south rim that's worth your time is the IMAX theater in Canyon Village, right near the airport. The show there is a special about the canyon. On that giant screen the great canyon is a once-in-a-lifetime experience.

The best part of the film is a segment filmed from an ultralight flying down a gorge into the bottom of the canyon. That is flight as you dreamed it on those warm summer nights when you were young. The final moments of the film are scenes of an ultralight flying above the canyon as the sun drops lower and lower. This scene will bring tears to your eyes.

As you leave the theater, ponder the fact that the flying the film depicts is now illegal.

*   *   *

Heading southeast out of Grand Canyon Airport, Humphreys Peak north of Flagstaff is at one o'clock. The *Queen* floats above the pine forest of the highlands as the Grand Canyon recedes to the north. Then finally I look and it's gone, hidden from view.

An old volcano, Humphreys Peak at 12,633 feet is well above me and today is hosting rain showers. Dark clouds obscure the peak. Here is a graphic illustration of the advantage that elevation bestows on living things in this desert country. Ahead of me and on my left in the lowland is the Painted Desert, and it's not getting a drop. Oh, there are clouds out there, most spawned by Humphreys, and rain is falling from some of them. Yet the hot dry air absorbs the raindrops after they have fallen just a couple thousand feet. Nowhere today but on the big mountain is liquid water reaching the ground. So the slopes of Humphreys are covered with trees.

Soon I am flying over a landscape that shows graphic evidence of a volcanic past. The Strawberry Crater Wilderness and Sunset Crater National Monument are two areas named after the biggest cones, but there are dozens, as well as numerous black lava flows.

I pick up I-40 going east from Flagstaff and follow it on the south side. The desert underneath the *Queen* is extraordinarily green this year, as green as I have ever seen it in August. Yet it is a hard, desolate land all the same. Even the names give you a taste of it. Canyon Diablo—Devil Canyon—is normally dry this time of year—its watercourse is San Francisco Wash. The village of Two Guns sits where the highway and railroad cross Canyon Diablo. Not Gloversville or Cooperstown, but Two Guns.

East of Two Guns and five or six miles south of the highway is Meteor Crater, which the first white men in this area thought was volcanic in origin. Nope. At least fifty thousand years ago and probably more a 300,000-ton meteor came into the atmosphere at so steep an angle that it escaped incineration. This crater is the impact point.

This eroded relic of an ancient catastrophe attracts me and I fly over it in the *Cannibal Queen*. From up here it doesn't look so big. But that crater is 4,000 feet in diameter and 600 feet deep. I've stood on the rim. Big as it is, it's still a dimple compared to the Grand Canyon, but then as meteors go, the one that hit here was a mere pebble.

Scientists say that if a meteor over six miles in diameter ever hits the earth, life on this planet will cease. So people who like to worry about things they can't do anything about want the federal government to spend hundreds of millions to keep an eye peeled skyward just in case. What all of us humans will do if the alarm is ever given isn't precisely explained.

The FBO at Winslow doesn't answer my calls, but after the third one the FBO at Holbrook does. I ask him if he has fuel. Yes. So I overfly Winslow and continue the 30 miles to Holbrook.

The wind is out of the west—I've been enjoying another tail-wind—so I enter on a right base for runway 21. As I flare the wind gets squirrelly, gusting from odd directions. This is the desert.

Inside the FBO office they have a board with photos of some of the niftier planes that have stopped here. On the board are three photos of a Waco biplane owned and flown by a popular singer that was badly smacked in a crash here last year. The prop was bent around the cowling, the gear wiped off, the lower wing crumpled like a rag, the fuselage deformed. This was no garden-variety goundloop.

The guy who pumped the gas explains: "What the singer told the FAA was this: A gust of wind caught him on landing, after he had touched down on the mains but before he got the tail wheel down. The plane probably weathercocked on him. So he added full power and honked it into the air.

"But he was too slow to fly and stalled. Maybe a gust or the wind shifted while he was just a few knots above a stall. What-ever, he fell maybe fifty feet and hit with full power on, which is why the prop is bent like that. Wiped off the gear, really bent everything there was to bend."

Looking at the photos, I think the pilot was lucky he hit in a flat attitude. I doubt if he stalled it 50 feet up—my guess is it fell about 20 feet. Much higher and the nose would have been more down at impact.

These pictures are a sobering lesson for a tail-wheel pilot. Once you pull the power to idle and begin the flare, never ever add power to go around. No matter what. It is better to groundloop at a low speed trying to get stopped than stall somewhere off the ground and drop it in. And in gusty, shifting winds, a stall is almost inevitable.

This story also illustrates the benefits of the three-point, full-stall landing. When the mains arrive on deck, you want the tail wheel down simultaneously or as soon thereafter as possible. Most tail wheels are steerable, so when coupled with the effect of the rudder, you can prevent the plane from weathercocking—if the tail wheel is on the ground and you are holding it down with full back stick. If it's up, all you have is rudder and you may not have enough.

Some tail-wheel pilots feel more comfortable with wheel landings in gusty conditions. A wheel landing is flown at a slightly higher approach speed than a full-stall—in the Queen, 85 MPH—and the plane is literally flown onto the runway at that speed. The mains touch while the tail is still up in the flight attitude. One then lets the plane decelerate while working stick and rudder to hold the plane straight and overcome the effects of crosswind and gusts. If everything goes right these landings work out. Yet if something goes wrong, such as too much wind or a misapplication of stick or rudder, the plane will be badly damaged in the resulting accident. Perhaps totally demolished.

The amount of dynamic energy varies with the square of the speed, so obviously an accident at 35 MPH will result in much less damage than one at 70 or 75. The old tail-wheel pros I have talked to recommend the full-stall landing, which is precisely why I use it exclusively.

Scrub off every knot you can before you put her on the ground, then if things go to hell, all you'll have to worry about is a scraped wingtip and damaged pride.

As I taxi out on the narrow taxiway that parallels the Holbrook runway, the waist-high sagebrush rubs against the underside of the Queen's wingtips. This gently rolling desert is covered with the stuff—this summer the plants are green, healthy and big. An off-field landing in this brush would probably set the Queen or any other light plane over on its nose or back.

East of Holbrook the land loses a lot of its greenish tinge and becomes pink and beige. Somewhere here is the Petrified Forest. Today I can't spot the park highway even with the aid of the chart. Maybe if I circled, but I don't have time.

I'm going to Albuquerque and park the *Queen.* John Weisbart has arranged for a hangar and will send one of his employees, Scott Olsen, to meet me in my Cessna T-210. I'll spend a week or so in Colorado on business, do some writing, wash my underwear and jeans.

I'm supposed to call John from Gallup, New Mexico, 110 nautical miles west of Albuquerque, and he'll launch Scott to meet me. Yet there are thunderstorms building in western New Mexico. I can see them plainly now, dark clouds with high tops.

There's one just north of Gallup as I make my approach. The airport at Gallup consists of a single runway, 6-24, lying in a valley with ridges on both sides. Field elevation is 6,469 feet above sea level. Temperature about 90. The wind is gusting and shifting from the northwest at about 12 knots as I make my approach to runway 24. I expect trouble on final and am ready when the wind flops to almost 90 degrees cross. The landing isn't pretty but it's safe.

Standing on the top of the front seat trickling fuel into the tank, I can plainly see rain falling from that boomer to the north. Another storm is off to the southeast. Eastward seems clear enough, but for how long? I feel vaguely uneasy.

Inside the terminal the FAA has a Flight Service Station. One man is working there today. In a few minutes he gets to me. He tells me nothing I don't already know, but I listen carefully anyway. Isolated thunderstorms across western New Mexico moving south at ten knots, chance of thunderstorms with 35 knots of wind and reduced ceilings and visibility all afternoon at Albuquerque. Thirty-five knots? Uh-huh.

I call John in Boulder from a pay phone in the lobby. He'll launch Scott. "No hurry," I tell John. "Tell Scott there's thunderstorms around and to be careful."

Outside I pause to smoke my pipe, look at the sky, and study the wind sock. Sixty, seventy degrees of crosswind, about twelve knots. The thunderstorm north of town is noticeably closer. The wall of rain is only a few miles north.

Time to get the hell out of Dodge.

The Flight Service specialist doesn't answer my calls as I taxi out. I decide to skip the run-up and taxi straight onto the runway. There is a Cessna 152 in the pattern on the downwind.

I feed in throttle and rudder as I add power. Stick forward and right. The Queen accelerates slowly. The air is hot and thin.

Come on, baby!

As the tail rises the wind increases dramatically and shifts farther right, toward the north. Uh-oh! The adrenaline smacks me.

Fifty MPH. Fifty-five.

I can feel the wind trying to shove the Queen sideways. I have left rudder crammed in and the stick almost full right.

Sixty!

The stick is full right when the left main wheel comes off. Only the right main is on the ground.

Sixty-five!

I ease in back stick and the right main breaks loose. The plane immediately goes sideways toward the left edge of the runway. This I counter by a gentle turn to the right—ten degrees, fifteen, twenty.

She's climbing slowly, very slowly. There's a hundred feet ... two hundred. The altimeter reads 6,700 feet. I have the Queen at 70 MPH and she's sluggish, doesn't want to accelerate or climb faster than this snail's pace. But she is going up.

The heart rate begins to slow. Made it!

If I turn south the wind climbing that ridge should give me a lift upward. I'll try it.

Gingerly I lower the left wing and keep the ball centered with rudder. The nose tracks around and I can see the ground begin to pass beneath faster as the wind starts to push. I keep the needle on the airspeed indicator right at 70.

The ridge is coming toward me, now dead ahead. Altitude 6,800. But the needle on the altimeter is *motionless*.

She's not climbing!

God! The air is descending here, not ascending! She's climbing, but only as fast as the air is going down!

The ridge ahead is getting closer. The combined velocity of

the moving air and the plane drives her at that ridge at a sickening rate.

She's still not climbing! Maybe 150 feet above the ground now. Why, oh, why did I ever leave that valley? Coonts, you are a fool. A crash here would serve you right. You've earned it.

Now the needle moves. Up 50 feet . . . now 100.

If I can't clear the ridge I'll chop the mixture and stall her in, minimize the damage.

But she's climbing. Agonizingly slow. Now 6,900 feet, now 7,000.

I decide to risk a turn to the east. If I can stop her progress southward I've saved this situation. Why didn't I think of that thirty seconds ago?

Now 7,100 feet. Wings level heading east. The land slowly falls away as the *Cannibal Queen* claws for the sky.

Now I am aware of the radio. The 152 is waving off. Too much crosswind. He asks the Flight Service specialist what the wind is.

"Ninety degrees off, eighteen gusting to twenty-one knots."

Mother of God! Twenty-one knots of crosswind! And I took off in that!

Still shaking, I fly eastward climbing slowly as the 152 pilot talks to the FAA man about the wind. Now it's out of the north, coming right out of that solid wall of rain and black cloud. The Cessna pilot decides to try an approach to runway 6.

I don't want to listen. I turn off the radio and meditate on the fortune that sometimes saves fools, sometimes destroys them.

Ten miles east I look back over my left shoulder. The storm is now over Gallup, the leading edge over the field. Behind the storm is clear sky. If I had just waited an hour, it would have passed completely.

I-40 takes me to Albuquerque. A desert storm looms over Mount Taylor north of my track and a couple darken the high ground to the south, but over the highway I have a relatively smooth ride. And Albuquerque is clear, with only a high scattered layer.

The man in the tower is advising airliners of wind shears east and west of the field as I make a sedate straight-in approach to runway 3, but he informs me that all is calm to the southwest.

"Thank heavens," I tell him.

There is only a little burble near the ground. The Queen settles onto her wheels thankfully. Or perhaps she is thanking whoever it is that has just delivered another sinner from the consequences of his folly.

25

THE AIRLINER DESCENDED THROUGH PUFFY CLOUDS INTO ALBU-
querque. Everyone aboard, including me, was reading newspaper accounts of the coup in the Soviet Union, but I lowered
my paper to look out the window and check the clouds. I
parked the *Cannibal Queen* in the hangar at Cutter Flying Service nine days ago and now I'm coming back to fly her. Gorbachev deposed, the Soviet Union on the brink of civil war, the
stock market down 95 points at 9 A.M., and I'm going flying in
an antique biplane.

The talking heads on television at the airport cafe in Denver
made me feel superfluous and gave this trip an air of unreality.
The black type of the newspaper congealed the mixture to guilt.
Maybe I should be at my office with the television on, sweating
World War III along with everyone else.

Newspapers and news broadcasts have an edge to them. That
harsh reminder of the real world is what we go on vacation to
escape, at least for a little while.

I tucked the newspaper and my guilt into the pocket of the
seat in front of me and left it there when I got off the plane.

After the line boy helped me roll the *Queen* into the sunlight
and fuel her, I had a major decision to make. Should I go east

through the mountain passes or south down the Rio Grande valley to El Paso, then east around the southern end of the mountains?

Decisions, decisions. I stood on the ramp and looked east. The cumulus clouds drifting eastward might not obscure the passes, but they would spawn thunderstorms that would be hard to circumnavigate in that rough country. South it is.

A gent named Steve Jones was carefully inspecting the Queen when I returned from settling the bill. We visited a moment and he told me he owned the blue and yellow Stearman I had seen in an open hangar on the trip over from the terminal.

"Been working on that plane for eighteen years. Haven't flown her yet. Was going to try it this morning but I had starter trouble. Seems like it's always one little thing after another."

Eighteen years! My God, he started on his plane in 1973.

"Got her in a basket from a guy in Phoenix. Been a hell of a job, but sooner or later I'll get the bugs worked out."

Eighteen years! If I were him I would have hired someone to haul the pile off to the dump years and years ago. Even if the pile were the *Cannibal Queen*. I don't have that kind of patience.

The *Queen*'s engine fired the instant I turned on the mags. She sprayed oily white smoke from her stack in a spectacular cloud. I leaned her all I dared but it still took a half minute before the white smoke ceased.

She's just glad to see me.

Mr. Jones waves good-bye and I hesitantly flap my hand as I let the *Queen* roll. Eighteen years! The man is not human.

Five minutes later she lifts off into the clear, high-desert air and I turn her south.

The ride south down the Rio Grande valley is bumpy, but not too much so. Cumulo puff-balls ride a couple thousand feet above me in a layer that runs all the way east to the mountain slopes. The valley floor is cultivated, irrigated with river water, but to the east and west lies arid rangeland good only for lean cattle with a camel or two somewhere in their bloodline. But the plains and mountains look unnaturally green this summer. The cattle must be loving it.

The sun coming through the gaps in the drifting clouds gives the land the look of pastels. No wonder several generations of artists have been enchanted by New Mexico. This place is enough to make Monet's knees quiver.

I encounter my first rainstorm as I approach Socorro. It is just west of town drifting east. I stay over the highway and get a spatter of drops for a few minutes, then I'm by.

Just north of Truth Or Consequences—that's a terrible name for a town. Only in America, Jack!—there's another one. This one has lightning ripping out the bottom and is in the middle of the valley. A restricted area lies just to the east, part of the White Sands Missile Range airspace, and I have no idea if it's hot or not. Still, I decide to try to squeeze between the storm and the restricted area.

As I approach, the monster continues to hurl thunderbolts at the ground. What one of those zillion-volt charges would do to the *Cannibal Queen* and her intrepid pilot is something to contemplate, so I contemplate it as I try to judge the speed of the storm eastward. On the leading edge, in front of the solid wall of rain and right above the route I will have to fly, is a nasty black, scalloped roll cloud. What if one of those lightning shots comes out of that?

I feel like a man racing a train to a railroad crossing. I'm getting closer, but is my 84 knots enough? Do I really want to find out? Is there hail in that malevolent brute?

I wheel the *Queen* on her right wing and fly straight west. Before I am abeam of the trailing western edge of the storm it closes off the sliver of airspace that I was going to fly through.

Lightning bolts continue to flay the earth as I pass behind the storm. And the ground over which it has passed is soaked, with standing water everywhere. The puddles seem to make an almost continuous sheet when viewed from my vantage point 2,000 feet overhead.

With the engine droning I fly on past the town and south down the valley. When you fly an airplane often or take a long flight, you learn how she reacts to every control input, every gust of air, you develop a feel for her. The *Queen* and I renew our relationship as the minutes pass and the country rolls by underneath.

The problems and concerns of the ground fade. Up here my world becomes the airplane, the instruments, the wind and sky. This is the charm that flying has always held for me. And once again it works—Soviet coups, bank balances, taxes, women, it all fades to insignificance as the Queen and I fly on through the summer sky.

The flying becomes the reality. I land only to fly on.

Perhaps it is escapism. Do I seek escape like the alcoholic or the hermit? The comparison seems unfair, and I am too much of an American male to wallow in self-analysis. The cockpit, the yellow wings, the way of an airplane in the sky are very pleasant, and that is enough.

The airport at Las Cruces is five miles west of the town, at 4,454 feet above the sea. Coming from the north you cross a hummock of high ground, with the highest peak at 5,890, to reach it. So you pull the throttle back and skim the tops of the bare ridges and voilà! there lies the airport on the plain.

The female on Unicom tells me the wind is calm, yet I am not surprised when I encounter seven or eight knots gusting from the southeast. Anything under ten knots is dead air to these folks out here in the desert. A Beech 99 airliner is circling for an approach as I turn final, so I clear the runway as soon as I can.

Inside the Southwest Aviation office the lady who owns the place comments on my nice plane, so I sit and we discuss old airplanes for a while. Then the weather. She says it has rained here or nearby for a few minutes every day since July 1. And it's unseasonably cool. What a summer!

A few more miles down the valley lies El Paso, at the very western tip of the Texas panhandle. Just across the Rio Grande lies Mexico.

I approach from the north at 7,500 feet and call El Paso Approach for a clearance through the ARSA, but the ridge just west of town is too high and he can't pick me up on radar. The controller tells me to call him again when I am over the race track. What track? Oh, there it is near the river, just a mile or two north of the Mexican border.

And then he picks up my IFF squawk and clears me through.

I turn east with the interstate and fly through the gap in the mountain that the river cut. I try to stay over the highway as I take my first good look at Juárez. The western side of Juárez consists of endless blocks of houses affixed to the eastern slope of the ridge I have just flown through. The streets are unpaved.

There are no traffic arteries, paved or unpaved. No trees. Not a one. Just hundreds of blocks of little houses on dirt streets baking in the sun.

In contrast, the suburbs of El Paso on the slopes north of the river have paved streets and lots of trees, and the houses are bigger, with driveways and occasionally swimming pools. Suburbanites cruise to and from their subdivisions on boulevards. Heaven forbid that they should have to waste time idling in a traffic jam.

Approach calls traffic, a jet airliner lifting off from El Paso International. I tally it, only to be told to avoid it.

Golly gee, mister, I'll sure as heck get out of the way if the crew of that jet plane is so foolish as to make a suicide run at this 84-knot Stearman, which will appear to them as a stationary yellow target. I'll do the only thing I can, which is roll the *Queen* on her back and pull her nose straight down.

I don't pop off to the controller, of course, but merely give him a respectful "Roger that."

The jet glides by well under me and turns westbound. I take no evasive action. But I am ready.

Just east of El Paso I hear Approach telling someone to watch for a Stearman eastbound climbing through 6,600 feet. Can't be me, of course, since I'm at 7,500. I think no more about it.

I-10 follows the valley of the Rio Grande for 50 miles southeast. The bottom of the valley on both sides of the river is covered with cultivated fields, but to the north and east lie gently rolling terrain and hills that rise to respectable little mountains, all of which this year are covered with green. But there are no trees. Even on the peaks, this country is normally too dry for trees.

To the southwest, across the river in the Mexican state of Chihuahua, one sees ranges of mountains separated by relatively flat country. And through the gap in the mountain chains, one sees a great sea of sand. Beyond the mountains and sand dunes are dry riverbeds, salt flats, arid hills and occasional villages. Normally that is one of the most inhospitable desert hells on this continent. It looks benign just now due to all the rain, but the sand sea is a giveaway.

Past Fort Hancock the highway turns east, and today two small thunderstorms stand sentinel. Following the highway I

283

go between them and across a low pass, then cross above the town of Sierra Blanca. This town is a monument to developers' hubris. Just east of the houses and paved streets is a huge section of dirt streets ready for development, a section bigger than the town of Sierra Blanca. It looks like a developer went crazy with borrowed money. Where the thousands of people will come from to buy lots and build homes in those sprawling subdivisions is a mystery, one that looks unsolvable from 7,500 feet on a Monday evening.

The divided highway and the occasional cluster of homes and gasoline stations every 30 miles are the only signs of life in this country. To my left I can see Guadalupe Peak at 8,749 feet, but beyond Guadalupe the sky is cloudy. To the right are more mountains and haze with a dark spot here and there. When one sees how empty this country is still, over a hundred years after the Indians were dispossessed, one wonders how a stone-age people survived here without horses or firearms or engines.

Imagine for a moment that you were here with your family on foot, and the highway and towns weren't. It's just you and your spouse and children finding water, finding food, finding shelter. The quest for these three necessities occupied your ancestors and your parents, will fill your life, and will fill the lives of your children and their children. These three things are all there are.

Most Americans can't imagine being in that situation. Yet just south of the Rio Grande are millions of people only one step removed from that.

I am thinking of survival when I survey the fuel sight-gauge and eye the chart. The towns—villages—are 30 miles or so apart, the airports more so. Ahead lies Van Horn with the Culberson County Airport and 80 miles beyond, the airport at Pecos. This empty land doesn't seem to be the place for a prudent man to try to stretch a tank of gas.

I call Van Horn on 122.8. No answer. My *Central States Flight Guide* is in the baggage compartment. Maybe the field is unattended. I call a second time.

After the third call I announce that I will overfly the field and look for the wind sock. Now someone answers. "Calling Van Horn, are you going to land?"

"Yes, if they have gas."

"They have it. A nice old lady runs the place."

I spot a column of smoke on the western edge of town trailing off to the northeast. "Looks like the wind is out of the southwest. I'll make a left downwind entry for the southwest runway."

"That's runway Two One," the man on the radio says. "I'm a mile behind you."

"You can go first if you want. I'm pretty slow."

"I'll follow you."

So I make the approach. Rolling out I look up and another biplane is crossing the field to the downwind. So that's who I was talking to.

I shut the *Queen* down by the fuel pump. One other plane is on the ramp. I am out of the cockpit in time to watch the biplane taxi in, and I recognize it. This plane is none other than the most-photographed Stearman in the world. The name on the side is that of its owner, airshow stunt pilot Earl Cherry.

When the engine dies I walk over. "You Earl Cherry?"

The sun-burned face grins at me. "No. I'm Bryan Regan. I work for Earl."

When he is out of the plane, we shake hands. "I followed you all the way from El Paso and couldn't catch you," he says. "I decided if you were landing here, I would too."

I am delighted. A beautiful day of flying topped off with an evening in the company of another gypsy of the sky—what a day!

Earl Cherry performed in an airshow at Naval Air Station Miramar in San Diego over the weekend, and Regan was flying the plane back to Lafayette, Louisiana, Cherry's home base. He started Sunday in Miramar and spent last night in Tucson. Today he caught up with the Jet Commander carrying Cherry and the rest of the entourage at El Paso and spent the afternoon helping repair an alternator. He told me all this as we fueled the planes and the FBO lady watched.

Her name was Rose Marie Budd. Rosebud. On her wall hung an autographed photo of Bryan at the controls of Cherry's Stearman, *General Smoke*. He'd been here before.

285

She proffered the keys to the courtesy car and we drove off for town trailing smoke, still talking and getting acquainted.

In his midthirties, Bryan Regan has one of the world's great flying jobs. He flies Cherry's Stearman to and from airshows and helps with the mechanical work. Ignoring the Red Baron Pizza pilots, who also give rides and airshow performances, Regan may be the only pilot in the nation being paid to fly a Stearman cross-country. Maybe the only one in the world.

Of course I was curious about *General Smoke.* The Pratt & Whitney R-985 500-HP engine burns 19 gallons per hour in cruise at 105 knots indicated, but to my surprise, the plane carries only a 46-gallon tank. "You get two hours and that's all you get," Bryan told me. "One time my first summer (this is his third season as a Stearman ferry pilot) I tried to stretch it. After I put in 45.1 gallons at the pump that time, I got religion. I even set it down on a road once, about thirty miles east of Van Horn, when the headwind got too bad. A truck driver gave me a ride to the crossroads filling station and helped me put enough gas in it to get to Van Horn."

Although the *General* is equipped with two VOR receivers and a Loran, it is not IFR capable. It lacks an artificial horizon indicator. The Loran is a new addition and is worth its weight in gold, Bryan felt. If my fuel situation were as critical as his, I would have to agree. Used for many years by ships to navigate at sea, Loran has only in the last ten years or so been married to a computer chip and adapted for use in airplanes.

"You know what IFR means, don't you?" Regan asked. "I follow roads."

We talked about landings. Bryan liked wheel landings when he first began flying the *General,* but now he is an advocate of the full-stall, three-point landing. This opinion jibed with my prejudices and I beamed complacently.

We finally got to bed around ten o'clock after discussing airshows and Cherry's female wingriders and the writer's life. I slept like a baby.

Tuesday we got an early start. After a 5 A.M. wake-up call and a careful look at the map on the Weather Channel, we ate breakfast in the same cafe where we'd had dinner, filled up

Rosebud's courtesy car and drove out to the airport. The morning was a cool 69 degrees here at 4,000 feet above sea level with not a cloud in the sky. Dew covered the *Cannibal Queen*.

We said our good-byes and Bryan fired up the *General* first. "I'll be here a little while yet," he informed me before he engaged the starter. "Takes a while to warm up eight gallons of oil."

And it did. While he was idling at the end of the runway, I said good-bye to Rosebud, finished my pipe, completed my preflight, and manned up. As I taxied out Bryan took the runway. He asked on the radio, "Steve, you ever been saluted by a Stearman?"

I confessed I hadn't.

As he rolled he toggled the *General*'s airshow smoke system. A cloud of white smoke poured from the exhaust and lingered in the morning air. Bryan used all those horses at his command to pull up in a sharp climbing left turn still trailing smoke. Heading eastbound he killed it.

"Thanks a lot," I told him, and meant it. As the *Queen* warmed up I watched *General Smoke* shrink to a dot. When the smoke had drifted clear of the runway I lined up the *Queen* and shoved the throttle forward. On the roll the water from the dew came pouring off the wings.

"Hey, Steve." Bryan from somewhere ahead. "I'm getting about ten knots of tailwind at five hundred feet." That's the value of a Loran.

I leveled off 500 feet above the ground and searched the sky ahead. Occasionally I got a glimpse of sun glinting off his top wing. The air was smooth and the green stubble on the land made it look hospitable. Below me trucks and cars poked along, but the *Cannibal Queen* navigated the azure at a blistering 100 MPH indicated. I waggled the stick to let her know how pleased with her I was. Two or three times Bryan and I exchanged words, just for company.

Thirty miles east of Van Horn, just past the filling station that Bryan once visited, the interstate split. I-10 continued straight east to Fort Stockton. I took I-20, the four-lane that headed northeast to Pecos and Odessa.

I was past Pecos when I heard Bryan call over Fort Stockton, but shortly afterward I had to switch frequencies. Good-bye, Bryan.

The largest collection of World War II airplanes in the world, over 150 of them, belongs to the Confederate Air Force. After a spirited competition between San Antonio and Midland-Odessa, the CAF decided to move from Harlingen, Texas, to Midland-Odessa. I dropped in to see how the move was coming and to squint at any odd treasures that might have arrived.

Alas, there was only one, a C-46, which was sitting out on the ramp. The manager of the Cutter Aviation FBO where I stopped, Chuck Davis, assured me that the C-46 was not a treasure.

"I got a couple thousand hours in a C-46, and believe me, it's one of the worst excuses for an airplane ever certified. The fuselage on the damn thing is too fat, so when you slow to landing speed the rudder and elevators become ineffective. So there you are, not landed yet and no longer flying, with no control. And it's too short-coupled. See how close together the main gear and tailwheel are. That's a great prescription for a groundloop in any kind of crosswind. The best anyone can manage in a C-46 is to arrive without crashing."

Chuck shook his head. "And the military back then was buying C-47s, real airplanes, as fast as they could get them. But there were never enough, so they flew the C-46s until the war was over, then got rid of the damned things. They were so cheap all the civilians bought them and flew them until they crashed or wore out, whichever occurred first. But they were always an abortion of an airplane."

Chuck was kind enough to take me over to the CAF's new office spaces for a look around. We met several people, including a gent and lady in their seventies accoutered in gray CAF jumpsuits covered with patches and pins. Both had colonel's eagles on their epaulets.

They had just driven down from Wichita, the man said. His name was Willard. He asked Chuck if he was a colonel, and Chuck said yes. So Willard shook hands with Chuck. Then he asked if I was a colonel, and I said no. So Willard didn't bother wasting a handshake on me and addressed all his remarks to Chuck.

"Yessir, they flew that C-46 here from Harlingen crammed full of people. Hadn't flown in four years, but they filled it up with people and flew it up here. I think they ought to have done some flying in it before they filled it up with folks. Four years is a long time."

Chuck agreed that four years is indeed a long time for an airplane to sit. Personally I didn't believe that the plane wasn't given a test flight before it was filled with passengers. Not being a colonel, I kept my opinion to myself.

"But they know what they're doing," Willard assured his fellow colonel. "Yessir. Me and the missus just came down to camp out and look around and get the feel of the place, y'know?"

After Willard and wife left, a lady gave us a tour of the offices. The folks that could have taken us into the hangars under renovation and construction were all at lunch, so we made do by stopping at one warehouse crammed to the eaves with World War II–vintage spare parts. That was only a small portion of the collection. They had a mountain of the stuff, they said, still waiting to be moved into two more warehouses the CAF had rented in the area.

Back in his office Chuck made some phone calls on my behalf. I had heard that a gentleman named Connie Edwards had a collection of airplanes at a private strip near Big Spring, and I wanted to stop in for a peek if I could wrangle an invite. Alas, Mr. Edwards was out of town for a couple days.

"Connie has a nice collection over there at his ranch," Chuck said. "Messerschmitt 108s and 109s, Spitfires, Hurricanes, P–51s, a lot of original, unrestored planes."

"I heard," I told him, "that these planes are just stacked in a hangar willy-nilly, lying on top of each other."

"Well, they let the air out of the tires of some so that they could overlap the wings, then the air went out of the tires of the others and they're resting on the first ones. Sure, there may be minor damage. But Connie's not running a museum. These are unrestored planes. They're dusty and dirty, all right, but nothing that soap and water couldn't cure. Then a competent mechanic could bring them back to airworthy status."

Chuck told me that Connie Edwards doesn't sell planes, but occasionally he'll trade a fighter for a Grumman amphibian,

289

which he also collects. He made a trade like that recently and the new owner of the fighter flew it to Chino for restoration.

He made another call, to the ranch belonging to Joe Mabee, and snagged me an invitation to visit. At 1:30 or 2 P.M.

"Joe Mabee is the colonel who heads the CAF board. There are colonels and there are colonels. He's sort of the colonel-general."

"What's out at his ranch?"

"You'll have to go look. I won't spoil the surprise."

So at 12:30 I said good-bye to Chuck and strapped into the *Cannibal Queen.* I might as well be a little early. Maybe the man who agreed to meet me, Tom Dollahite, would be early too.

He was standing on the ramp when I taxied up to Mabee's hangar on his private strip 20 miles north of Midland International. Along with him was a man named Ken Shugart, who I eventually figured out was a world-class aircraft restoration expert. Together they showed me the treasures of Joe Mabee's hangar.

I'll tell you about them in the order in which I saw them. Centered in the door was an AT-11 wearing two R-985 Pratt & Whitneys that didn't look that clean when they came new from the factory. Ken is restoring this aircraft, and when he is finished, it will be better than new. It will also, Tom told me, have an authentic cockpit. But the cabin will be pressurized and outfitted with a bar and comfy chairs, perfect for joyrides for people whose idea of aerial adventure is a Learjet.

Behind the AT-11 was a Hellcat fuselage without an engine. It's owned by the CAF and is awaiting its turn for Ken's attention. Joe Mabee agreed to foot the bill for the aircraft's total restoration. "There's only three Hellcats flying in the world," Ken told me. "This will be the fourth one."

He showed me the engine sitting on a stand. There he is bringing the exhaust and induction systems back to military specs. "They customized this thing and raced it at Reno, but it was uncompetitive. Probably would have performed better stock. Of course the CAF wants it stock."

In the adjoining hangar were completely restored aircraft, scrumptious delights that turned me green with envy. Standing there staring at those toys, I wished I were Joe Mabee.

The world's newest P-51, with just 30 flight hours on it, sat there gleaming in raw aluminum. They're still researching the paint scheme.

Not far away was probably the world's lowest-time Harvard, with a mere 1,300 hours on its airframe. Mabee bought it in Canada in its present, perfect, original condition for exactly $8,000. True, that was a few years back, but . . .

$8,000?

The plane has never been restored. It doesn't need it. I fought back the envy, but I confess, it got the better of me. If I were a Catholic I would have needed a priest right then.

There's just no justice in this world. No one calls me offering to sell like-new nifty airplanes for $8,000. No one! I'd buy them if they did. But nooo, they call guys like Joe Mabee. Is that fair or what?

I stood there staring at an immaculate P-40. What can I say? Robert Scott and Tex Hill should come look.

Parked in front of the P-40 was a T-34 from the shop of a former cop in Kansas who restored his first T-34 for fun, Tom said, and got so many appreciative comments he decided to try to make a living at it. He bought every T-34 airframe and all the spare parts he could find and went into the business. And he makes his own parts. I suspect all top-notch restoration experts have to.

In the back of the hangar was the finest Grumman Wildcat I ever laid eyes on. This one was restored by two machinists in Chicago who got her someplace and decided to make her restoration their life's work. The craftsmanship is sublime, equal to the best that any living soul could do.

And there was a replica Nakajima Type 97 Kate torpedo-bomber built from AT-6 and BT-13 fuselages for the filming of the movie *Tora! Tora! Tora!* This one is owned by Ken Shugart, who bought the pieces in Los Angeles and rebuilt it here. He paid $8,000 (there's that number again!) for the parts, which were spread all over Los Angeles in the homes of volunteers who were polishing them. The owners apparently realized the enormity of the project and sold the plane. The man who sold it to Ken had all the names and addresses on a Rolodex and spent two days phoning. All the parts didn't come in, but the major subassemblies did. Ken made the rest of the parts himself.

The resemblance between this replica and the real McCoy is only superficial. The real Kate had a wingspan of 51 feet and a fuselage 34 feet long. The big wing was necessary to carry a load of bombs or a Long Lance torpedo. The dimensions of the replica are reversed, with the fuselage much longer than the shortened wings. And instead of a double-row radial that develops 1,020 horsepower, the replica wears a single-row 600-HP mill. But she doesn't have to carry bombs or deck-run from an aircraft carrier.

Skipping the replica hoopla, this plane is a big, brand-new, one-of-a-kind, all-metal low-wing monoplane with retractable gear and a respectable radial engine. Not a bad prescription for a fun machine.

"She cruises at 185 miles per hour true," Ken said, "and is a real pussycat in the air. Impossible to stall. The stall is just a gentle mushing. She's an absolute delight to fly."

She's also expensive to fly and insure, so Ken is thinking about selling her. I didn't ask him the price. I just might be able to borrow or steal enough. And I don't even own a hangar to house her.

But wouldn't it be a kick? Fly to airshows in a replica Nakajima Kate, maybe work up an act with some guy who owns a P-40 and stage mock dogfights. The cockpit holds a pilot and two passengers seated all in a row, so I could take two girl-friends along. Imagine pulling up to gas pumps around the country with that big rising sun emblazoned on the fuselage!

Perhaps I could get a Colorado Mazda car dealer to sponsor me, buy me some gas if I put his logo on the wings and flew over his dealership on sale days. Imagine the ads on TV, with me and the dealer all decked out as kamikaze pilots and sitting in the Kate, which the announcer could lie and call a Zero. We could recruit a bunch of hot women and drape them on the wings wearing bikinis. Thong bikinis. We could . . .

Naw!

Tom Dollahite led me over to the last hangar to see the latest acquisition, a Grumman Avenger. She sat at the back of the hangar with her wings folded and her bomb bay door open.

This is a huge plane, with a giant four-bladed prop. God Almighty, she's big! On the other side of the hangar on a dolly sat the upper turret.

"Joe has a rather novel approach to buying aircraft," Tom said. "He buys them FOB the ranch, so the seller has to get it here to get paid. Avoids a lot of problems for us."

"The seller flew this thing here?"

"Yep."

We climbed up and peered into the cockpit.

I could fly this plane! Honest. If George Bush could do it, I sure as hell can. I could get that big prop spinning and taxi her out and feed in the throttle and rudder and—

"She flies like a big Piper Cub," Tom said.

Ah me. . . . Why couldn't I have been rich?

I almost asked Tom what it will cost to restore this Avenger, but I didn't. If you have to ask. . . . No sense dreaming.

I thanked Tom and Ken for their time and strapped on the Queen. I took off to the south, right over the hangars full of fighters. But they weren't flying. The *Cannibal Queen* was.

On my way east to Sweetwater I got to thinking about the Confederate Air Force. Founded in 1957 by five ex–fighter pilots who had just pooled their resources and acquired a military-surplus P-51 Mustang for $2,500, the CAF has grown exponentially to over 150 aircraft and 8,000 members who donate money, labor and expertise to keep the warbirds flying.

Many of the members, I suspect, are World War II veterans of advancing years, like Willard from Wichita in his natty gray jumpsuit. These people donate millions of dollars and spend uncounted hours washing, fixing, polishing and so forth. A large number of them do it, I suspect, to recapture a bit of the sparkle from the golden days of their youth, when they were young and a part of the greatest conglomeration of national power ever assembled on the planet.

What will happen to the CAF when these veterans pass from the scene, as will inevitably happen in the next few years? Can the CAF find enough members who will donate enough money and labor without the nostalgia impetus? I don't know.

Joe Mabee and the other colonel-generals will have their hands full in the next few years keeping this organization going.

I suspect that as the years go by more and more of these planes will have to be retired to permanent static-display status as money and manpower dry up.

In Sweetwater the FBO had a Texas magazine lying on the table. The cover touted a story inside listing the hundred richest Texans. You needed net assets of $130 million to get on the list. I looked to see if Connie Edwards or Joe Mabee made it. Nope. Probably squandered their piles on airplanes.

Just like me.

But then, I wouldn't have made a list of the ten thousand richest Texans, even if I lived here and didn't own anything with an engine except a motorcycle.

26

M<small>Y WAKE-UP CALL CAME AT 5:30, BEFORE DAWN. S</small>WEETWATER, Texas, is on the western edge of the Central Time Zone, so the sun rises late here. It's up but hidden by clouds on the eastern horizon when I complete my preflight and strap into the *Queen*. I'm going to do some flying today, a lot I hope, and go all the way to Savannah, Tennessee, 80 miles east of Memphis. If the weather cooperates.

Avenger Field in Sweetwater lies 2,385 feet above sea level. Built in 1929, during World War II this field was home to the WASPs, women pilots who ferried fighters and bombers around the country for the military. Today it's home to Bob Sears Airshows, an outfit that puts on aerial acts at airshows à la Earl Cherry.

But this morning I am the only person moving at the airport. The shabby old Beech 18 that was dripping oil beside the gas pump when I landed last night is gone. Only the stains on the asphalt remain. The owner and pilot of that antique was lying on his back under the airplane when we talked. He was a college instructor in Hawaii and had owned the twin-Beech for three years. He worked on it all summer and was trying to get the FAA to sign it off for a flight across the Pacific to Hawaii.

295

He installed racks of 55-gallon drums in the cabin and plumbed them to deliver extra fuel, and he rigged up a system to oil the engines in flight.

I stood there staring at the Beech. It badly needed the attention of someone like Ken Shugart. I thanked my stars that I wasn't going to fly across 2,300 nautical miles of open ocean in this clapped-out twin-engine prop, one that cruised at 150 knots indicated and had no autopilot.

"What are you going to do with it when you get it to Hawaii?" I asked.

"Haul skydivers."

"Uh-huh."

"Had our problems getting started. An aux fuel tank ruptured yesterday when we climbed to eighty-five hundred feet for a test. Sand daubers had plugged up the vent line. Found the rupture this morning when we tried to fill the tank and it ran out all over." He gestured to the great stain on the asphalt and sighed. "I'll put in one more drum and go without the aux tank. If I can just get the FAA to sign off the fuel mods. I keep telling them I can just disconnect the lines and call the drums cargo, but they may want to inspect the whole rig. I been talking to them all day."

"Long way to Hawaii."

"Oh, we'll make it. Got to be there Monday when classes start."

That was yesterday afternoon. Now he's gone. Maybe up to Lubbock to have the FAA inspect the plane, or on to San Diego.

This morning the temperature is in the low 70s and my leather jacket feels good, but yesterday evening when I landed the temperature was 101 degrees. I am gradually coming down off the spine of the continent as I go east. So the temperature and humidity increase as I descend.

There is a stiff southwest wind blowing about 12 to 15 knots, but one of the runways points dead into it. I taxi out thinking about college teachers flying worn-out twin-Beeches across the ocean.

Sand daubers!

With no wind he will need a minimum of 16 hours to make the hop. Allowing for adverse winds and a little reserve, he should have fuel for 20 hours. Two Pratt & Whitney R-985s at

20 gallons an hour each—absolute minimum—40 times 20. He needs 800 gallons of fuel, and God only knows how much oil. That's 4,800 pounds of fuel alone.

If he loses an engine before he burns off part of that load, he's history. Or if his homemade plumbing rig springs a leak, or the plane fills with fumes, or the oil filler system craps out.

I line up the *Cannibal Queen* with the runway and run up the engine. The prop cycles properly and the mags check out. Trim set. Controls free. Okay, here we go. Throttle forward and feed in right rudder, now a touch of left. Tail up . . . and almost . . . yes, she's flying.

But the college instructor and his twin-Beech—that's what aviation is all about, isn't it? If he wants to risk his life flying an old airplane across the Pacific so that he can earn a few dollars hauling skydivers aloft, who are we to say that is foolish? Who are we to deny him permission to go? It's his life and his plane. After all, Lindbergh made it and he didn't have an FAA inspector sign off his fuel system.

I level at 3,500 feet and pull the power back. Soon I have stabilized at 97 MPH at 2,000 RPM and 21.5 inches. That is very good! And I have a crisp quartering tailwind out of the southwest and smooth air. My cup is full.

Thank God I need no one's permission to fly. If I kill myself the world will keep on turning. They'll have a memorial service, the lawyers will divide my worldly possessions, such as they are, and the people who care about me will miss me. That's all any of us ever get. And it will happen for every one of us sooner or later no matter how the cards fall. If I crash the only real effect on the cosmos will be the loss of one irreplaceable Stearman, but this rock will keep spinning on its axis and the sun will rise tomorrow, as usual.

In the meantime . . .

East of Abilene the land below is dotted with ponds and little lakes, all full. A cool, wet summer . . . I suspect this coming winter will be a real dilly. That Philippine volcano blew a lot of dust into the atmosphere and the sunsets have been spectacular lately. That dust should have a cooling effect.

There are clouds ahead, a high layer. By the time I cross Eastland and strike off east-southeast away from the highway shafts of sunlight are illumining the haze underneath. The air here is moist. Already the land is a thousand feet lower than it was in Sweetwater.

The land has trees on it now in woodlots and odd abandoned places. Over Stephenville I decide the sunlight shafts look like the pillars of heaven, and I scrawl that phrase on the chart. But soon the pillars disappear as the sky above solidifies. It's gloomy to the northeast toward Dallas–Fort Worth. I came south to avoid the TCA, that sprawling toadstool of controlled airspace, and now I can see I avoided bad weather. Well, the forecast was for showers and isolated thunderstorms today in east Texas, which was one reason I started so early.

I once spent four months in Texas, May through August 1969. I was a flight student at Naval Air Station Kingsville flying F-9 Cougars, midfifties-vintage swept-wing jet fighters. The engines had centrifugal compressors instead of axial ones so they were nothing to brag about even before the Navy de-rated them, taking a percent or two RPM off the top end, to make them last. And the final indignity, the Navy painted the fighters white and red to minimize the possibility of midair collisions. Still, they were jet fighters, some of them single-seat. For most of us these were the only single-seat jet fighters we would ever be fortunate enough to get our grubby hands on.

Looking back you can see how crazy it was: Uncle Sam provided hundreds of twenty-three-year-old boy-men just out of college with real, genuine, honest-to-God jet fighters armed with four 20-mm cannons and real bullets and ordered them to fly these machines all over south Texas and have the time of their lives. And picked up the tab for everything. And paid these kids for doing it.

The coin had a slimy side, of course—there was a truly shitty little war going on in Southeast Asia and later on we would be expected to go do our bit to win the thing for our side. You may remember that one—we lost it. The war killed some of these kids and cost others, the ones shot down and imprisoned as POWs, a price higher than any human should have to pay.

All that lay in a hazy future during my F-9 Texas summer.

I remember the heat. We manned airplanes baking on the concrete in the south Texas sun and humidity and almost melted before we got into the air. The planes had to be coaxed off the runway—climb-outs were long, leisurely affairs. The air conditioning in the cockpit merely delayed the onset of heat exhaustion. But the flying! Strafing with real ammo, air-to-air gunnery, dropping bombs, dogfighting, carrier qualifying, formation, low-level navigation, aerobatics—the flying was as good as flying can be.

Everyone said an F-9 would not go supersonic. I had to try. I climbed to about 30,000 feet and with the throttle cobbed, rolled her on her back and pointed the nose straight down. She smacked into the Mach buffet and would not cut through it. At 10,000 feet I glumly retarded the throttle and pulled out. For once everyone was right.

In Vietnam I missed those F-9s with their four 20-mm cannons in the nose. At night we would fly our A-6s at 400 feet over the Red River delta of North Vietnam and attack targets we located by radar. The North Vietnamese liked to line up antiaircraft guns along roads and dikes and open fire when they heard the sound of our engines. As the muzzle-flashes strobed and the tracers poured skyward, I wished the A-6 had a couple of those 20s. If we had been able to occasionally lower the nose and put a burst or two into an antiaircraft gun position, we might have had a lot less flak to fly through. Maybe fewer guys killed. Alas, guns were too low-tech for the A-6.

And maybe that's good. If A-6s had had guns, I was young enough and foolish enough to have tried to duel the guns at night at 400 feet over the delta. I wanted to. The gunners were trying to kill me and I desperately wanted to kill them.

That's what you remember most vividly about war—that urge to kill.

Vietnam was long ago. So was my F-9 summer. Back when I was very young.

On days off I drove around, visited little Texas towns like Beeville, Alice, Uvalde.... Small towns in Texas are like oysters, you either develop a taste for them or you don't. I liked them. I liked the shady streets and the old cars and the soda-pop machines with glass bottles and the girls with the go-to-hell looks. It's still there—all of it. Texas is still Texas.

Passing Lake Whitney today the land below confuses me. Throughout the Midwest and Great Plains the land is surveyed into east-west, north-south tracts. Here the boundaries run

299

about 240-060 magnetic. All the cultivated fields and fences and farm roads are skewed 30 degrees. Flying by the compass, it's disconcerting to look out and see the land out of kilter. Wonder why they did that?

Two hours after leaving Sweetwater I see Corsicana, Texas, looming ahead. I locate the field without difficulty and announce that I am making a straight-in to runway 16. The wind is out of the west, about 90 degrees cross, at about 12. I look at the chart and double-check the field elevation. Yep, only 448 feet.

The Unicom freq, 122.8, is relatively busy with people announcing their location in the pattern and the runways they are going to use, but it seems few of them ever state what airport they are at. There are only three or four Unicom freqs, so in congested areas it is not uncommon to hear traffic from five or six airports on one frequency. Some of these pilots remember to state the airport but they mumble it, and the Queen's radio is not very good.

On final I spot a twin about to take off in the opposite direction on the runway I am landing on. He announces with disgust in his voice that he will hold for the Stearman. Sorry, Jack, but if you had said you were at Corsicana, I would have gladly gotten out of your way. Now you can wait for this kite to float in.

Ray Rodgers runs the FBO at Corsicana. A tall, lean Texan, he plunks his feet on his desk and sighs as he looks out the window at the Queen sitting by the pump.

"God, I learned to fly in one of those things," he said with a wistful look on his face. "It was out at Charlie Wyche's ranch. I was friends with his son. We got to flying Charlie's brand-new Taylorcraft and he about had a fit. We hadn't taken any lessons or anything and it was all illegal, but Charlie didn't care about that. He was upset because he had paid $1,875 for that Taylorcraft and he didn't want it wrecked. So he said if we wanted to fly, to go fly one of those $75 Stearmans. So we did. Taught ourselves to fly it."

"Seventy-five bucks?"

"Yep. He went over to Pyote and bid on a lot of Stearmans. Got 250 of them for $75 each. They hauled in planes from all over and auctioned them off there at Pyote. Now Charlie brought those Stearmans back to his ranch and took the engines off and stored them in a barn. He stored the wings in another barn and stacked the fuselages on their noses down the fence rows. He bought 'em on speculation. Figured all the fliers returning from the war would buy 'em. So me and his boy had our very own $75 Stearman and we flew it all over Charlie's ranch that summer."

"How old were you then?"

"Sixteen. I was sixteen. Of course, nowadays nobody in his right mind would let a sixteen-year-old kid fly a Stearman. Worth too much." He sighed again and glanced out the window at the *Cannibal Queen*.

"Whatever happened to all those planes?"

"Well, Charlie finally sold the fuselages and wings to some outfit up in Tulsa. They were making dusters out of 'em. They didn't want the engines but Charlie made them take 'em. He didn't want the engines either."

By the time I reach Tyler at least half the land below is covered by trees. East of Shreveport the land is all trees, with only here and there a pasture, roads like ribbons, towns hidden by the trees on their streets.

East of Shreveport I encounter my first clouds at 3,500 feet, so I descend to 1,500. Visibility is ten to twelve miles, a clear day in this part of the world.

Descending into Ruston, Louisiana, 30 miles west of Monroe, I get my first good whiff of the sticky-sweet odor from the pulp mills. Welcome back to the South!

Ruston only has one north-south runway with a parallel taxiway on the eastern side of it, but coming in I keep hearing people talking on Unicom about runway 34 Right and 34 Left. As I make the left downwind I am searching without success for the second runway.

Have I got the right town? Appears so. The right airport? Well, this one is where the map says Ruston's airport is and it has just the one runway depicted on the sectional chart. So what the devil is this right and left stuff?

On the ground I find out when a Cessna comes floating in and lands on the taxiway. *That's 34 Right, fella!*

301

Airborne again, I level the Queen at 1,500 feet and head northeast for Arkansas. My route takes me northwest of Monroe, across Bayou D'Arbonne and the town of Farmerville. (Yes, Farmerville! And no, I have no idea what possessed these people to name it that. Maybe there was a banker or merchant named Guido McGillicuddy Farmer that they wanted to honor. Maybe they were tired of farmer and salesmen jokes. Good Lord, who can say?) Somewhere past Farmerville I cross the route that David and I used in June to get to Monroe.

But the clouds are coming down. Now they're just above my head. Visibility still pretty good though.

But I am descending to stay out of the clouds. I'm flying a compass course, 040, and the way ahead looks gloomy. Oh well, the tank is full of gasoline—why not give it a try?

The land below me is swamp with large trees growing here and there. Looks like miserable country for a forced landing, but the worst of it is that there are no landmarks or highways.

When I pass over a river I look left and can make out a lake to the northwest. Good. That's the reservoir at Felsenthal. I'm on course for Crossett. But I'm down to 500 feet. Visibility down to two or three miles. Where in the heck is this town? If I miss it by much I'll never see it.

But I hit it dead on. The first thing I see is a road leading north. I follow that until I catch sight of the pulp mill. Whew, that smell! But the land looks firm enough under all those trees. I seem to have cleared the swamp.

But is this Crossett? And how low does this fog go? Should I turn around?

There's an airport just east of here. I'll land there and call Flight Service. That's a good plan. I turn and follow the highway leading true east. Minutes pass. It's misting rain and the stuff collects and flows along the windscreens.

But the airport isn't there!

Either I'm on the wrong road or that town wasn't Crossett. It might have been Hamburg, ten miles away. But I was on course. Or was I?

When I hit a decently wide two-lane highway running north and south, I swing the Queen north. Wrong choice. The fog ahead goes all the way to the ground. I lower the left wing to turn her and glance out the right side—at absolutely nothing.

302

Momentarily disoriented, I look left. The ground is still there, but I'm too high. I drop her some and roll out heading south. I'm going to fly south out of this stuff.

Just south of the Arkansas line the clouds lift. I am back at a thousand feet when I sight the town of Bastrop. If it is Bastrop. It should be, but what if it isn't?

I fly around the water tower of the pulp mill and look for a name. A forest products company! Whatever happened to civic pride?

But there's an airport where Bastrop's is depicted. Okay. I give them a call.

No answer. Terrific! But they have the name of the town painted on the runway. "Bastrop." If I ever manage an airport, I'm going to do that.

I fly over and can't find the wind sock. When it goes bad, it all goes bad. I set up for the northern runway, 34, just like at Ruston. On final I have the power at idle and I'm floating. The wind's behind me.

I go around and come in on runway 16. The wind is out of the south. Tiny crosswind.

The line boy motions me over to a pump on the side of the mat. "We're about out of gas," he tells me. "The truck is supposed to be here this afternoon but he hasn't showed up yet."

"Got any left?"

"Maybe a little."

"Well, let's put it in and see if it's enough."

We drain the tank into the Queen. She could hold another gallon or two, but that'll do.

I go inside and call Flight Service.

"Go east," the man on the phone says. "You won't have any problems. Scattered showers maybe, but the ceiling at Greenville, Mississippi, is fourteen thousand feet. Ten thousand at Greenwood. Memphis has scattered showers around, ceiling at ten. Should be okay."

"I had a little trouble flying through Arkansas."

"Yeah, well, they've had rain and fog this afternoon. That stuff is moving southeast at ten knots. Shouldn't be a factor."

It isn't. I cross the Mississippi River at 1,500 feet just north of Lake Providence and angle a little north of Rolling Fork. Then I point more north and fly across Belzoni. A rain shower dampens the Queen but the clouds are high, at least 10,000 feet. Below is the Mississippi bottomland, flat as a pancake and intensely cultivated, cut up by meandering rivers that occasionally looped back on themselves and made crescent lakes. Spotted here and there are ponds in series, catfish farms.

I land at Greenwood, Mississippi, because they have a Flight Service Station on the field and I want a look at the prognosis charts. Before I can shut down the man in the nonfederal tower asks, "We have a new man here in the tower. You have time to give him a ride?"

The request is unexpected. I'm tired and it's after 5 P.M., and I do want to get to Savannah tonight. But what the hell is the rush? Why not? Wasn't fun the object of this whole trip? "Send him out."

His name is Ed Pitcock. "It's like cockpit," he informs me, "but reversed."

"You ever been up in an open cockpit plane, Ed?"

"No."

"This'll be the most fun you ever had with your clothes on. We won't do any aerobatics, just fly around a little and give you a taste of it."

And that is what we do. Gentle turns and pirouettes in the afternoon sky. I let Ed fly some. He experiments while I sit back and relax. I've been in this seat almost eight hours already today, but having someone up front who has never seen it makes it all fresh and beautiful.

The air is dead calm. I set the power and let the Queen descend at exactly 80 MPH. The flare works out perfectly and we squeak on all three wheels.

Amen!

Savannah, Tennessee, is not on the Mississippi bottomland. It's on the drainage of the Tennessee River, a heavily wooded area of low, rolling hills. Nearby is the Shiloh battlefield, which I have come to visit.

I arrive just as the sun is setting. No one answers on Unicom. No doubt they've locked up for the night. I fly over the runway and look for the wind sock. Looks like a light breeze out of the northwest.

I swing out for a left downwind and set the power at twelve

inches. The air is so smooth that the Queen comes around the turn like she was on rails, which I confess delights me. After 9.4 hours of flying today, I want one more good landing and then I will be content.

The saint in charge of landings happens to be a former U.S. naval aviator named Roger Ball. He smacked the back end of the ship one bad Navy night and ended up in the spud locker, but they saved his bones and a couple miracles are attributed to them. So he got promoted to saint. That's why every U.S. Navy landing Signal Officer says "Roger Ball" when you tell him who you are and how much fuel you have. He's really praying.

Tonight Saint Roger grants my wish. He gives me a bona fide greaser.

A Cessna Citation, a twin-engine business jet, sat on the ramp in front of the FBO. The crew watched me taxi in and maneuver myself into a tiedown spot. When I came strolling over they assured me the place was indeed locked up tighter than John Sununu's hatband.

"Watched you come in," one of them told me. "Boy, that Stearman was pretty against the dark sky with the last rays of the sun on it."

"She's a good ol' gal."

They broke out the catered food that their client today didn't eat and beer all around. We ate it using the Citation's wing as a table. Stale ham-and-cheese sandwiches and potato chips. I've never eaten better.

And they gave me news. (A) Savannah didn't have a taxi service. (B) Every motel in town was full. (C) The coup in the Soviet Union was over. Gorby's back.

"Over?"

"Yeah. They say they caught some of those commie clowns on the way to the airport. Guess they were taking the first flight to Mexico. One of them shot himself."

How about that!

Their names were Bill Greenwald and Chuck Davis. We got acquainted over beer as the twilight faded to darkness. They've read my books. They're truly great guys.

And they called their office in Columbus, Ohio, and the duty dog there got them rooms at the Pickwick Inn, a hotel run by the State of Tennessee at the Pickwick Dam 15 miles south of town. The inn sent a van. Bill and Chuck invited me to ride along.

When we got there the Pickwick had an extra room for me.

The morning papers were full of the collapse of the attempted coup in the Soviet Union. In a twist straight from a fairy tale, freedom and democracy triumphed over the forces of darkness, forces led by the most inept group of would-be dictators that has ranted and postured on the world stage in many a year.

Communism is as dead as Vladimir Lenin. Like him, it will probably be mummified and displayed in a Moscow mausoleum as a reminder of the bad old days. Lenin they'll probably just bury. He richly deserves it.

So today around the globe people are euphoric. The stock market's up, nuclear war looks more and more inconceivable, the human race's chances of surviving on this lonely pebble in space look better and better.

Of course, the bloom will soon be off the rose as people in Eastern Europe and the Soviet Union come to realize that democracy is no panacea, that free elections don't create jobs, food, housing, clothing or meaningful lives. All democracy does is place power in the hands of people who are accountable. Those with power can still misuse it, still make grievous errors. Democracy is a thing worth dying for, but I don't think that the people of the Soviet Union yet realize it. For them, now, democracy is simply the promise of a better life.

After reading the paper this morning I rented a car and drove out to the Shiloh National Military Park, which is run by the National Park Service. This was my first visit to Shiloh, long delayed and long anticipated.

Perhaps I should fill you in on the battle that was fought around the little log Shiloh Church above Pittsburg Landing on April 6 and 7, 1862. Forty thousand Union troops under Major General U. S. Grant had ascended the Tennessee River and disembarked at Pittsburg Landing on the west side of the river. They were awaiting the arrival of an additional 25,000 men under Major General Don Carlos Buell, and when assembled, would march the 24 miles southwest to Corinth, Mississippi, where 44,000 Confederate soldiers under General P. G. T. Beauregard were guarding the railroad junction of the Memphis & Charleston and the Mobile & Ohio. Beauregard knew Grant's army was coming, so he suggested to his superior officer, Albert Sidney Johnston, that the Confederates march to Pittsburg Landing and smite the Yankees before the entire Federal host assembled.

General Johnston came to Corinth, looked the situation over, and concluded Beauregard's advice was sound. Indeed, it was the only course open to the Confederate defenders. Outnumbered and ill-equipped, the Confederates were doomed if they waited for the Federals to assemble and march to Corinth for an assault.

For the first and only time in his military career, U. S. Grant was caught by a surprise attack. He had underestimated his opponent. That was a mistake he would never repeat.

After a sloppy march and a two-day delay in front of the Federal army that Beauregard thought must now be on full alert, the Confederates hit the Yankees with a clumsy attack just before dawn on Sunday, April 6. The soldiers on both sides were green as grass, but while they lacked experience they had ardor aplenty. The Confederates hit hard, repeatedly, driven by Johnston, Beauregard and Braxton Bragg, three of the most determined warriors who ever fought on this continent.

They came oh so close, but in the end they just didn't have enough to deliver the knockout punch. And the Confederates hadn't counted on the steel in Ulysses S. Grant. Some of his officers counseled retreat that Sunday night. According to Bruce Catton, Grant snapped, "Retreat? No. I propose to attack at daylight and whip them."

Catton added that William T. Sherman found Grant standing under a tree in the rain late that night—his headquarters had been converted into a hospital—and said, "Well, Grant, we've had the devil's own day, haven't we?"

"Yes," Grant said, and puffed on his cigar. "Yes. Lick 'em tomorrow, though."

That night the remainder of Buell's men arrived. Deducting the previous day's casualties, Grant's army now numbered 55,000. The next day Grant drove them forward and recaptured

the ground he had lost. Fought out, with Albert Sidney Johnston dead and 15,000 other men dead, wounded or missing,
the Confederates retreated to Corinth Monday night. Grant tried
to follow, but he had no cavalry and his troops were fought out
too.

The Federals had 3,500 men killed and another 6,600
wounded. In addition, the Confederates captured about 2,500
Union soldiers. At the time this was the bloodiest battle ever
fought on this continent and the long casualty lists stunned
people north and south who had thought this would be a short,
easy war.

Amazingly, the battle was fought by raw troops, some of
whom had never even fired their muskets before. Some of the
inexperienced volunteers cut and ran at the first volley, but
most dug in their heels and fought savagely. A lot of them
fought to the death.

The irony of the battle was the aftermath, which presented
the Union with a golden opportunity. With the whipped Confederate Army camped at Corinth, the more numerous Federals
could have bagged the whole lot if they had moved fast and
decisively. The entire Confederate military situation in the west
had come unhinged.

To his credit, U. S. Grant saw this opportunity and wanted
to seize it with both hands. But it was not to be. His superior
officer, Major General Henry Wager Halleck, came to Pittsburg
Landing on April 11 and took personal command. Halleck frit-
tered away three weeks waiting for reinforcements. When he
had gathered his host, 128,000 fighting men, he dug his way to
Corinth, entrenching every step of the way. It took him a month
to move his army 24 miles. Beauregard burned the military
supplies he couldn't carry and marched away before Halleck
arrived, seven weeks after the Battle of Shiloh.

Yet the opportunity still existed! With this vast army the
Federals could have marched anywhere on the continent and
the Confederates could have done nothing about it. The Union
Army could have smashed New Orleans, sacked Mobile, burned
Vicksburg. Even better, they could have chased and cornered
and gutted Beauregard's army, the only Confederate army west
of the Alleghenies. But Halleck wanted territory. This military
genius divided up his forces and garrisoned every hamlet on

the railroad, which gave the Confederates invaluable time and allowed the Civil War to drag on for three more years, consuming half a million lives. The obscene, bloody infernos of Fredericksburg, Gettysburg, Stone's River, Chickamauga, and the Wilderness all lay in the future.

Frustrated, Grant almost quit the Army. Fortunately William T. Sherman talked him out of it.

We today are lucky that the war didn't end in the summer of 1862. In the furnace of war Abraham Lincoln converted a war to suppress a rebellion into a social revolution, freed the slaves, and forced the nation onto the road that would lead, in the fullness of time, to a multiracial society with the rights of every citizen guaranteed by a supreme federal government. It took years of gunfire and rivers of blood to accomplish those miracles.

The Shiloh battlefield today is a park full of stately oaks and well-paved drives, with little monuments and markers and old cannons scattered everywhere. Armed with a map of the battlefield you drive around and stop at each numbered marker where a recorded message or a park ranger will tell you all about it.

I took in the park ranger's short guided walk at the Sunken Road and the Hornet's Nest, the site of the stand that the Union soldiers made from 10:30 A.M. until almost 5 P.M. that fateful Sunday that gave Grant time to prepare his defensive line close to Pittsburg Landing, the time that Grant absolutely had to have to prevent a rout.

The Johnny Rebs assaulted the Sunken Road and Hornet's Nest position *eleven* times without success. One survivor wrote that all he could see in the thick pall of gunsmoke were the continuous sheets of fire from muzzle blasts. The rebels finally blasted the Federals out of this position with a two-hour barrage from 62 cannons.

Of course today no traces of the battle remain. The gore and body parts and shattered trees are all gone. The men who fought here—those who died, those who were maimed, those who survived—all of them are now dead and well on their way to becoming dust. And this was a gorgeous summer morning. The early morning fog had burned off and it was cool for August, only in the mid-eighties. The sunlight filtering through the trees

309

and illuminating fields where once bodies laid in windrows gave the place the atmosphere of a cathedral. Other people felt it too. Everyone talked in low, respectful tones.

There weren't many people there. I had most of the tour stops all to myself. Just me, a gentle breeze and the cicadas in the trees singing to the spirits of thousands of dead soldiers.

I could almost hear the muskets and cannons roar, hear the shouting men and feel the adrenaline surge. Shoulder to shoulder in the dense smoke as bullets came like leaden hail and men fell left and right, most of these men stood their ground and fought to the bitter end. Amid the screams. Amid the stench. Fought here on the doorstep of hell.

I was deeply moved.

I stopped at each of the other tour stops and looked around, but Ulysses S. Grant was on my mind. He's one of my heroes. An Ohio boy who hated West Point but stuck to graduate, he served in the Mexican War, as did Robert E. Lee. But Lee was a gallant staff officer and Grant was a quartermaster. Grant resigned from the Army at the age of thirty to avoid a court-martial for drunkenness. He failed at farming and was clerking in his father's leather-goods store in Galena, Illinois, when the war broke out. Three years later, at the age of forty-two, he was commander of all the nation's armies.

Grant was a small, disheveled man who couldn't look neat or play a role if his life depended upon it. But he had common sense and never panicked, and he may well have been the best soldier this nation ever produced. Sending men forward into the inferno wasn't easy for him—he could not eat meat unless it was burned black.

Here at Shiloh Grant saw the true face of war for the first time—unspeakable violence, carnage, courage, terror, selflessness and selfishness, all the best and all the worst in man.

And he endured. We'll lick 'em tomorrow.

Before I left the park I went into the national cemetery on the knoll just up from the landing. Union soldiers killed at Shiloh are buried here. Over 3,500 of them. Other U.S. soldiers from other wars have also been interred here. The Confederate soldiers who died at Shiloh still lie in four mass graves.

The graves of the Shiloh dead in the national cemetery are obvious. These men were originally buried right where they had fallen. When moved here the majority of the bodies could not be identified. Now those graves are marked with a small square post that has a number on it. Nothing else. Some of the graves are marked with stones that bear the name and state of the decedent. A few conventional slabs bear the inscription, "Unknown U.S. Soldier." And a few, the most eloquent of all, simply state, "U.S. Soldier."

I got a can of soda pop from a machine in the bookstore and sat on the porch drinking it. The quintessential American tourist and his spouse and sister-in-law came out of the visitors' center and got into their car for the tour. Everyone fastened seatbelts and kept the windows up. Air conditioning. And off they went, driving slowly, just as I had done.

The greatest risk to life and limb that most people face today is riding in a car without their seatbelt fastened. They put it on before the car is moved from the driveway. Which is as it should be.

But these belted, air-conditioned people—these are the descendants of the soldiers in this cemetery and their comrades, men who felt so deeply about the fate of our republic that they were willing to fight, willing to kill and willing to die. They were willing to lie in a soldier's grave.

Antiwar activists like to tell us that there is nothing left worth fighting for. Pacifists tell us that there is nothing worth killing for. Draft evaders tell us there is nothing worth dying for.

Let them come and preach amid these tombstones. On a Sunday morning in April or on a sunny August day. They freely exercise their freedom of speech in this constitutional democracy these men gave their lives to preserve. Let them preach here.

311

27
_____

Saturday morning I'm flying again. By the time I get the car returned to the agency in Savannah and get the plane loaded and fueled, it's 9:45. The sun came up red this morning and faded from time to time—some clouds and lots of haze.

I find out how much haze when I lift off. I can see three, maybe four miles. Yuck! But the sky is clear above.

I fly west to Pittsburg Landing on the Tennessee and take a look at the national cemetery and the park. The only way one can distinguish the landing now is because there is a parking area between the trees on the bank. There wasn't much there in 1862 either.

The Tennessee River will lead me north. It will meander a bit on its way to the Ohio, but I'm in no hurry. Sooner or later I'd like to get to Oshkosh, Wisconsin, yet the Oshkosh airport will be there whenever I arrive.

This kind of leisure is foreign to me. Like everyone else I arrange my life to meet deadlines and commitments. Since I began flying civilian planes I have used them mostly for transportation. "I'll be there tomorrow afternoon about three. Meet me at the airport." That type of thing. So this summer trip is a vacation. In a week or two I'll be back in the office using my watch to regulate my life. Perhaps that's for the best. Still, I don't know that I would turn down an offer from Donald Trump if he wanted to adopt me. If he offered a good allowance and picked up my American Express bill every month, I'd be tempted.

The Tennessee River is a bit unique in that it doesn't flow through a single city or town of any size between Savannah, 15 miles north of the Mississippi state line, and the Ohio River, 100 nautical miles north. Small towns lie several miles away from the river on either side, but the river is a scenic boater's paradise.

A fellow could put a boat into the water at Nashville and descend the Cumberland all the way to the dams just south of the Ohio, cross to the Tennessee through a channel, then go up the Tennessee to the Pickwick Dam, just above Savannah. No doubt a lot of people do that for a summer vacation.

The river and land are gorgeous from a thousand feet overhead. The winding river and the farms and wooded areas all look very peaceful.

The visibility has increased to about seven miles by the time I reach Paducah, Kentucky, on the Ohio. The airport ATIS says the temperature is 84 degrees, but the humidity makes it seem boiling hot.

The FBO's line boy at Paducah's Barkley Regional at first denies that his employers own a five-gallon bucket, so I'll have to go on up the road to change the oil in the *Queen*. Then he decides maybe they do and produces one, plus four gallons of the right weight of new oil.

Two hours later I have the job done and the *Queen* buttoned up. I'm sweating like a tent-meeting evangelist wrestling with the Lord on a hot summer night. I gulp down a soda pop and stand in front of the FBO's air conditioner, but the perspiration doesn't slow down for almost 15 minutes. I'm hot, sweaty and filthy. Too bad the *Queen* doesn't appreciate the lengths I go to to preserve her engine.

Flying north over Illinois I latch onto an interstate and sit thinking about tent meetings. They had one in Savannah last night. I drove by and looked through the rolled-up tent flaps at the rapt crowd and the preacher with his shirtsleeves up and tie pulled down. I've never been to a tent revival, although they're popular and common throughout the South and I spent some time there when I was in the Navy. I guess I never thought my faith needed reviving. And I have trouble visualizing myself swaying and singing and shouting Amens as some inspired Elmer Gantry works himself into a lather for my benefit.

Sweaty public religion is a part of the rural South. Except when it turns into TV preachers bilking the gullible, I don't suppose it does anyone any harm and it undeniably makes a lot of people feel good.

Savannah had a lot more going on besides a tent meeting that Friday night as the moon rose all orange and swollen. In the motel parking lots people were checking the boats on their trailers. A group of young people were working out at the karate academy in a Main Street storefront across from the courthouse. McDonald's was serving burgers and fries, and teenagers were cruising. In the modest blue-collar homes of eastern Savannah young men were drinking beer around pickups parked in front yards while old men sat rocking on their porches.

All these people doing precisely what they wanted to do on a Friday night in August; somehow it's all very normal and, in a way, comforting. Life goes on.

At Salem, Illinois, my highway zags off to the northeast, so I drop to 500 feet and latch onto a powerline running the 50 miles north to Pana.

The visibility has improved to about twelve miles and I'm in the mood for a power line. I really don't need it, of course, since Pana is due north and the section lines would take me there even if I didn't have a compass. Power lines are difficult to follow because they are hard to see from the air and you have to get low to do it. And not all the power lines are on the sectional charts.

But the prospect of zipping along at a couple hundred feet above ripe farmland is enticing. I keep my eye peeled for birds. They're there. At my low speed—84 knots—I just have time to see and avoid them. At twice this speed I wouldn't.

Cows lying down chewing their cud look up as I pass overhead but don't get up. Cattle are used to engine noise, which is a man noise. Sailplanes and balloons frighten them. They're too much like big, silent birds that might be hungry enough to strap on a calf.

Two or three hundred feet above a fertile prairie is precisely where a Stearman should be. Here her pace seems fast, here the scale is right.

I sing. The snoring of the engine is the perfect accompaniment for my fractured baritone and butchered lyrics. This is much better than a shower. "O-oh dar-ling, a love like this is hard to find. Don't make me wait for luvvvvv. . . ."

I stopped for fuel at Decatur. I was sitting on the bench outside having an antisocial smoke when a Piper Colt shut down on the mat and the pilot came over carrying his logbook.

"You on a solo cross-country?" I asked.

"Yep. Looking for someone to sign my book."

"Better ask inside. I'm just passing through."

When he came back out he dropped onto the bench beside me. He farms seed corn, he said, and needs only to complete his ten hours of cross-country work prior to taking the flying test for his private pilot's license. "Passed the written a while back. Want to get the license before that expires. But it's tough finding the time. And flying's expensive."

"It'll be worth it. You'll see. When you don't need to hire a flight instructor or get permission to fly, it'll be a whole new ball game."

People like this man in his late thirties with a modest amount of discretionary income are the future of general aviation. Are there enough of them? If general aviation loses the common man, the politicians will drive the last nail into the coffin lid. Aviation will become just cattle-car airliners and warbirds for the filthy rich.

Some people feel that the Experimental Aircraft Association—the EAA—at Oshkosh is the best way to keep Joe Public in aviation. I have my doubts, but I'm going to Oshkosh to take a look.

The Rockford ATIS is scratchy. Maybe it's my radio receiver or maybe the woman who made the tape enunciated poorly, but after listening through three repetitions I still don't understand what the wind is.

Oh well.

I'm tired. The sun, wind and engine noise have taken their

toll. No doubt the two hours of sweating on the ramp in Paducah has contributed. So I'm just sitting here with my mind in neutral watching the world go by and the sun drop into the haze on the western horizon. I'll never make it to Oshkosh before dark, so I'll land at Rockford and spend the night.

I call Approach when I am about 15 miles out. The controller clears me to make a left downwind entry to runway 18. Okay.

And another plane calls, a Cherokee 32 miles southeast.

Finally Approach asks me if I have the field in sight.

Yes. "Eleven o'clock and five or six miles."

"Go to Tower."

Tower's reply to my call is short and to the point. "Runway 18, cleared to land."

I descend to the downwind and shove the prop to full increase, adjust the trim, nudge the mixture up. Landing checklist complete. Gear is welded, no flaps, no hook, no boost pump, no flaperon pop-up, no thrust reversers.

As I start the turn to base, the Cherokee calls base.

What?

"Stearman's turning left base," I remind everyone.

This wakes up the guy in the tower. "Where are you on base, Cherokee?"

"Four miles out."

Turning final I realize I have a problem. There's a hell of a crosswind here. Now I remember that I never got the ATIS information clearly.

"Tower, say your wind."

"One Zero Zero at ten."

Feels like twelve to fifteen. Eighty degrees off runway heading. I've got a gob of right rudder and left aileron crammed in and still I'm drifting.

Damn that jerk! They've got a runway pointed right into this hurricane and he gave a goddamn ground-looping biplane runway 18 to crash on!

I start to add power to go around and hesitate. If I go around I can ream out that lazy bugger on the air, and I'm tempted. But the challenge of landing the *Cannibal Queen* in a healthy crosswind is irresistible.

I flatten the glide and lower the left wing. I want the left main wheel to touch first, then as the right comes down the tail must also. My speed must be just right, the angle perfect.

No grass to help. This is pavement.

I juggle the power and rudder and stick and watch the pavement come closer, closer . . . little back stick, throttle closed . . .

And we're there! The left main touches and I catch the swerve as the right tire and tail wheel kiss. Stick full left. Another little swerve and gentle brakes and whew!

Parking the Queen the glow of a good landing fades. I crabbed my way north along highways since leaving Paducah, fighting an easterly wind, and the crab got worse the last hour into Rockford. I paid no attention.

And when Approach said runway 18, I assumed the wind was out of the south!

I could have asked, of course, and never did. I was tired, complacent. The wheels had stopped turning.

And I should have gone around and landed into the wind on a different runway. What if I had dragged a wingtip or ground-looped? After six hours of flying, all wrung out, that's no time to try to prove you're as good as Eddie Rickenbacker. The government built those other runways for guys like you to use, if only you're smart enough to ask for one when the disciple in the tower is asleep at the switch.

Dammit, you know the rule. It's written in blood. *Never take a chance if you don't have to.*

I walk toward the FBO thoroughly disgusted with myself.

The weather Sunday is a carbon copy of Saturday—visibility about ten miles in haze and no clouds anywhere. By 10 A.M. I am flying north at 3,500 feet, bound for Oshkosh. The first town of any size north of Rockford is Janesville, Wisconsin, so when the TRSA that guards Rockford spits me out, I dial in the tower freq to get permission to fly through the Janesville airport traffic area.

The first thing I hear is some guy giving the tower controller a rundown on an airshow performance. No, this is a request. This is all the stuff he wants the tower to let him do right now!

Are they having an airshow?

It sounds like a circus, something right out of *Those Magnificent Men in Their Flying Machines.* Pipers and Cessnas coming and going, a flight of four T-34s practicing an airshow routine, a flight of two Stearmans somewhere in the pattern, two more Stearmans inbound, some guy that can barely speak English ten miles east and inbound, an AT-6 doing circles north of the field, and somebody lost, can't find the field. Through all of this the tower controller stays cool, keeps them coming, doesn't use foul language. I'm impressed. The tower at O'Hare must have sent their best pro to the big leagues, Janesville.

I stare out of my cockpit at the saturated airspace around this little airport in Wisconsin. Planes everywhere—T-34s spewing smoke, planes landing, taking off, Holy Toledo! If it's like this on Sunday morning, what are Saturdays like? Doesn't anyone around here play golf?

If it's bumper cars in Janesville, what will it be like in Oshkosh, the home of the EAA? Will I find a hundred weird planes in the same little chunk of airspace?

No. Oshkosh is properly somnolent this Sunday morning. Two other planes leave while I am inbound, but I have the field all to myself. The tower controller gives me runway 22, right into the teeth of the ten-knot wind from the southwest.

I park the *Cannibal Queen* at Basler Aviation and stroll toward the office. A man preflighting a Cessna 172 wants to chat, so I pause to visit.

It is obvious he is a little shook. He is a student on his first solo cross-county and he got slightly lost getting here. He asked for help and was assigned a discrete IFF squawk, but the fifth time the controller told him to recycle the transponder he found he had it in standby all along. So now, safely connected with the firma, he wants someone to talk to and I am the only one around.

"Oshkosh is an easy field, y'know, because it's right here by Lake Winnebago. But the haze is so bad I couldn't see the lake."

Uh-huh. Using pilotage sounds so doggone easy—you have the chart and you can see the ground, so how could anyone get lost? Well, it's easy. Easy for an old hand and easier still for a student trying it for the first time. The problem is that charts are constructed of symbols—they depict reality but they are not photographs. The skill is transposing the symbols to the real world, and vice versa.

I talk to the student a bit and wonder if he really should go on alone, yet I hesitate to suggest he call his flight instructor. Maybe I should. I don't because I think he is learning something by flailing around the sky making basic mistakes. As long as he doesn't drive it into the ground, what could happen to him in this flat countryside dotted with airports? An instructor has to kick them out of the nest sometime, and apparently his has concluded that today is the day.

I know how the student feels. Everyone who ever learned to fly has had days like this. It all sounds so easy . . .

The EAA was founded in Oshkosh in 1953 by Paul Poberezny to assist people interested in designing or building an airplane at home, i.e., a home-built. The FAA licenses do-it-yourself aircraft in the "experimental" category, a nice little exception to the rules that require commercial builders to spend millions getting a design certified for sale to the public. The growth of enterprise liability lawsuits against general aviation aircraft manufacturers in the 1960s, '70s and into the '80s, and the resulting decisions by Piper, Beech and Cessna to stop or drastically curtail the manufacture of single-engine airplanes spurred the EAA's growth.

Today the EAA proclaims itself as "*the* Sport Aviation Association." And it is. It puts on the world's biggest annual airshow the first week in August here at Oshkosh, it lobbies hard in Washington on general aviation issues, and it still provides technical advice to all those people busy in their garages or tee-hangars building their own flying machines. It also publishes a neat monthly magazine, *Sport Aviation*, which is automatically sent to every EAA member.

The focus of the EAA has always been on light civilian aircraft. Their new museum complex on one side of the Oshkosh airport has an F-86 mounted on a pedestal out front, an F-80 parked around back and a World War II hangar exhibit. Still, military flying machines are somehow out of place here. The strength of the museum is civilian antiques from the 1920s and 1930s and a breathtaking display of home-builts.

The Wright brothers were the first home-builders. Their Flyer was a home-built, and had the FAA been around then, presumably the feds would have given it an experimental certificate. Of course, the brothers would have then tried to get the Flyer

319

certificated in the unrestricted category so they could make and sell other aircraft of the Flyer type. The resulting hassle would have probably bankrupted them.

Entrepreneurs today avoid the certification problem by selling only the plans for successful aircraft. Some also sell prefabricated parts, but you, the buyer and user, must build the darn thing yourself. That's the rub. That's also the only reason the designers and parts fabricators can stay in business—legally you are the manufacturer of your home-built, so if you crash it your widow has no one to sue.

One of the first home-builders without higher aspirations was a Minnesota automobile mechanic named Bernard H. Pietenpol, who got the bug in 1922. Aircraft engines were expensive then too, so Mr. Pietenpol used the engine from a Model T Ford in his first plane. And his second. When he needed an engine for his third the Model A was out; Mr. Pietenpol found that engine an adequate source of power. His Pietenpol Aircamper cruised at 70 MPH with two people aboard, but you had to build it yourself in your own barn and fly it from your own pasture.

Pietenpol designed and built 24 aircraft during his lifetime, the final one with an engine from a Chevrolet Corvair. He thought this engine excellent for aircraft use.

Pietenpol was obviously something of a mechanical genius. He gave up auto mechanics but taught himself radio, and television when that came along, and made his living repairing these devices. Building airplanes was his hobby. His hangar and two of his aircraft are at the EAA museum.

Another fellow who showed what a home-builder could do was Donald P. Taylor, who built something called a Thorp T-18 and proceeded to fly it around the world in 1976. He took two months to make the journey, flying 24,627 miles in 171.5 hours. Taylor's plane is in the museum.

"I did it," Taylor said, "to prove the individual still counts for something in this world—that a little guy can still go out alone and accomplish something no one has done before."

The latest home-builders to fly into the pages of the record books have the big record, the one the experts said would never fall. They flew their craft, *Voyager*, nonstop around the world on one tank of gas. Yes, Burt and Dick Rutan and Jeane Yeager were home-builders. Designed by Burt Rutan, the plane was constructed of space-age composites and took six years to build, about the norm for a home-built. Then Dick Rutan and Jeane Yeager flew it nonstop around the globe.

The EAA museum has a full-scale replica of the fuselage of *Voyager*. The composite material is half the weight of steel and five times as strong. But you have to mold the parts and cook them: the family oven probably isn't big enough.

You say you want to own your own plane? You're tired of renting. But forty-year-old fabric-covered tail-draggers don't turn you on and used Cessnas, Mooneys, Pipers and Beeches seem out of financial reach or too stodgy. What's left? Build your own. You say you're not a mechanical genius like Bernard Pietenpol or a world-class aeronautical engineer like Burt Rutan? Can you do it?

The average American probably tinkered with cars when he was young and maybe even overhauled a lawn mower or two. Today he takes the car to Jiffy Lube. If the lawn mower needs anything more than a new blade or sparkplug, it goes to the shop. Mr. Average owns a few hand tools—pliers, some wrenches, a couple screwdrivers and a hammer—and he gets them out for minor fix-up jobs around the house. Rebuilding an antique car would be a stupendous project for Mr. Average.

To successfully build an airplane you must be an incurable tinkerer. You must like to work with your hands and be fairly good at it. Most successful home-builders are professional mechanics or engineers—many have airframe and powerplant mechanic's licenses from the FAA. These are the people with big red professional tool cases from Sears filled with thousands of dollars' worth of tools that they know how to use. The planes they build are usually carefully constructed. Building the plane is the challenge.

Right there is the problem. The people who want to fly the planes can't build them. Fortunately the people who can build them aren't all that interested in flying them. Stories of builders spending six or eight years building the plane of their dreams, flying it two or three times, then selling it, are legion. Happens all the time. But in this imperfect world there are a lot more flyers than there are builders.

One of the goals of the EAA is to design a plane that is so easy and cheap to construct that Mr. Average can get in on the fun. The fun of building.

I don't think it will ever happen. Mr. Average is never going to spend all of his spare time for two or three or six years in his garage or out at the airport working like a slave so he can go fly someday when it's finished.

There is a place for home-builders, and the EAA has done a magnificent job fulfilling their needs. And it has become a powerful, much-needed voice in general aviation. But if general aviation is going to be saved, we need legislation that relieves aircraft manufacturers of the unlimited strict liability they currently face. In effect, a company that manufactures and sells an aircraft to the public today guarantees it for the life of the plane, literally forever. How much must they charge to purchase insurance to cover that risk? How much will the judgments be ten years from now? Twenty? Thirty? Fifty?

No one knows the answers. Mooney seems to be the only healthy company manufacturing single-engine planes. You will pay at least $150,000 for a Mooney, so they are bought mainly by upscale professional people. Cessna today builds only business jets. At this writing Piper is in bankruptcy and not making anything. A few planes still trickle from the Beechcraft factory, and a few little companies build specialty planes—mainly new production of forty or fifty-year old designs—but only Aerospatiale, a French firm, has even attempted to design and manufacture new airframes using the latest technology. There have been no new engines for thirty years.

The Beech Bonanza, considered by many as the best aerial carriage available to middle-class Americans, has been manufactured essentially unchanged since 1947. Depending on the model you select, you will pay between $178,000 and $300,000 for a new one today. Over $400,000 if you want the top-of-the-line model with all the electronic goodies. Middle-class? Okay, if you can afford one of these you are at least dusty rich. Yet all that money doesn't change the fact you are getting the technological equivalent of a 1947 Buick.

Imagine an automobile industry in which innovation ceased in the 1950s and most major production lines halted in 1986. The general aviation industry is dying—federal regulation and the legal system have driven it to the lip of the grave where it is waiting to expire and fall in. Soon it will be extinct. Like the dodo bird.

Behind the main EAA museum is Pioneer Airport, three regular hangars full of antiques from the 1920s and '30s facing a grass runway. On days when the crosswind is not too bad you can get a ride here in a genuine Ford Tri-motor. The only other Tri-motor that I know about still flying passengers is one owned by Scenic Airlines at Grand Canyon Airport, Arizona.

In these hangars are some truly rare airplanes. The one that froze me in my tracks was a Ford Flivver, only two of which were ever built. Henry Ford wanted to follow up the Tri-motor with a cheap aerial Model T that Everyman could own and fly, and this was his attempt. One of them crashed in Florida, killing the test pilot, and the project was abandoned in 1928. The other one is in the Henry Ford Museum in Dearborn, Michigan. This is a replica. It's a fabric-covered, low-wing monoplane with an open cockpit that holds just one person, the pilot. It's small.

I stared at it, trying as Henry Ford must have done to envision a sky filled with tens of thousands of these aerial Flivvers. The vision was beyond my power of imagination, just as it was beyond Henry's.

The hangars hold several Stinsons, some rare Fairchilds, a Jenny, and lots of other neat stuff. Most of these planes have a tag dangling from the prop that warns you not to turn it—the engine is "pickled." To preserve the engine, they drain out the oil and squirt it full of something like Cosmoline.

These airplanes don't fly. This isn't a flying museum. The EAA doesn't have the money or manpower to fly and maintain most of these airplanes. The planes reminded me of steam locomotives in railroad museums, the fireboxes eternally cold, the steam whistles never to sound again, the great driving wheels welded in place. Somehow it's a little sad.

Inside one of the hangars I got into a conversation with a volunteer who had spent the summer mocking up Stearman wing ribs and explaining the process to visitors.

He had an idea, he said, for selling Stearman wing ribs arranged around a U.S. eagle or shield. He thought people would buy something like that and wanted my opinion. Not really. He wanted me to nod, so I did.

The wing ribs were built of cheap wood and kid's school

glue to save money, yet to my untrained eye they looked work-manlike and carefully done. This gentleman was one of the builders.

And he found a great place to spend the summer, here in a hangar amid these beautiful old airplanes, talking to people interested in aviation, watching the Tri-motor come and go with loads of joyriders. Don't you envy him a little?

Outside sitting on the grass in the sun was the most beautiful biplane I've ever seen, a blue Lincoln-Page wearing a 100-HP Kinner five-cylinder radial. The lines are just so perfect. Rare? This is the only Lincoln-Page I ever laid eyes on, and maybe the only one left. Period.

I walked back across the grass strip and went through the museum, stopping to commune for a moment with the EAA's Stearman. This monster was donated or loaned to the EAA by Joe C. Hughes, an airshow stunt pilot. She wears a brute of an engine, a Pratt & Whitney R-1340 Wasp with a governor that limits it to 650 horsepower.

I saw Hughes and his wingwalking partner, Gordon McCollam, do their act with this plane at the Canadian National Airshow in 1974 or '75. At the climax of their show Hughes would make an inverted pass down the runway and McCollam on the top wing would grab a ribbon stretched between two poles. Then one summer turbulence or wind shear caught the plane during one of these performances and McCollam was killed. The FAA now forbids inverted passes at low altitudes with wingwalkers.

McCollam's death was a tragedy, of course, one that was probably extraordinarily difficult for Hughes to learn to live with. Yet his magnificent Stearman still reeks of that airshow magic that has inspired Americans since barnstormers performed in Jennys on summer weekends over a pasture on the edge of town. Bands playing, balloons and smoke trails aloft in a blue summer sky, the throb of unmuffled exhausts as planes sweep by overhead—these images still stir us deeply.

Flight is the promise of vigorous life, a life in which infinite possibilities are within the grasp of determined men and women of vision.

If we pickle the engines and relegate it all to museums in the name of the great safety pooh-bah, we will be a poorer people.

28

FROM THE WINDOW OF MY HOTEL ROOM I COULD SEE THE HAZE.
Thick.

I ate breakfast watching the flags on the sidewalk on the
banks of the Fox River whip in the wind. A wind out of the
southwest.

The Flight Service briefer summed it up: "Three miles visibility in haze in Oshkosh but improving as you go north. Winds
ten to twelve out of the southwest at Oshkosh and getting
stronger farther north. Thirty percent chance of thunderstorms
across your route of flight today."

Winds aloft?

"At three thousand, southwest at twenty-five, then thirty near
Lake Superior."

The wind whips my hair as I go through the preflight ritual
on the parking mat at the airport. Aviation is full of rituals,
even more so than formal religion, which gives it a flavor that
is timeless. You begin each morning with sacramental coffee,
usually at the same time you are chanting the liturgy with the
FAA weather priest.

Out on the mat, at the altar of flight, you approach your
airplane, this mechanical steed that will transport you into the

325

heavens. Every morning you check everything you can see, inspect this, touch that, peer here, look there. You examine the oil level on the dipstick, you swing the prop through to ensure that an oil lock has not developed in a cylinder, you arrange the charts in the cockpit just so, you put every switch in its proper position, you start the engine and listen to the predictable, familiar sound, you examine every instrument for any deviation from the norm, you waggle the controls in the same way you do every time.

The rituals assure you that the machine and you are both ready. They ensure you are in control, that the flight will go as planned, that this is not your last day of life, that you will sleep in a bed tonight with your health and your hopes and your petty vices safely intact. Ancient mariners used to burn thighbones on the headland and spill wine before they cast off. I perform my solemn rites for exactly the same reasons.

This morning, with the gods satisfied and my soul prepared, I mumble the holy words to the ground controller and the tower controller in turn and stroke the throttle. The miracle occurs. I fly.

The air is like soup. I climb to 3,500 feet and point the Queen northeast. The wind squirts me along faster than a politician's promise.

The first problem is the airport traffic area at Menasha, just north of Oshkosh. I give the tower a call. "Stay clear of the traffic area. The field is IFR with a partial obscuration."

Oh, great!

I could climb, but in this goo I risk losing sight of the ground if I go much higher. I can barely see it now. I'll circle the Menasha airport to the east, over the edge of Lake Winnebago. I glance east. There's nothing there. The haze merges with the water and there is no horizon. Nor, looking down, is there much of a surface. Quickly I look left at the land to reestablish my spatial orientation.

Okay, no over-water stuff today.

I sneak along the shoreline, a fast sneak with the wind behind me, and then pick up the four-lane toward Green Bay as I talk to Green Bay Approach. They clear me through their airspace.

The four-lane squeezes down to two lanes north of Green Bay. I have a ten degree crab in and still I'm bucketing along,

326

but the poor visibility keeps me busy trying to stay found. Abrams, Stiles, Lena, Coleman, I tick them off one by one. I also use my pencil to try to measure the distances. It appears I've done about 76 miles from Oshkosh to Coleman in 43 minutes. How many knots is that? More than a hundred.

I'm going under a cloud layer. The gauzy sun disappears and the haze turns gloomy. I decide to go lower. At 2,500 feet I am bouncing in the cockpit. I can see better but the ride is definitely worse.

Approaching Iron Mountain, Michigan, the clouds are behind and the visibility has improved to about six miles. The wind is fierce out of the southwest at about 15 or 20.

Runway 18 is as close to the wind as they have, so I get to practice my crosswind landing technique. I get the Queen onto the runway without altering her appearance, but the landing is nothing to brag about. Upon shutdown I check the time—1.4 hours from engine start in Oshkosh. Then I stand up in the cockpit and strip off the jacket. This place is hotter than Mississippi was.

Well, it was a nice tailwind. While it lasted. Westward from here it's a headwind.

Life's like that.

Ten minutes after I landed at Iron Mountain I had two spectators photographing the plane. The first man to arrive said he was out in his yard when he heard the Queen. "I knew it was a radial the minute I heard it. Sure enough, a yellow biplane. So I grabbed the camera and came on out to the airport."

The second man to arrive had a passenger as well as his camera. He had just finished mowing the lawn of an apartment house when he saw the Queen go over. "I try to take photos of all the interesting planes that land here. This is the only Stearman this summer besides the Red Baron Pizza plane that gave rides to all the grocers."

"No," the first man said. "There was that fellow from Illinois that brought up a Stearman for the airshow."

"Yes, that's right. Good airshow too. Weather was a little crummy but they flew away. The P-51 was the best act, I thought. Boy, I liked the sound of that engine."

If ever three guys deserved Stearman rides, here they stood. I watched the wind sock whipping through twenty or thirty

327

degrees and decided not to tempt my luck. Rockford was a sobering lesson. So I paid for the gas and oil, shook hands all around, and taxied the *Queen* out.

The three were still on the mat as I lifted off. I turned the *Queen* to go over them and waved like a man possessed. They waved back with every arm.

The FAA says the *Cannibal Queen* is mine. She must be, since everyone sends me the bills. Yet in a larger sense, she isn't. She's just mine to fly for a while, for as long as my turn lasts. Like every wonderful old airplane she really belongs to everyone who sees her. Everyone who hears the engine and looks up and catches the sun glinting on yellow wings. Everyone who feels somehow richer, more alive because he saw her in the sky.

I fly westward at 2,500 feet in a bobbing, corkscrewing airplane that has to be pointed at least twenty degrees south of the desired course. The hot, gusty, malevolent wind is out of character this far north, amid this great hardwood forest that is already showing tinges of fall color.

The hills roll gently and the forest covers everything. Cold creeks and streams meander through the wilderness. Ernest Hemingway loved these forests and wrote a series of short stories set here for *Boy's Life* magazine. These stories were among the first he managed to get published. They've been republished in collections and are worth your time, even if you're politically correct and think you don't like Ernest Hemingway. The Nick Adams stories will surprise you.

I've always wondered why the environmentalists and conservationists haven't latched onto Hemingway's work. No writer I know of in this century had a more profound love for the outdoors or expressed it better then Hemingway. I guess he played the writer role too macho and that image still gets in the way of what he wrote. Which is a shame.

After an hour and a half of flying I am feeling the first twinges of airsickness. Not nausea, just a general malaise that will progress to nausea if I don't get this bucking pig on the ground so that I can give my inner ear a break.

The first airport ahead is Ironwood, Michigan, but the runway is oriented east and west. I give them a call. Winds 200 degrees at 11 gusting to 21.

Now *that* is a crosswind! Fifty degrees off, 11 to 21.

I set myself up for a straight-in, then decide to overfly the field and get a good look.

The wind sock is flopping from south to southwest, standing straight out. There is a taxiway pointed straight south that I could use, yet it's narrow and if I landed on it someone might have a cow unless I claimed I had an emergency. Most of the folks at these little airports wouldn't care, but you never know.

I circle for a left downwind and set the *Queen* up. Coming down final I have in almost full right rudder and left stick. Still I'm drifting right. I lower the left wing. That stops the drift, yet now the wing is down too far. I add power to flatten the glide angle and work on holding her stable.

I can't do it. The wind is shifting directions and gusting and the *Queen*'s bucking like a pony at the county fair. I wave off and tell the Unicom man I'm going on down the road.

I would try it if I had to, but I don't. Ashland, Wisconsin, is just 30 miles west and they have a runway pointed southwest.

The Ashland Unicom man says the wind is blowing at 34 knots.

Thirty-four?

Yeah, but it's within ten degrees of runway 22 at Ashland.

I'm flying into the eye of a hurricane. Every wind report is worse than the last one.

At Ashland I flatten the glide angle with power—I've got lots of excess runway—and concentrate on getting her to light on all three at the same time. I don't concentrate hard enough and the mains touch first. She bounces as I try to pull the tail down. Now the tail touches, then the mains.

And with the power at idle, she is instantly down to taxi speed. "An arrested landing," I comment on the radio.

"Yeah," said the Unicom man, "but we liked the second landing best." Then he hastens to add, "None of us could have done it any better."

They can't fool me. They all think they could. If they didn't think that, they shouldn't be flying airplanes. Flying is an assortment of skills that one must acquire, practice, and try to perfect.

If you aren't proud of your skill, you don't work hard enough at it.

I'll be honest—Steve Coonts is the world's finest pilot still strapping them to his ass.

Ashland lies on an inlet on the southern shore of Lake Superior. The air temperature in the high 90s is unusual, rare. Sitting in his new log cabin office, the airport manager shakes his head in amazement.

The log cabin is a piece of work. The logs are big, fitted tightly, and the rafters inside are bolted together. This structure was built to endure harsh winters for a lot of years. The airport manager at Bryce Canyon, Utah, needs an office like this to complement his 1936-vintage log hangar.

Run your hands over the logs, finger the imperfections in the wood, examine how the logs are notched and fitted together. Built to last, like the Stearman.

Soon I am on my way again with the freshwater inland sea of Lake Superior on my right. Storms over the lake make it look dark and gray. The lake ends in a point at Duluth, Minnesota, and I fly slowly on, out across the Minnesota lake country, "the land of ten thousand lakes." I believe it. The flat, forested land is pockmarked with lakes as far as the eye can see (about twelve miles in this haze), dimpled like the surface of a golf ball. There are too many lakes and they all look alike, so it is impossible to use these things for navigation. As usual, I'm stuck with roads and towns and the occasional railroad track.

The wind is still blowing ferociously and the Queen is still bucking. When I land at Brainerd, Minnesota, the temperature is 96 degrees. Inside the office building the line boy offers to call a motel that will send a car but I ask him to wait a little bit. I've had too much flying. I need to sit awhile on something that doesn't move.

The coffeepot is still on. I pour myself a cup and sit looking out the window at the runways and the treeline beyond and the big sky covering everything.

The next morning I'm 40 minutes west of Brainerd under indefinite clouds, headed for Fargo and bucking a wind from the southwest, when I spot it. Yes, an airport with three—count them, three—grass runways!

I quickly check the chart. Yep, it's a public field, right here at Wadena, Minnesota. And, glory be, they have a runway pointed right into that southwest wind. Now that is a piece of luck.

Quicker than a pickpocket can snag a wallet I have the power back and am banking into a left downwind for the southwest runway. No one answers my Unicom call, but that's normal. It's a public field and there are no cattle on the runway, so here I come.

The *Cannibal Queen* likes grass. Invariably she gives me her best landings on the green stuff. She does this time too, a perfect three-point that will be something to think about this winter on cold, snowy evenings.

Safely on the ground, I look about like a lucky K-Mart shopper. The grass is mowed like a PGA fairway and the areas between runways have just been hayed. The rolls of hay lie safely off the runways, which are outlined with bright yellow markers.

At the south end of the field is a little office and three or four hangars. I taxi over to the office and the two fuel pumps. Now which is which? One will probably contain 100 octane, which I am feeding the *Queen*, and the other will contain automobile gasoline—mogas—for airplanes that can use it. The pumps are so old and weathered I can't tell one from another, so I park the *Queen* by the one against the building and kill the engine.

No one comes out. After the unstrapping ceremony, I get out the camera and photograph the *Queen* with the grass runways in the background. This chore takes a couple minutes. There are two cars behind the building, but still no signs of life.

Finally I try the office door. It's unlocked. Inside is a counter with an honor-system snack box, comfortable chairs, lots of flying magazines, a pop machine and a restroom. I use the restroom and go back outside for a smoke.

When I have been here a quarter of an hour I go back inside and inspect the place more closely. A lot of flying stories have been told in this room, crops discussed, the fortunes of the high school football team, the weather endlessly. On the wall a half-page clipping from a newspaper published in April 1990 informs me that Frank Pothen, the manager and operator of the Wadena Airport, just turned eighty years old. The story has a photo of Mr. Pothen at the controls of his Piper Colt in which he still gives flight instruction. He first soloed on May 22, 1931, and, according to the FAA, is believed to be the oldest active pilot in Minnesota.

But he isn't here. Probably went flying. Or to town for coffee. And left the place unlocked. After all, this is Wadena, not L.A. or the Bad Apple. The folks in the cafe on Main Street will probably tell you—this is God's country, full of honest folk. Then the waitress will say she hasn't locked her door in years. And the guy on the next stool will tell you he still leaves the keys in his car. Who would steal it?

Indeed. Who?

Rumbling thunder brings me back outside. A storm three or four miles north is tossing lightning bolts at the ground. Some rain is falling up that way. And there's a boomer to the west. They're partially embedded in the haze but the lightning flashes give them away.

I sit listening to the thunder and watching the storms and the wind sock as my pipe smoke hurries away on the wind.

This hasn't been a wet summer here. The grass is dry and yellowish and the dirt has the consistency of dust.

According to the newspaper, Mr. Pothen has managed this airport for over twenty years. That's a lot of flight students, a lot of thunderstorms, snows in the winter, wet springs, summer afternoons with baseball on the radio, gorgeous falls with touchdowns and halftime bands.

Sixty years of flying. . . . I wonder if Mr. Pothen regrets any of it. Does he wish he had flown for an airline, or perhaps farmed a little place ten miles out of town? I wonder . . .

Money and material possessions are not the measure of a life well lived. Fame? That's smoke on the wind.

Looking at the *Queen*, almost a half century old, against the grass runways and thinking about Mr. Pothen, I can't help but take inventory of my own life, my career. As much as I love flying, I long ago concluded that I didn't want to spend my life doing it. I didn't like law, which is merely helping people settle disputes, all of which boil down to money—how much? If you help rich people settle theirs you make a lot of it. But.

Writing books seems like an occupation more likely to make a lasting impression, until you're in it and find out that the shelf life of a paperback novel is about a month. That's it—a month on the shelf and the ones that haven't sold are recycled into grocery bags. Hardcovers? Go to your library and look at all the best-sellers of yesteryear that nobody reads today.

Before I get very much older I am going to build a house, one made of stone and brick and logs. I'm going to build it with my own hands on a mountain where I can watch the storms and look at the stars at night. That is what I want to do with my life.

Sound silly? I suppose.

I'm going to do it someday.

There's blue sky to the northwest between the thunderstorms, in the direction I have to go. I knock out my pipe and climb into the Queen.

The southwest runway points straight at Wadena, so I go over town climbing at full power. It's a nice little town, like a thousand others that I've flown over this summer. It could be in Texas or California or Illinois or anywhere. But it's here, in Minnesota, with a little airport that has never been paved and an eighty-one-year-old active pilot as the airport manager. So it's special.

Passing between the two boomers the Queen gets a light rinse, not enough to even wet the plane thoroughly. No turbulence. On the other side of the shower the sky clears and the wind shifts to the southeast. Now it's a tailwind. This was the front the briefer mentioned this morning. And a thin line of scattered thunderstorms was the whole shebang.

The sun comes out and shines on the Queen's wings. They look brilliant against the greens of the land.

Flying west into Fargo, North Dakota, I notice the trees are no longer a forest. They're in groves and woodlots between cultivated fields and hayfields. This is the eastern edge of the Great Plains. The western edge is the first upslope of the Rockies.

This will be the fourth time this summer I have flown the Great Plains. This southeast wind will probably shift to the southwest, yet even so, the Great Plains will be worth it. Once a great sea of grass that supported millions of buffalo and thousands of Indians, today the plains are America's breadbasket.

Here the grain that feeds America and a large portion of the rest of the world is grown as the seasons cycle by with their sun, rain and snow. As old as the planet, this cycle is life to the people here, far from big cities and big city worries. Every hour the local radio stations give the information that these people need—the weather and the farm report. Natives of the big cities of the East regard the plains as merely dreary stretches to pass through, which in a way is sad even if it is understandable. This is America's beating heart.

I stop for fuel at Jamestown on the western edge of the intensely cultivated Red River valley, only nine-tenths of an hour west of Fargo. At the *Queen's* modest rate of progress the airports with fuel west of here are far apart. And the wind has shifted, now straight out of the south. I'll be bucking it southwestward.

Still, leaving Jamestown I climb to 6,500 feet. The visibility is up to about 30 miles. The scale out here is huge, the landmarks far apart just like everything else, so I must get up where I can see.

From almost a mile above the earth the view is spectacular, although limited by the haze. I follow a two-lane highway south, one with ranches arranged a mile or so apart. Thirty minutes south of Jamestown the road doglegs east at the town of Edgeley, but I am through with it. I strike off southwest for the town of Mobridge, South Dakota, on the Missouri River. I pass over an area used only for grazing before I get back to wheat country.

Southwest of Ashley I follow an abandoned railroad right-of-way that is going in my direction. Not too many years ago the railroad was the only way to market wheat and cattle, corn and hogs. It was also the best way to travel and the carrier that delivered fuel, clothes, spare parts and machinery, and goodies from Sears & Roebuck. Then after World War II the roads out here were improved and trucks and cars became practical. Finally trucks could do it cheaper than trains, so an era ended.

The Missouri River in this section of South Dakota is a lake. They dammed the river 70 miles south of Mobridge at Pierre, so today the Missouri here is wider than the Mississippi and long arms of water reach up the valleys. Yet all this water is between empty hills covered with yellow grass this late in the summer. A few roads, a rare house, and nothing else. Not a tree anywhere. Not one.

These hills must look almost exactly as they did to Lewis and Clark when they came up this river on their way west to the Pacific, back in 1805. Thomas Jefferson sent them to find out what the United States had just paid France fifteen million bucks for. And Lewis and Clark found out: oceans of grass, mountains with glaciers, great huge valleys so big they stun the human eye. The United States had purchased an empire.

Today Mobridge is a small town on the main drag east and west, U.S. Route 12. But Route 12 is not an interstate, not four lanes. It's precisely two lanes of blacktop threading its way westward from Aberdeen and crossing the river here on a bridge, the bridge that gave the town its name.

They just repaved the runway at the airport. It looks nice, but I'm too busy fighting the 70-degree, 15-knot crosswind to appreciate it. The landing isn't pretty.

The fuel man isn't in the office. The only person there, a flight instructor waiting for a student, tells me he has been called. When the fuel man arrives we gas the plane, then he loans me his elderly Buick for the two mile jaunt into town.

Signs on the edge of town proclaim that Mobridge is the Walleye capital of the world, "the Oasis of the Oahe." They call the river Lake Oahe. The temperature on the bank clock reads 96 degrees.

Rick's Cafe in the heart of downtown Mobridge is the first eatery I see. Sure enough, they have a wall covered with big movie posters and publicity shots from *Casablanca*. I eat a bowl of chili with Humphrey Bogart smoldering over my shoulder.

Halfway through a hamburger it occurs to me that I have just landed in the 48th State since I left Boulder on June 8. South Dakota was the last one.

So I've done it! I've flown over and landed in all 48 of the contiguous United States in the *Cannibal Queen*. In one summer.

I haven't crashed. I haven't had a major breakdown. I haven't run out of gas and landed in some farmer's potato field. I've left two credit cards behind and had to call and have them mailed home. I've trashed four pairs of socks and bought more.

I've gone through 17 rolls of film and maybe have three decent photographs.

Why? Because I always wanted to.

I am a little happy and a little sad. If only there were four or five more states!

Climbing out of Mobridge I fly south along the western shore of the lake, south almost to Pierre. I don't see a boat. Not a single boat, a single wake, which amazes me. This lake must be a big secret. You folks in Tennessee and New York—bring your boat here and you'll have a huge lake all to yourself.

West of the river the hills are virgin prairie grass. In the valley of the Cheyenne River a few ranchers are raising irrigated hay, but mostly the land looks as it probably did when the first white trappers saw it in the early 1800s.

The Cheyenne turns south, so I follow the Belle Fourche River westward for a few minutes. Finally I realize that I can see the sun reflecting on the hangars of Ellsworth Air Force Base at Rapid City, 40 miles away. I turn in that direction.

The temperature at Rapid City is 103 when I land, a new record. Unloading the Queen and wiping her down drains what energy I have left.

The air conditioning in the FBO's office feels good. I stand in front of the blower and slowly come back from the sky.

29

THE FIRST SIX MILES OF THE ROAD FROM RAPID CITY TO MOUNT Rushmore has an eclectic mix of tourist traps. There is a water-slide emporium, two go-kart tracks, an aquarium, an antique car place that looks deserted, a factory making "genuine Mt. Rushmore gold and diamond jewelry," and—saving the best for last—something called Reptile Gardens.

Taking your youngster to Reptile Gardens may well prove to be the highlight of your vacation. Here he or she can watch mesmerized as lizards eat bugs and snakes swallow mice. Then hourly for the next week you will be treated to the same question over and over again: "Why can't I have a snake?" Put Reptile Gardens down as a must-see on your vacation list.

After the last of the tourist traps the road climbs more steeply and winds up canyons into the Black Hills, which, in the finest tradition of American names, are neither black nor hills. They are mountains covered with pine trees with some aspen salted in.

As a youngster I first became aware of the gigantic sculptured faces on Mount Rushmore when I watched Cary Grant in a business suit—he always wore a suit and tie—climb down Lincoln's nose in the Alfred Hitchcock thriller *North by Northwest*. Remember that scene?

The faces of George Washington, Thomas Jefferson, Theodore Roosevelt and Abraham Lincoln are carved together in the granite cliff just below the mountaintop. Working haphazardly as funds and weather allowed, sculptor Gutzon Borglum and his crew spent fourteen years creating this masterpiece, and believe me, it *is* a masterpiece. You view the sculpture by looking up from overlooks on a hillside across the creek. The necessity to raise your head and gaze upward converts you to a mere peasant in the presence of magnificent greatness, which is no doubt precisely the emotion that Borglum intended you to have.

Obviously Borglum was a world-class sculptor when he started this project at the age of sixty, in 1927. George Washington has the prominent place, on a projection of the cliff that allowed Borglum to do almost a complete bust. To Washington's left, your right, and recessed slightly is Jefferson. On to the right in a crevice that makes the face the least prominent is Theodore Roosevelt. Lincoln is on the extreme right, on another projection of the cliff, but this bust is tied in with the others by the way Lincoln faces, which is almost toward Washington.

This is the world's largest sculpture. More important, it is one of the best, set here amid the wind and pines and clouds of the Black Hills.

The morning I was there a lusty wind sang in the pines. Not many people, which sort of surprised me this late in the summer with Labor Day just around the corner. I had the windy observation deck all to myself for the first ten minutes I was there, then six or seven other people arrived.

There are cracks in the faces, cracks visible with the naked eye. In the visitor's center are photographs from the 1930s of the workmen using jackhammers on the faces; the cracks were there then too, imperfections in the rock. Apparently water gets into the cracks during the winter and freezes, so the cracks are getting worse. Even carved into living granite, memorials made by man are attacked by the forces of nature in the oldest process on earth, erosion.

The completed sculpture was dedicated on October 31, 1941, just five weeks before the Japanese attacked Pearl Harbor and the nation plunged headlong into the maelstrom of World War II. So the sculpture is fifty years old this year, a year older than the *Cannibal Queen*.

338

Washington's and Lincoln's presence on the mountain need no explanation. They are easily the two most important Americans who have yet drawn breath. The author of the Declaration of Independence and champion of the common man, Jefferson penned these words: "We hold these Truths to be self-evident, that all Men are created equal, that they are endowed by their Creator with certain unalienable Rights, that among these are Life, Liberty, and the Pursuit of Happiness—That to secure these Rights, Governments are instituted among Men, deriving their just Powers from the Consent of the Governed. . . ." That sentence alone qualified him for the cliff, even if he hadn't slickered the French out of half a continent when he was President or introduced ice cream to America.

Teddy Roosevelt got his mug up there because Borglum liked his style. T.R. was not a great president. One needs great events, great challenges, and great enemies if one is to impress the historians. Teddy's tragedy was that the nation was at peace and prosperous throughout his presidency.

Yet he wanted to be great. In the visitor's center is this quote: "Far better it is to dare mighty things, to win glorious triumphs, even though checkered by failure, than to take ranks with those poor spirits who neither enjoy much nor suffer much, because they live in the gray twilight that knows not victory nor defeat." Teddy took his own advice: he seized life with both hands, and Borglum liked that. I do too.

There are no plans to carve more faces on Rushmore, yet there is room for a couple and the federal deficit is so big we'd never miss the money. Of course, we could always rescind the latest 25 percent pay raise our 535 congresspeople awarded themselves and use those dollars. They're not giving us anything for our money—why not spend it on something worthwhile?

My candidates for the cliff are Franklin Roosevelt and Martin Luther King, Jr. Although each man had his smirches, I think history will ultimately conclude they were the two greatest Americans of this century.

Roosevelt had the crises his cousin Teddy lacked—the Great Depression and World War II. During his twelve years in office he indelibly stamped his personality and character upon America and our way of life.

339

King used unforgettable words, personal courage and leadership to forever alter race relations in this country. He forced Americans to attempt to make Jefferson's ideal our reality. We should put him up there on the cliff with Tom and Abe.

Sitting at the overlook pondering those faces in the granite, one wonders if the sculptures will outlast the republic to which these men contributed so much. Our institutions look permanent to us only because of the perspective from which we are forced to view them—one day at a time during short human lives.

The Soviet Union lasted a mere seventy-two or seventy-three years. The Soviet people are toppling the statues, destroying the icons, shattering the institutions that looked so permanent even a month ago.

If financial bankruptcy is the harbinger of moral and political bankruptcy, the United States is well on its way down the road that leads to extinction. Our politicians regard elected office as a lifelong career offering power, prestige and wealth. They win it by selling their "friendship" to economic enterprises that contribute campaign money. They use their victory to live in a style that most Americans can't even envision—great salaries, fantastic pensions, annual expense accounts of $640,000 each, exemptions from the laws they pass to regulate everyone else, a staggering list of perks—they're like characters out of Gibbon. They make themselves impervious to attack by supplying government checks to the middle and working classes, checks the government must borrow ever-increasing sums of money to cover. Will our members of Congress, like the Soviet parliamentarians this August, someday find that they represent no one but themselves?

I don't know. The genius of the democratic system is that it is self-correcting, that it gives us precisely the government we want, no more, no less. But is this what we want? If it is we're in big trouble.

I wish I had a time machine. I would zip three or four hundred years into the future, pop into a bookstore if they still have those archaic institutions, and grab a handful of history books. I confess, I'm one of those people who cheats and scans the final chapter first to see how it all turned out.

Of course, I could just come to Mount Rushmore in my time

machine to see if three or four hundred years from now the inhabitants of this continent still revere Washington and Lincoln. Will those presidents still be looking at distant horizons, or will a future generation have used explosives or artillery to obliterate a hated symbol of a dead past? Those faces on the cliff would tell me everything I really needed to know.

Later that morning I strapped on the *Cannibal Queen* for the final two legs of my Stearman summer—Rapid City to Torrington, Wyoming, and from there to Boulder. With the temperature at 88 degrees and no wind, I committed lift.

After flying by Rushmore and snapping the camera, I wandered around the Black Hills a little looking for the mountain that is being carved as a statue of Crazy Horse, the great war chief of the Sioux. And I found it, about fifteen miles southwest of Rushmore and six miles or so north of the town of Custer. Irony never comes in little pills, but in great doses.

When finished, this tribute to the American Indian will be the world's largest sculpture. The figure has yet to emerge from the stone but they are hard at it. Maybe in a few years . . .

Flying south across the high plains I tried to put my Stearman summer in perspective. I have flown a long way. From an airplane almost a half-century old, I have seen America.

Without permission from anyone, without a flight plan or a destination, you can fly any airworthy machine anywhere in the nation. There are some rules and regulations, of course, and while they are sometimes tiresome and intrusive, they are not onerous.

In this America of 1991 almost every town of any size has an airport and someone at the airport has fuel to sell. Down the road will be a motel that will give you a clean room for a reasonable price. Nearby will be a restaurant that serves palatable food. Unless you are extraordinarily unlucky, you will not be assaulted, robbed or ripped off. You will be treated with courtesy and respect by friendly people who will urge you to return someday. And they will mean it!

I never know just what to say when people ask me where my home is. My house is in Boulder, Colorado, but my home is the United States. Everywhere in the United States. I am as much at home in Savannah and St. Francis and Rockland as I am in Boulder. This entire nation is where my heart is.

Often the problems that make news threaten to overwhelm me. The foolishness, the stupidity, the shortsightedness, the naked self-interest at the expense of the public interest, these things sometimes lead me to despair of my fellow citizens and our future. But from 2,000 feet above the ground individual hills lose their identity and the lay of the land becomes apparent. Our nation has weathered its first two centuries well. From this altitude that is plain. The future ... well, the future belongs to those yet unborn. They will have to spread their own wings.

As this summer draws to a close the Soviet Union is in meltdown. Only one thing is certain—the people of the Soviet Union and Eastern Europe are emerging from darkness into light. What will come next no one knows. Perhaps anarchy, perhaps chaos, starvation, civil war or even a new political system that rests, in Jefferson's immortal words, "on the consent of the governed."

We free people wish the Soviets and Eastern Europeans well. We wish for them and all the people of the earth the life, liberty and freedom to pursue their concept of happiness that we ourselves enjoy.

And I wish the same for you.

I catch my first glimpse of the Front Range while I am still over Cheyenne. Thunderstorms are drifting east off the Rockies. One with a base of solid, opaque rain lit by strobes of lightning rests over the Cache la Poudre. In the next half hour or so it will drift down on Fort Collins.

And one is just east of Boulder. I point the right wing of the *Cannibal Queen* at the ground and corkscrew down at three Gs. Then I roll and pull some to the left. I right her and chop the throttle for a stall. She shudders and pitches forward and I smartly give her forward stick. Now roll and pull as the speed increases.

She responds crisply. The stick and rudder bring instant responses as the sunlight highlights the dancing yellow wings against the gray vagueness of the storm.

She has been on a long flight, visited every state. She has

delighted people from coast to coast and carried many aloft on flights they aren't likely to forget.

Now it's over.

I'm tired of living out of a soft bag and sleeping in motel beds, so in a way I'm glad. But there will be no more strange airports or fog in mountain valleys, no more unanswered calls asking the direction of the wind, no more low passes searching for wind socks, no more inviting grass runways.

Still, I have lived it. For that I am truly thankful.

Maybe when he is my age and remembers how it was, my son, David, will grin and be thankful too. Good memories, those are the best things you can give a kid.

After a few minutes of whifferdills I cut the power and point the *Cannibal Queen* toward home, down there under the trailing edge of that storm.

The wind is out of the southwest at four or five knots and a gentle rain is falling. I make a fair landing.

If only I had a little more practice I could get good at landings. Really. All I need is some confidence, and a little practice would give me some. I need to get out to the airport and do a couple dozen landings. Maybe this Saturday.

I shut her down by the hangar and am wiping the oil off her nose and belly when the mechanics come out and welcome me home. Together we look the *Queen* over and poke this and prod that.

She's in good shape. I think she'll fly another 49 years, at least. Perhaps someday one of my grandchildren will use the *Cannibal Queen* for a Stearman summer. That's certainly one of the infinite number of possibilities.

After I get my gear unloaded and we get the *Queen* inside, out of the misting rain, I take the time to inspect the little plane I acquired in April, a Breezy.

The Breezy is a homebuilt, yet it doesn't look like you expect an airplane to look. Most airplanes you sit *in,* this one you sit *on.* It has no fuselage, merely a triangular-cross-section framework of welded tubular steel. On this framework hang conventional wings and a tail. Power is provided by a 140-HP pusher engine. The pilot and passenger sit in tandem in front of the wings and engine, out there in front of everything, on seats bolted to the framework. There is no canopy, no windshield, no fuselage, no cockpit. But it flies!

The Breezy looks like what you might get if an ultralight had carnal knowledge of the *Cannibal Queen*.

This one was constructed in 1972 by a high school welding teacher, probably with the help of his students. It was never flown enough, however—a mere two hundred hours in nineteen years—and neglect and corrosion have taken their toll. We're restoring it—overhauling the engine, replacing corroded tubing, re-covering the wings with new fabric, and so on. When it's finished in a month or two it'll be better than new.

And I'll get to fly it first!

It'll be a kick. I'll be sitting on that chair out in front of the whole shebang with a stick and throttle and rudder and darn near nothing else, my nose splitting the breeze. I'll be grinning so much my teeth will get splattered with bugs.

I'm going to need a name for it, something catchy.

Maybe next summer I'll fly it around the country. Or to Oshkosh. Or West Virginia. Or . . .

But that will be another story.